Friends or Strangers

FRIENDS
OR
STRANGERS

The Impact of Immigrants
on the U. S. Economy

GEORGE J. BORJAS

Basic Books, Inc., Publishers   New York

Library of Congress Cataloging-in-Publication Data

Borjas, George J.
    Friends or strangers: the impact of immigrants on the U.S.
economy / George J. Borjas.
    Includes bibliographical references.
    ISBN 0-465-02567-6
    1. United States—Emigration and immigration—Economic aspects.
2. Alien labor—United States. 3. Labor supply—United States.
 I. Title.
JV6471.B674 1990   89–43093
331.6'2'0973—dc20   CIP

To the memory of my father

CONTENTS

PREFACE

THIS BOOK analyzes the impact of immigration on the American economy. In many ways, it is not the book I intended to write when I first began thinking about this problem in 1980. To my surprise, many of my preconceptions about the immigrant experience simply did not stand up to the rigorous scrutiny of the data.

The study, therefore, is not driven by a passionate belief in some dogmatic axioms about how immigrants benefit or impair the economic opportunities of natives in the United States. Instead, it is driven by the desire to present a systematic and objective analysis of the available data, within the framework provided by the methodology and tools of modern economics. It is my hope that readers will find these arguments and the empirical evidence as persuasive as I did.

In conducting the research, I benefited from comments and suggestions made by many friends and colleagues. I owe my greatest debt to Richard Freeman and Marta Tienda. Their enthusiasm and constructive reactions were an important source of encouragement during the long gestation period. I am also particularly grateful to Stephen Bronars and Stephen Trejo, with whom I discussed practically all aspects of the work reported here. These discussions sharpened my arguments and helped me understand the implications of the approach that I advocate.

In addition, my work benefited from comments made by Orley Ashenfelter, Gary Becker, Charles Brown, Ronald Ehrenberg, Matthew Goldberg, Daniel Hamermesh, James Heckman, Larry Katz, Larry Kenny, Douglas Massey, Jacob Mincer, Sherwin Rosen, Robert Topel, and Finis Welch. Finally, I would like to acknowledge the research assistance of Wei-Jang Huang, Conrad Mir, Larry Singell, and particularly Bernt Bratsberg. Their hard work and devotion greatly simplified my task.

I have been extremely fortunate to have had a number of institutions fund my research during the past decade. These are the Department of Labor, the Rockefeller Foundation, the W. E. Upjohn Institute for Employment Research, the Sloan Foundation, the National Institute of Child Health and Human Development, and the National Science Foundation. Without their financial support, it would have been impossible for me to devote my time and energy to this project. In addition, a grant from the Ford Foundation gave me the opportunity to spend the 1988–89 academic year at the Cambridge, Massachusetts, office of the National Bureau of Economic Research. The intellectually exciting and friendly environment at the NBER provided just the right setting for writing and completing this book.

I have dedicated this book to the memory of my father. Although he died in 1961, the book touches upon topics that were dear to his heart.

PART I

IMMIGRANTS IN THE UNITED STATES: AN OVERVIEW

CHAPTER 1

Who Comes: How the Immigration Market Works

THE UNITED STATES has been populated by peoples from many different national origins, races, religions, cultures, and languages. According to the Immigration and Naturalization Service (INS), 54 million persons chose to immigrate to the United States between 1820 and 1987.[1] Although the many groups of immigrants making up this population flow differed in practically every aspect of their cultural, social, and economic backgrounds, they had a common vision: the belief that the United States offered better opportunities for themselves and for their children than did their countries of origin.

This vision was shared by many of their compatriots who never migrated to the United States. There is, therefore, another bond uniting the immigrant population. Immigrants not only had the dream; they were also willing to incur the often considerable costs associated with international migration in order to realize their vision. So these 54 million immigrants are not typical individuals. People willing to make a costly and uncertain investment in the American dream are quite different from the millions who chose not to migrate at all, or who chose to migrate elsewhere. In an important sense, the American experience is the story of how these very different peoples, united by their search for a better life and by the stake in their investment, interacted, adapted, and built a country.

Despite the fact that almost all of us are immigrants or descendants of immigrants, American history is characterized by a never-ending debate over when to pull the ladder in.[2] The political debate over how many and which kinds of immigrants to admit has been and remains heated and is often tainted with racial (if not racist) overtones. Even Benjamin Franklin wrote that German immigrants "are generally the most stupid of their own nation . . . it is almost impossible to remove any prejudices they entertain."[3]

Because the economic and social value of admitting certain groups of immigrants was questioned even at the time of the country's birth, it is a remarkable characteristic of American history that no federal statutes restricted immigration throughout the first century after independence.[4] Anyone with the will, courage, and financial resources to cross the oceans or the borders could begin a new life in this country. It was only in the 1880s that U.S. immigration policy began to restrict the number, race, and national-origin composition of the immigrant flow.

Two arguments are typically used to justify and legitimize these restrictions. The first is that immigrants have an adverse impact on the earnings and employment opportunities of native-born Americans. For example, the influential People's Party platform of 1882 stated, "We condemn . . . the present system, which opens up our ports to the pauper and criminal classes of the world, and crowds out our wage earners."[5] It seems that little has changed in the past hundred years. Today the same accusations are hurled at illegal aliens, at boat people originating in Southeast Asia and Cuba, and at other unskilled immigrants.

It is also argued that immigrants find it hard to adapt or assimilate in the United States because of their very different cultural, political, and economic backgrounds. This view, in turn, raises fears that a large number of unassimilated immigrants will splinter the country's national identity. Colorado's ex-governor Richard Lamm and Gary Imhoff make the case concisely: "I love America, and I want to save and preserve it. . . . Civilizations rise and civilizations fall—and there are certain universal pathologies that characterize the fall of history's civilizations. Ethnic, racial, and religious differences can become such a pathology; they can grow, fester, and eventually splinter a society."[6]

Moreover, immigrants who are not well integrated in the American economy may form a permanent underclass, further straining the provision of public services and exacerbating social problems in the United States. The growth of this unassimilated underclass could lead to a worsening of the problems of poverty and crime in American cities, to political upheavals caused by the presence of large groups of persons who lack even the most basic familiarity with the English language, and to significant increases in the costs of maintaining the welfare state.

From this perspective, restrictions on the number and types of immigrants are necessary because both the economic health and the national identity of our country are in jeopardy.

It may well be that these are valid hypotheses. Proponents of these views, however, often base their arguments more on perceptions or ad hoc theorizing than on solid empirical evidence demonstrating the validity of their conjectures. Surprising as it may seem, until very recently there was virtually no systematic empirical research of the issues at the core of the debate over immigration policy. This neglect was due to the lack of data sources allowing researchers to study the impact of immigrants on native labor markets, the adjustment process experienced by the foreign-born in the United States, and the effects of changes in immigration policy on the skill composition of immigrant flows.[7]

A classic (and disturbing) example of how difficult it is to learn even the most basic information about key aspects of the immigrant population occurred in 1979. The Carter administration was considering retaliatory measures against Iran after the hostage crisis began. It asked the INS how many Iranian students were enrolled in American universities. The INS was unable to provide an answer during the 444 days of the crisis, and to this day it remains unable to provide that statistic.[8]

Of course, the lack of solid evidence does not silence debate over immigration policy. Instead, it allows stereotypical impressions about the immigrant experience and the role immigrants play in the economy to flourish. These stereotypes adjust over time as the national origin and cultural background of immigrants change. The modern view of the immigrant experience differs from the earlier, racially tainted portrait by containing both favorable and unfavorable impressions of the immigrant. Among the axioms of the current conventional wisdom are the following:

- Immigrants have a significant adverse impact on the earnings and employment opportunities of the native-born. By crowding out natives from the labor market, immigrants take jobs away from natives.
- Legal immigrants are, on average, highly skilled and hard-working people and tend to be relatively successful in the labor market.
- There may be as many as 10 million illegal aliens. They tend to be single men working in agricultural jobs, and they have an adverse impact on the labor market opportunities of less skilled natives.

• Current U.S. immigration policy is a ticking population time bomb. By allowing current immigrants to sponsor the entry of their relatives, who in turn can sponsor the entry of additional relatives, practically everyone in the world could eventually qualify for entry into the United States.

These impressions about the immigrant experience are widespread. They are also false. This is one of the main lessons of the literature that has recently developed in economics and other social sciences, specifically addressing questions at the core of the debate over immigration policy. The rapid growth of this literature in the last decade is mainly attributable to the fact that immigration flows are now at near-record levels. The immigration question is once again at the center of public attention.

As table 1.1 indicates, immigration is rapidly becoming an important component of demographic change in the United States. The size of the immigrant flow reached a record high of 8.8 million immigrants per decade in the 1901–1910 period. Because of the Great Depression, it sank to a low of half a million immigrants in the 1930s. Since then, the immigrant flow has increased steadily at the rate of about 1 million persons per decade. As a consequence of the increasing size of the immigrant flow and the declining birth rate among American women, the ratio of immigrants to births began to rise in the 1960s, and it is now

TABLE 1.1

Immigrant Flow into the United States, 1901–1987

Period	Immigrants Admitted (In Millions)	Immigrant Flow as Percent of Births	Percent of U.S. Population That Is Foreign-Born
1901–1910	8.8	—	14.2
1911–1920	5.7	19.9	13.6
1921–1930	4.1	14.4	12.1
1931–1940	.5	2.2	10.1
1941–1950	1.0	3.3	8.2
1951–1960	2.5	6.2	6.0
1961–1970	3.3	8.5	5.0
1971–1980	4.5	13.5	5.5
1981–1987	4.1	15.8	6.0

SOURCE: Adapted from George J. Borjas and Marta Tienda, "The Economic Consequences of Immigration," *Science* 235 (February 6, 1987): 646. Copyright © 1987 by the American Association for the Advancement of Science. Data on births obtained from U.S. National Center for Health Statistics, *Vital Statistics of the United States* (Washington, D.C.: Government Printing Office, annual); and U.S. Bureau of the Census, *Historical Statistics of the United States, Colonial Times to 1970* (Washington, D.C.: Government Printing Office, 1975), p. 49.

approaching the high levels reached in the early part of the century. Further, although the percentage of the U.S. population that is foreign-born is only 6 percent today as compared to 14 percent in the early 1900s, this percentage has also begun to increase in recent years.

Today, however (unlike earlier times), the debate over immigration policy need not be conducted in a vacuum of empirical evidence. The recent literature makes use of a large number of recently available data sets. These data contain detailed information on the demographic characteristics and labor market experiences of hundreds of thousands of immigrants and natives. This book brings together and summarizes the evidence on the question, what role do immigrants play in the U.S. economy?

The emphasis on the economic consequences of immigration is not meant to imply that other aspects of the immigrant experience, such as cultural adaptation and participation in the political process, are less important. The economic focus of recent research on the immigrant experience arises because so much of the current debate over immigration policy emphasizes economic issues: job displacement, immigrant adaptation in the labor market, and immigrant participation in welfare programs.

A unifying hypothesis of the research summarized in this book is that immigrants choose to come to the United States. The immigrant flow is composed of the pool of persons who are attracted by the earnings, employment, and welfare opportunities provided by the American economy, who are willing to incur the costs associated with immigration, and who are able to gain entry into the country. Changes in immigration policy, like changes in economic conditions and migration costs, alter the size and skill characteristics of the group of persons attracted to the United States; hence they change the role immigrants play in the U.S. economy.

In a sense, the United States competes with other countries, such as the home countries of migrants and other potential host countries, for the immigrant's human and physical capital.[9] International trade involves not only the movement of goods and services among countries, but also the movement of people. Just as countries compete in a worldwide market in which goods and services are exchanged, they also compete in an immigration market. By presenting a specific set of economic opportunities and by pursuing an immigration policy that prevents the entry of some persons but encourages the entry of others, the United States makes a particular type of "offer" in the immigration market. The attractiveness of the American offer, relative to the offers of other countries, determines the size and composition of the immigrant flow entering the United States. This approach to the study of immigration yields a number of new insights and results that can play a central role in the ongoing debate over immigration policy.

Three key questions guide the analysis: Which types of immigrants does the United States attract? What is the impact of these immigrants on the U.S. economy? And is the United States competitive in the immigration market? The empirical evidence presented in this book indicates that the skill composition of the immigrant flow entering the United States has deteriorated significantly in the past two or three decades; that this decay in immigrant skills justifies a reassessment of the economic benefits and costs of immigration; and that major reforms in immigration policy may be needed to reestablish American competitiveness in this important marketplace.

What Do Markets Do?

Markets are the institutions that regulate transactions among individuals. In some markets, goods such as bicycles or cars are exchanged between buyers and sellers. A free-enterprise economy uses prices to allocate the scarce goods among the many persons wishing to own them. Only those persons willing and able to pay the going price get the goods. Other markets, such as the labor market, guide the allocation of labor among different firms. In these markets, transactions involve the exchange of monetary compensation from buyer to seller for the good being purchased.

There are also markets in which the transactions do not necessarily involve the direct exchange of money between the parties. One example is the market for political ideas, where politicians "sell" their ideologies and political platforms to voters, and (in modern democracies) voters "buy" or reject these ideas through their votes. Similarly, in the marriage market individuals search for and find spouses by offering a package of personal traits and living standards that other players in the market find attractive.[10]

All markets share two features. They provide the rules of the game in which exchanges are made, and the interaction of players in the marketplace determines a certain allocation of the scarce resources among competing uses. In other words, only a subset of persons will own the limited number of bicycles; firms and employees will be "married" in a particular sorting of workers to jobs; and some politicians will win while others will lose.

The main theme of this book is that there also exists an immigration market allocating persons wishing to leave their current countries of residence among the few host countries willing to admit them. Potential migrants, like workers looking for a job, are looking for the best country they can live in. Host countries, like firms looking for specific types of workers, set immigration policies so that they can attract specific types of migrants. Just as the labor market guides the allocation of workers to firms, the immigration market guides the allocation of persons to countries.

The existence of an immigration market implies that countries compete for the physical and human capital of immigrants, that the particular sorting of persons and countries depends on how the offers to potential migrants differ among the competing countries, and that there will be winners and losers in this competition. Changes in the parameters guiding transactions in the immigration market, such as immigration policies and economic conditions in the competing countries, alter the size, origin, and skill composition of immigrant flows to the United States. This approach, therefore, directly tackles the central questions in the debate over immigration policy: How competitive is the United States in the immigration market? And how can immigration policy be changed to increase our competitiveness?

The Nature of the Immigration Market

There are three sets of players in the immigration market: the people contemplating whether to leave their home countries, the governments of immigrants' home countries, and the governments of the various potential host countries. All of these players enter the immigration market with different objectives, and it is the interaction among them that leads to a particular sorting of immigrants among the various host countries.

Persons residing in any country of origin consider the possibility of remaining there or of migrating to one of a number of host countries. Individuals make the immigration decision by comparing the values of the various alternatives, and they choose the country that makes them best off considering the financial and legal constraints regulating the international migration process.

These constraints include the individual's financial resources. After all, international migration is costly. The costs include direct expenditures, such as the out-of-pocket expenses associated with the transportation of the immigrant and his family to their new home, along with indirect costs, such as the income losses associated with unemployment spells that occur as immigrants look for work in the new country. Because only persons who have accumulated sufficient wealth and savings can afford to migrate, the potential migrant's financial resources obviously influence the immigration decision.

Potential host countries are also important players in the immigration market, for they can encourage, discourage, or prevent the entry of certain groups of persons. In particular, potential host countries are characterized by a specific set of economic opportunities. These income and employment opportunities can be described in terms of the existing income distribution, whereby certain types of skills are highly rewarded and other types are not; whereby jobs are easily available in some industries but scarce in others; whereby some occupations are in high demand, but high levels of unemployment persist in others; whereby persons who experience relatively poor labor market outcomes are subsidized by the welfare state, while persons who experience favorable outcomes are heavily taxed. These differences in income and employment opportunities by skill, industry, and occupation imply that the attractiveness of the economic "offer" made by a host country will differ among potential migrants. Some will find the offers lucrative, others will not.

Host countries also regulate the size and composition of the immigrant flow by imposing restrictions on entry according to the potential migrant's skills, wealth, occupation, political background, moral rectitude, national origin, or family relationships with current residents. These regulations generate additional variations in migration costs among potential migrants. For example, current U.S. immigration policy makes immigration costs almost prohibitive for persons who do not already have relatives residing here. Other host countries, such as Australia and Canada, have a "point system" in which potential immigrants are screened and graded on the basis of their educational attainment, age, occupation, and other demographic characteristics, and only those individuals who score highly can enter the country. Immigration policies, by their very nature, impose different entry costs on different people and act as a screening device to filter out "undesirable" persons from the applicant pool.

Thus, through their immigration policies and their offers of economic opportunities, host countries compete for the human and physical capital of the potential migrants. Certain kinds of immigration policies, such as those that make it easy to migrate if the visa applicant has relatives in the host country, attract different kinds of persons than policies that award entry visas based on the applicant's educational attainment or occupation. Similarly, host countries in which economic and labor market conditions favor certain skills attract different types of immigrants than host countries that reward other skills.

The competition among host countries for "desirable" immigrants is clearly illustrated by a recent example. Australia's immigration policy has provisions designed specifically to attract people with substantial physical and investment capital.[11] In particular, the Business Migration Program provides unrestricted entry to persons who are willing to invest a minimum of $500,000 (Australian dollars) in an Australian business venture or who are willing to start their own businesses in Australia with a minimum of $100,000.[12]

Obviously, this policy is an important enticement for prosperous persons wishing to leave Hong Kong before 1997, when the territory will be incorporated into the People's Republic of China. The political and economic uncertainty clouding Hong Kong's future creates incentives for the wealthy and the highly skilled to settle elsewhere. Some host countries, such as Australia, perceive significant economic benefits from attracting these individuals and enact immigration policies designed to draw these types of persons. In a very real sense, Australia is now in the business of selling entry visas to wealthy persons.

It may seem somewhat callous that some host countries literally sell visas in the immigration market. But the fact is that all host countries are in the same business, regardless of whether they do it for monetary rewards. The United States also "sells" visas to potential migrants, but it uses an extremely peculiar pricing system. We literally give visas away to persons who have close relatives in the country and, with a few exceptions, charge a prohibitively high price to persons who do not.

The home countries of potential migrants are the last major players in the immigration market. Their economies also provide a certain set of income and employment opportunities to their residents, and their emigration policies regulate the size and skill composition of the outgoing flow. In some countries, like the United States, citizens are free to leave the country whenever they wish, for any duration, and for whatever reason. In other countries, emigration statutes impose large costs and penalties on potential emigrants and make it very difficult for residents to migrate elsewhere. Moreover, such restrictions often control not only the size but also the skill composition of the emigrant flow. For instance, the Soviet Union long prevented the exit of any persons who worked in sensitive government jobs, and Cuba prohibited the exit of persons in the age group subject to military service.

Economists typically assume that individuals behave in ways that maximize their well-being. In the context of the immigration market, this means that after potential migrants compare the feasible alternatives, they choose the country that provides the best economic opportunities. There exists a close analogy between the immigration market and the job market. Like persons looking for work, potential migrants enter the market, receive offers from competing host countries and their home country, compare the offers, and make a migration decision. The information gathered in the immigration market leads many to conclude that they are better off staying where they are. Others decide that conditions in some foreign country are better than at home, and these persons are the ones who make up international migration flows. A subset of these immigrants find that the U.S. offer was more attractive than the offers of competing host countries, and these make up the pool of foreign-born persons in the United States.

The immigration market approach reveals the link between the components of the American offer, in terms of both economic characteristics and the visa-allocation system dictated by U.S. immigration policy, and the size and composition of the immigrant flow entering the country. As economic conditions in the United States change (relative to those in other countries), different types of persons find it economically beneficial to immigrate. Similarly, whenever Congress changes important aspects of immigration policy, immigration costs are altered for many potential migrants, and a different immigrant flow enters the United States. To assess the benefits and costs of alternative immigration policies, therefore, it is necessary to determine how key components of America's offer in the immigration market affect the incentives of potential migrants. Analysis of the link between the nature of the offer and the types of immigrants attracted to the United States would then indicate the types of policy changes required to increase American competitiveness in this marketplace.

If we assume that individuals move in response to better economic opportunities, it is evident that differences in average income levels among countries are a prime determinant of the size and direction of immigrant flows. Immigrants tend to gravitate from low-income countries to high-income countries. Further, the greater the income differential between the countries, the larger the size of the population flow. For instance, the wage differential between Mexico and the United States is the largest income gap between any two contiguous countries in the world. It should not be too surprising, therefore, that large migration flows originate in Mexico and move toward the United States, instead of the other way around.

In addition, the size and direction of the flow depend on immigration costs, both of leaving the source country and of entering a particular host country. The number of immigrants originating in a country that imposes high penalties on emigration will be small, for few persons can afford these costs. Similarly, the number of immigrants entering any host country depends on the costs of migrating there, for again few persons can afford to enter the country if substantial entry penalties are imposed, or if high transportation costs are associated with the move.[13]

This approach explicitly assumes that immigration is the result of a search for better economic opportunities. Some immigrants, however, move for other reasons, such as persons seeking refuge from political or religious persecution. In fact, the United States experienced a substantial increase in the number of political refugees entering its borders in the past few decades. About 20 percent of the 4 million persons who immigrated legally between 1981 and 1987 were classified as refugees or "asylees."[14] Although I have not yet addressed the determinants of this type of flow, the discussion can easily be expanded to allow for politically motivated immigration. In subsequent chapters, I shall present a complete discussion of the refugee aspects of international migration.

In addition to the implications about the size and direction of population flows, the immigration market approach can also tell us much about the skill composition of the immigrant pool. For instance, about 10 percent of Jamaica's population now resides in the United States.[15] Obviously, income differentials between the two countries are sufficiently large to generate a sizable population flow. It is not enough, however, to know that 10 percent of Jamaicans find it beneficial to migrate to the United States. Perhaps more important is the question, *which* 10 percent? Are the immigrants drawn from the pool of skilled workers, or are they drawn from the unskilled? Any assessment of the role immigrants play in the American economy crucially depends on the answer to this question.

Clearly, persons emigrating from a particular country are "self-selected" from that country's population. The very fact that some persons choose to migrate, while others do not, implies that immigrants differ in significant ways from the rest of the population. Moreover, the immigrant flow that eventually reaches the United States is doubly self-selected. It contains persons who found it profitable to leave their home countries *and* who found it unprofitable (or were unable) to migrate elsewhere.

Put succinctly, these immigrants differ from the average person both in the country they came from and in the United States. The self-selected sample of immigrants may be dominated by relatively unskilled persons, who find it worthwhile to migrate to the United States but who also find it difficult to assimilate into the country and enter the economic mainstream. Alternatively, the immigrant pool may be composed of persons who are highly skilled and ambitious, who are very able and hard working, and who may be an important source of economic growth for the United States.

The type of skill sorting that occurs as people move to whichever country makes them the best offer is far from obvious. Nevertheless, it is one of the most important questions that must be addressed by policy makers: after all, the economic benefits of immigration clearly depend on it. The immigration of unskilled workers may allow American manufacturers and farmers to fill menial jobs that require few skills with relatively low-wage labor. By contrast, the immigration of skilled workers helps staff universities, hospitals, and scientific laboratories. In addition, the immigration of the unskilled will have a different impact on native labor market conditions, on tax revenues, and on the costs of social programs than the immigration of the skilled.

The main determinant of the skill sorting generated by the immigration market is the fact that countries competing in this marketplace attach different values to workers' skills. For instance, in practically all countries, higher education levels are associated with higher earnings. College-educated persons are better paid than persons with a high school diploma, who in turn earn more than persons who only completed grammar school.[16] But the rate at which earnings increase with additional schooling, or the rate of return to schooling, is not the same for all countries.[17] In a well-known study of international differences in the rate of return to schooling, economist George Psacharopoulos reports that an additional year of higher education increases earnings by only 5 percent in Germany, by 15 percent in the United States, and by 29 percent in Mexico.[18]

Because people migrate in search of better economic opportunities, highly educated workers have much to gain by moving to countries that pay a higher price for their skills. As long as income differentials among countries are large enough to justify migration, highly educated workers naturally gravitate to countries in which the rate of return to education is high. Workers with little schooling have little to gain by immigrating to such countries, and because immigration is costly they are much less likely to move there. Therefore, the sorting of persons in the immigration market leads to the allocation of highly educated workers to countries that have high rates of return to education.[19]

In short, workers offering their human capital to employers in different countries behave in exactly the same way as firms selling their goods. Both parties sell to the highest bidder. The immigration market, therefore, generates a nonrandom sorting of educational skills among the various countries. The American offer in the immigration market will be particularly attractive to highly educated immigrants or to immigrants with certain types of schooling if the rate of return to that schooling is higher here than in the country of origin. But the United States is less likely to attract educated immigrants if the workers originate in countries that value their education more.

Of course, the skills and productivities of individuals depend on many factors other than education, including demographic characteristics such as age, family background, health, and marital status. Moreover, even among workers who have the same demographic characteristics, there is substantial variation in productivity and skills. After all, individuals also differ in unobserved traits, such as ability, drive, and motivation, which have a major impact on the individual's productivity and earning capacity. In fact, more than two-thirds of all variation in wage rates among individuals cannot be explained in terms of differences in observed demographic characteristics and are probably caused by differences in these unobserved traits.[20] Immigrants are likely to be self-selected on the basis of all of these characteristics. The immigration market approach implies that particular traits are allocated to countries in which their economies happen to value them, because a country's offer is particularly lucrative to persons with those traits.

The determinants of international differences in income distributions have not been carefully studied, so that little is known about how the rewards to the various skill characteristics vary among countries. But international differences in these rewards generate substantial variation in the amount of inequality exhibited by the income distributions of the countries participating in the immigration market.[21] There is a strong positive correlation between the extent of income inequality in a particular country and the rate of return to schooling in that country.[22] Countries with highly dispersed income distributions pay relatively higher returns to education and presumably to other skill characteristics than do countries with more egalitarian income distributions. Therefore, it is useful to think of income inequality as a summary measure of the returns to skills in a country.[23]

To see how the amount of income inequality in the country of origin affects the type of immigrant attracted by the United States, consider two alternative source countries, one with a relatively egalitarian income distribution, such as Sweden, and one with a substantial amount of income inequality, such as Mexico.[24]

Should highly skilled Swedes immigrate to the United States? They can choose to remain in their birthplace but find that their earnings opportunities are severely constrained by the fact that Sweden, relative to the United States, has an egalitarian income distribution. Put differently, highly skilled Swedes do not earn much more than those less skilled. In addition, because of the almost confiscatory tax rates at higher income levels, the income distribution in Sweden narrows even more relative to that in the United States.[25] Therefore, highly skilled Swedes find that their earnings opportunities would increase substantially if they migrated to the United States. By the same token, unskilled Swedes find that their economy protects them from the poor labor market outcomes that would likely befall them if they were to migrate to the United States. Because the United States, relative to Sweden, does not insure unskilled workers against the possibility of low earnings, unskilled Swedes would experience a decline in their economic well-being if they were to migrate to the United States. Therefore, the self-selection of the immigrant pool ensures that the typical immigrant originating in Sweden is highly skilled.

This argument says nothing about the size of the migration flow. In fact, few Swedes migrate to the United States because income differentials between the two countries are too small to cover the costs of immigration. But the sorting generated by the immigration market suggests that those who do migrate tend to be skilled. So an important implication of the immigration market approach is that the United States is likely to attract relatively skilled persons from countries with egalitarian income distributions, because these countries reward skills less than we do.

Should a highly skilled Mexican immigrate to the United States? Mexico has substantially more income inequality than the United States. Skilled Mexicans find that the Mexican income distribution greatly rewards those skills, while unskilled Mexicans have little protection from poor labor market outcomes. As long as they can afford to migrate, unskilled Mexicans have the most incentive to come to the United States and skilled Mexicans the least, so Mexicans in the United States are likely to be unskilled. This point suggests that the

United States attracts relatively unskilled persons from countries that have highly disperse income distributions, because these countries reward skills more than we do.

In the end, persons are matched with countries that reward the specific skills they have to offer: this is the central implication of the immigration market approach. As long as individuals migrate to take advantage of different economic opportunities among countries, there is no reason to presume that the United States will always attract the "best and the brightest" or to presume that the United States will be continually flooded with the least skilled persons of the source countries.

The skill composition of the foreign-born population in the United States thus depends on how our offer of economic opportunity compares to the offers made by other host countries and by the individual's home country. Immigrants originating in some source countries are likely to be substantially more skilled than immigrants originating in other countries. Changes in U.S. immigration policy that lead to wholesale redistribution of visas among source countries, therefore, will have a major impact on the skill composition of the immigrant flow. Moreover, as economic conditions in the United States, in competing host countries, and in the source countries change, the skill composition of the immigrant flow also changes. The competitiveness of America's offer in the immigration market, therefore, largely determines the economic impact of immigration on the United States.

Conclusions of the Analysis

This book analyzes the immigrant's role in the American economy. The conceptual framework provided by the immigration market approach ties together the many strands of discussion and provides a coherent interpretation of the data presented.

The essence of the empirical evidence summarized here is that because of changes in U.S. immigration policy and because of changing economic and political conditions both here and abroad, the United States is currently attracting relatively unskilled immigrants. For the most part, these immigrants have little chance of attaining economic parity with natives during their lifetimes. Although these immigrants do not greatly affect the earnings and employment opportunities of natives, they may have an even greater long-run economic impact because of their relatively high poverty rates and propensities for participation in the welfare system and because national income and tax revenues are substantially lower than they would have been if the United States had attracted a more skilled immigrant flow. In short, the United States is losing the international competition for skilled workers to other host countries such as Australia and Canada, and this fact imposes costs on the American economy.

America's poor performance in the immigration market, therefore, suggests a need for reevaluation of our immigration policy. Among the specific findings that lead to this conclusion are:

1. Immigrants in the United States have a small impact on the earnings and employment opportunities of natives. A 10-percent increase in the number of immigrants decreases the average wage of natives by at most .2 percent and has little effect on the labor force participation rates and employment opportunities of practically all native groups. Moreover, despite all of the concern about the displacement effects of illegal immigration, the available evidence suggests that illegal aliens also have a minor impact on the earnings and employment opportunities of natives.

2. Immigrants do, however, have a significant effect on the earnings and employment opportunities of foreign-born persons already residing in the United States. A 10-percent increase in the number of immigrants decreases the wage of foreign-born persons by at least 2 percent.

3. There are 3 to 4 million illegal aliens in the United States. Contrary to the common stereotype, most undocumented workers are not single men living on their own and working in the agricultural fields of the Southwest and California. Like their legal counterparts, illegal aliens are typically men and women who live with their immediate families and who work in nonagricultural jobs. Illegal aliens have lower earnings than their legal counterparts. This wage differential is not due to employer exploitation of undocumented workers, but rather to the fact that illegal aliens are less skilled, on average, than legal immigrants.

4. The skills of immigrants entering the United States have declined during the past few decades. More recent immigrant waves have relatively less schooling, lower earnings, lower labor force participation rates, and higher poverty rates than earlier waves had at similar stages of their assimilation into the country. Therefore, the nature of the skill sorting generated by the immigration market has deteriorated substantially in recent years.

5. Upon entry into the U.S. labor market, immigrants do not perform as well as natives. Over time, the differences between the two groups in labor force participation rates, unemployment rates, hours of work, and hourly wages narrow, but the rate of convergence in some of these measures of labor market success is relatively small. It is very unlikely, for instance, that the typical immigrant who entered the United States in the 1970s will reach earnings parity with natives during his lifetime. The assimilation experience is not sufficient for recent immigrant waves to overcome their initial economic disadvantage.

6. Although these results describe the experiences of the typical immigrant, there are great differences in labor market characteristics among national-origin groups. Generally, immigrants originating in Western Europe are more successful in the U.S. labor market than immigrants originating in Asia and Latin America. This finding partly reflects the fact that immigrants originating in countries with egalitarian income distributions tend to be more skilled than immigrants originating in countries with substantial income dispersion. In addition, the skills of persons originating in advanced, industrialized economies are more easily transferable to the U.S. labor market than are the skills of persons originating in the less developed countries.

7. The fact that the new immigrants are less skilled than the old is responsible for a significant reduction in the potential national income of the United States. If the persons who migrated between 1975 and 1979 had been as skilled as those who came in the early 1960s, national income would be at least $6 billion higher in every single year of the immigrants' working life. The accumulation of these losses over time, combined with the continuing entry of unskilled immigrant flows, implies that the long-run reduction in national income and the corresponding losses in tax revenues may be substantial. There are large

economic costs associated with America's poor performance in the immigration market.

8. Because recent immigrant waves are relatively unskilled, they are more likely to participate in the welfare system than earlier waves were. In addition, the immigrant family has a higher probability of participating in the welfare system the longer the family has resided in the United States. The assimilation process leads not only to an increase in income opportunities in the labor market, but also to an increase in the opportunities available through the welfare system. The unfavorable skill sorting generated by current conditions in the immigration market, therefore, has an impact on the economy through its adverse effect on the costs of income-transfer programs and the potential development of a welfare underclass among many immigrant groups.

9. An important consequence of immigration is the creation and growth of immigrant enclaves in many American cities. These enclaves generate significant economic opportunities for immigrants, either because many immigrants start businesses in order to cater to members of their national-origin group or because the immigrant entrepreneurs often hire their conationals. The fact that immigrants have higher self-employment rates than natives is largely due to the rapid growth of these immigrant enclaves. Immigrant entrepreneurs, however, are not particularly successful. They have lower incomes than comparable immigrants employed in salaried jobs. Moreover, immigrants who remain in the enclave and work in immigrant-owned firms tend to be paid less than immigrants who leave the enclave and enter the economic mainstream.

10. Contrary to popular belief, the number of relatives sponsored by an immigrant currently residing in the United States is relatively small. Thus, there is little reason to suspect that the size of the immigrant flow will eventually explode because of the family-reunification provisions in current immigration policy. Further, the family context of the immigration decision has conflicting impacts on the skill composition of the immigrant flow. Because only a fixed number of visas is available, allocating a large fraction of these visas to relatives of U.S. residents implies that many highly skilled applicants cannot enter the United States simply because they lack these family ties. But the

21

empirical evidence indicates that persons who migrate as part of a family unit are more skilled than single or unattached immigrants.

11. The United States is only one of several countries competing for the physical and human capital of immigrants. As compared to two other potential host countries—Australia and Canada—the United States now attracts the least skilled immigrants. The situation was almost the reverse in the early 1960s, when the United States attracted immigrants who were as skilled as (if not more skilled than) the competing host countries.

In sum, the nature of America's offer in the immigration market has changed substantially in the past two or three decades, and as a result the immigrant flow entering the United States has become less and less skilled. Although the immigration of unskilled workers may help fill menial jobs at relatively low wages and leads to lower prices for the goods they produce and higher real incomes for American consumers, this type of immigration also imposes substantial costs on the American economy. The fundamental question facing policy makers is whether these costs exceed the benefits of unskilled immigration. If so, in order to draw a more skilled immigrant flow the United States will have to alter its offer to potential migrants.

The immigration market approach suggests that the United States attracts the types of persons who find the American offer most lucrative (relative to offers provided by competing countries). The INS cannot force persons to come here; it can only award entry visas to those who find it profitable to migrate in the first place. This fact has important implications for immigration policy. It implies that economic conditions in source countries and in competing host countries play a role in determining the national-origin and skill composition of the immigrant flow. Thus, it would seem that the economic impact of immigration depends on factors that are beyond the reach of American immigration policy. Nevertheless, the United States can influence economic conditions abroad through such economic policies as import restrictions, foreign aid, and debt repayment subsidies, as well as through its participation in the programs of the World Bank and the International Monetary Fund. These economic policies, which are often ignored in discussions of immigration policy, partly determine the attractiveness of America's offer in the immigration market and the role immigrants play in the United States.

The immigration market approach also implies that the skill composition of the immigrant flow depends on how the American economy rewards skills relative to other countries. Factors that influence how skills are rewarded in the United States, such as the tax structure, the generosity of social insurance programs, and the extent of interindustry and interoccupational wage differentials, affect the nature of the sorting of immigrants among competing countries. Again, domestic government programs that are often regarded as being unrelated to immigration policy, such as subsidies to particular industries or an overhaul of the income-tax system, change America's offer in the immigration market and influence the impact of immigrants on the economy.

A central implication of the immigration market approach, therefore, is that there is a close link between the economic policies pursued by the U.S. government and the size and skill composition of the immigrant flow. Government programs that affect economic conditions both here and abroad are important policy tools, and they can be used effectively to alter the sorting generated by the immigration market. Conversely, reforms in the visa-allocation system that ignore the important link between economic policy and the nature of America's offer in the immigration market may not be successful in attracting more skilled immigrants to the United States.

It is important to stress that these findings and conclusions are not based on conjectures or ad hoc theorizing about the role immigrants play in the American economy. Rather, they are the result of systematic analysis, by myself and by many other researchers, of many data sources—including INS administrative data, U.S. censuses, and censuses from other host countries such as Australia and Canada—that describe the economic experiences of immigrants and natives in the United States and in other host countries.

Nevertheless, it is wise to admit at the outset that this research, like practically all research in social science, is open to a number of important criticisms. Unlike physical scientists, social scientists cannot conduct controlled experiments on the economy. There is no way of knowing what the economy would have looked like if immigration had been prohibited or if a different immigration policy had been pursued. The analyst must address the questions raised in the debate over immigration policy by studying the imperfect data that are available.

A good example of this type of indirect inference is the way in which economists attempt to measure the impact of immigrants on the native labor market. We do not know what the earnings and employment opportunities of natives would have been in a world without immigration. Instead, we infer that if job displacement occurs, the labor market outcomes experienced by natives should be less favorable in localities in which immigrants tend to reside than in localities with relatively few immigrants. Existing data allow these types of comparisons among U.S. cities, and it is from these comparisons that we draw conclusions about the impact of immigrants on the native labor market.

Needless to say, although this methodology is useful, it is not flawless. There are many other reasons why labor market conditions for natives vary among localities. The validity of the inference thus depends on being able to control for these other factors. Throughout the study, therefore, I will note the possible problems with the underlying research, the ways in which these problems can be corrected, and the sensitivity of the findings to these corrections. This approach, I believe, informs the reader of technical weaknesses in the analysis and of the robustness of the conclusions, and it allows the reader to make his own judgment regarding the validity of the research.

The next three chapters paint a portrait of immigration in the United States. Chapter 2 begins with a brief history of American immigration policy. Chapter 3 profiles the characteristics of the typical foreign-born person residing in the United States and describes, in very broad terms, the labor market experiences of immigrants during the past five decades. Chapter 4 discusses the size and skill composition of the illegal flows that are the focus of so much concern.

The middle section of the book reviews the body of empirical research on the role immigrants play in the economy. Chapter 5 documents the impact of immigration on the earnings and employment opportunities of natives; chapter 6 analyzes how immigrant earnings are determined and how these earnings change as a result of the assimilation process; chapter 7 discusses the reasons for the sizable decline in skills among successive immigrant waves in the past two or three decades; chapter 8 reviews the impact of the changing skill composition on immigrant employment and poverty; and chapter 9 summarizes the impact of these trends on immigrant participation in the welfare system. The next two chapters analyze additional aspects of the immigrant experience: the economic importance of immigrant entrepreneurship and immigrant enclaves (chapter 10), and the role played by the family in the immigration process (chapter 11).

The final section of the book begins with a discussion of American competitiveness in the immigration market. Chapter 12 compares the foreign-born populations in the United States with the foreign-born populations in two other host countries (Australia and Canada) and documents how changes in policy and economic conditions alter the sorting of immigrant skills among host countries. Chapter 13 concludes the study by discussing the broad implications of the findings for American immigration policy.

CHAPTER 2

American Immigration Policy

THROUGH its immigration policies, the United States is an important player in the immigration market. It can prevent, restrict, or encourage the entry of certain classes of persons, and it can deport undesirable aliens. As historian E. P. Hutchinson writes in his comprehensive review of U.S. immigration policy, "The desire to pick and choose between the applicants for admission has pervaded the thinking of the immigration policy makers."[1]

The characteristics of persons who are denied entry into the United States have varied over time, in response to changes in political and economic conditions. Drastic shifts in the country's perception of the value of particular immigrant groups can occur swiftly. For instance, the 1864 Republican Party platform stated that "foreign immigration, which in the past has added so much to the wealth, development of resources, and increase of power to the nation . . . should be fostered and encouraged by a liberal and just policy."[2] Only twelve years later, the Republican Party platform recommended that "it is the immediate duty of Congress to fully investigate the effect of the immigration and importation of Mongolians upon the moral and material interests of the country," while the Democratic Party platform denounced a policy that "tolerates a revival of the coolie-trade in Mongolian women imported for immoral purposes, and Mongolian men held to perform servile labor contracts."[3]

This chapter reviews briefly the history of U.S. immigration policy and describes the existing statutes in some detail. By documenting the institutional framework in which immigration takes place, the discussion depicts key components of the U.S. offer in the immigration market. Finally, the chapter explains how changes in immigration policy, and the corresponding changes in the parameters of the U.S. offer, have had a major impact on immigration market outcomes.

U.S. Immigration Policy Before 1965

The Aliens Act of 1798 was the first attempt by the federal government to regulate immigration into the United States.[4] In this unenforced and short-lived law (it was not renewed after its two-year term), the federal government legalized the deportation of any alien deemed "dangerous" to the peace and safety of the country.

After this brief flirtation with regulation, no federal restrictions on immigration existed for nearly a century. Although some states, particularly New York and Massachusetts, tried to control the entry of immigrants through the imposition of head taxes, the Supreme Court in major decisions in 1849 and 1883 declared these taxes unconstitutional and held that Congress had sole power over the regulation of immigration.[5]

The first successful wave of restrictionism occurred in the 1870s, in response to the entry of large numbers of Chinese immigrants into the western states. Public attitudes about immigration, as reflected by the platitudes in the typical political party platforms quoted above, changed very rapidly. The intensity of the anti-Chinese feelings is evident in the 1876 California Legislature's xenophobic report on immigration:

During their entire settlement in California they have never adapted themselves to our habits, mode of dress, or our educational system, have never learned the sanctity of an oath, never desired to become citizens, or to perform the duties of citizenship, never discovered the difference between right and wrong, never ceased the worship of their idol gods, or advanced a step beyond the traditions of their native hive. Impregnable to all the influences of our Anglo-Saxon life, they remain the same stolid Asiatics that have floated on the rivers and slaved in the fields of China for thirty centuries of time.[6]

Responding to these political pressures, Congress moved to ban the entry of certain classes of persons into the United States. The first restrictions in 1875 prohibited the entry of prostitutes and convicts. In 1882, Congress suspended the immigration of Chinese laborers and added idiots, lunatics, and persons likely to become public charges to the list of "excludables." By 1917, the list included persons with tuberculosis, polygamists, political radicals, and practically all persons born in Asia. An important lesson of this experience, one that recurs throughout the history of American immigration policy, is that successful demands for immigration restrictions usually arise when the new immigrants differ from the older immigrants.

As these restrictions were enacted and the immigrant flow from Asia was completely cut off, a major change occurred in the national-origin composition of European immigrants. Traditionally, the immigrant flow had originated in northwestern European countries, such as the United Kingdom and Germany. Economic and political factors shifted the origin of the immigrant flow toward southern and eastern European countries, such as Italy, Poland, and Russia. This shift in the national-origin mix of the immigrant pool had a predictable impact on public attitudes to immigration. The new immigrants, it was argued, were not as intelligent or productive as the older "Nordic" immigrants. Francis Walker, president of the Massachusetts Institute of Technology and the first president of the American Economic Association, vividly summarized this hypothesis: the new immigrants, he wrote, "are beaten men from beaten races; representing the worst failures in the struggle for existence. . . . They have none of the ideas and aptitudes which . . . belong to those who are descended from the tribes that met under the oak trees of old Germany to make laws and choose chieftains."[7]

To address the widespread perception that something was wrong with the melting pot, for "an inconveniently large portion of the new immigration floats around in unsightly indigestible lumps," Congress enacted a series of laws in the 1920s designed to preserve the ethnic makeup of the U.S. population.[8] Thus was born the national-origins quota system.[9] The number of entry visas allocated to countries in the Eastern Hemisphere depended on their representation in the national-origin composition of the U.S. population in 1920. In particular, the fraction of visas allocated to any particular country was the same as the fraction of persons of that national origin in the U.S. population.[10] Further, Congress for the first time set a limit of 150,000 on the number of immigrants who would be admitted annually from the Eastern Hemisphere.

Because the ancestors of the great majority of U.S. residents originated in northwestern Europe, the United Kingdom was allocated 65,721 visas (almost half of all available visas) and Germany was allocated 25,957 visas, while Italy was allocated 5,802 and Russia, 2,784.[11] Little wonder that upon passage of one of the laws institutionalizing the national-origins quota system, the *Los Angeles Times* headline for April 13, 1924, read, "Nordic Victory Is Seen in Drastic Restrictions," or that President Calvin Coolidge proclaimed, "America must be kept American."[12]

These statutes began another tradition in the history of U.S. immigration policy. Countries in the Western Hemisphere were exempt from the quotas and faced no numerical restrictions on the number of visas, presumably because of the close economic and political ties between the United States and its geographic neighbors. Visas for Western Hemisphere applicants were awarded on a first-come, first-served basis as long as the persons satisfied the growing list of health, moral, and political requirements.

A review of immigration policy in the immediate postwar period led to the reaffirmation of the national-origins quota system in the Immigration and Nationality Act of 1952 (also known as the McCarran–Walter Act). In addition, the 1952 statutes included a preference system as a means of allocating quota visas among the Eastern Hemisphere applicants.[13] First preference was given to applicants whose skills were "needed urgently" in the country, and half of all visas were allocated to such persons. The remaining visas were allocated to relatives of U.S. residents.

Finally, Congress kept expanding the list of grounds on which applicants for entry could be excluded or resident aliens could be deported. By 1952, there were thirty-one possible grounds for exclusion. They included mental retardation, psychosis, drug addiction, prostitution, contagious diseases, convictions of crimes involving moral turpitude, and likelihood of becoming a public charge. Similarly, by 1952 there were eighteen possible grounds for deportation, including the eviction of persons who were excludable at the time of entry but somehow evaded the authorities, members of subversive classes, those guilty of immoral behavior, and drug addicts.

U.S. Immigration Policy Today

A mélange of laws, regulations, and private bills diminished the importance of the national-origins quota system over time. In their review of immigration policy, Elliott and Franklin Abrams conclude that "although the national origins system was theoretically the heart of American immigration policy until 1965, by the 1950s two thirds of all immigrants were being admitted under exceptions to it. The quota law had become an anachronism."[14]

The 1965 amendments to the Immigration and Nationality Act (and subsequent revisions in the immigration laws through the 1980s) are the key statutes that regulate the process of legal immigration into the United States today. Table 2.1 summarizes the main components of current law and reports the number of legal immigrants admitted in 1987 under the various provisions.

Congress passed the 1965 amendments at a time when the civil-rights movement was at its peak, and the legislation can be interpreted

TABLE 2.1

U.S. Immigration Law and Number of Immigrants Admitted in 1987

Preference	Number Admitted (in 1,000s)
Immigrants Subject to Numerical Restrictions (270,000 Visas)	
First: Unmarried adult children of U.S. citizens and their children (20 percent of visas are allocated to this category)	11.4
Second: Spouses and unmarried children of permanent resident aliens and their children (26 percent and any visas not used above)	110.8
Third: Professional or highly skilled persons and their spouses and children (10 percent)	26.9
Fourth: Married children of U.S. citizens and their spouses and children (10 percent and any visas not used above)	20.7
Fifth: Siblings of adult U.S. citizens and their spouses and children (24 percent and any visas not used above)	69.0
Sixth: Needed skilled and unskilled workers and their spouses and children (10 percent)	27.0
Nonpreference and other (visas not used above, and other special admissions)	5.4
Subtotal	271.1
Immigrants Not Subject to Numerical Restrictions	
Spouses, parents, and minor children of adult U.S. citizens	218.6
Refugees and asylees	96.5
Other	15.3
Subtotal	330.4
TOTAL	601.5

SOURCE: U.S. Immigration and Naturalization Service, *Statistical Yearbook of the Immigration and Naturalization Service, 1987* (Washington, D.C.: Government Printing Office, 1988), pp. 8–11. The numbers admitted under each provision of the law do not add up to the total because of rounding error.

as one in the series of civil-rights statutes that were enacted during that period. The bill, President Lyndon Johnson said at the signing ceremony, "repairs a deep and painful flaw in the fabric of American justice."[15] In particular, the 1965 amendments abolished the discriminatory national-origins quota system. In combination with subsequent revisions in the law, the amendments permit the entry of 270,000 persons per year, with no more than 20,000 immigrants originating in any particular country of origin.[16]

The legislation also institutionalized the humanitarian goal of family reunification as the central objective of U.S. immigration policy through several provisions. First, the preference system in the 1965 amendments (as revised by subsequent legislation) requires that 80 percent of the 270,000 numerically limited visas go to "close" relatives of U.S. citizens or residents. These close relatives include unmarried adult children of U.S. citizens, siblings of adult U.S. citizens, and spouses of resident aliens.

The remaining 20 percent of the visas are allocated to persons on the basis of their skills. It is worth noting, however, that a large number of the 54,000 visas allocated to the skill preferences are given to the families of the principals, the persons qualifying for the visa. The net impact of the kinship bias in the preference system is that in 1987 only 9 percent of the 270,000 numerically restricted visas were received by persons who qualified to enter the United States because of their skills.[17] In addition, as a result of the fifth preference, which allocates visas to brothers-in-law and sisters-in-law of adult U.S. citizens, the 1965 amendments establish a system in which the number of persons who qualify for entry into the United States will increase exponentially over time. As a congressman exclaimed during the hearings reviewing the legislation: "Don't we see now with the operation of this law that immigration per se begets immigration?"[18]

Finally, parents, spouses, and minor children of adult U.S. citizens can bypass the numerical restrictions specified in the legislation. These "immediate" relatives automatically qualify for entry into the United States and need not apply for one of the 270,000 numerically limited visas. As table 2.1 shows, more immigrants (218,600) entered under this single provision of the law than entered under all of the family-reunification preferences combined (211,900). Due to the combination of the kinship bias in the preference system and the unregulated entry available to immediate relatives, only 4 percent of the legal immigrants admitted in 1987 actually entered the United States because of their skills.[19]

It is conceivable that some of the framers of the 1965 amendments saw the family-reunification provisions as a way of preserving the status quo in the national-origin mix of the U.S. population, without having to resort to explicit racial or national-origin restrictions. Because at most 20 percent of the visas are allocated to applicants without relatives in the U.S., no major changes in the national-origin mix of the population were foreseen.

For instance, Attorney General Robert Kennedy, when asked about the prospect of Asian immigration under the 1965 amendments, responded that "it would be approximately 5,000, Mr. Chairman, after which immigration from that source would virtually disappear; 5,000 immigrants could come in the first year, but we do not expect that there would be any great influx after that."[20] Similarly, Attorney General Nicholas Katzenbach predicted that "if you look at the present immigration figures from Western Hemisphere countries there is not much pressure to come to the United States from these countries. There are in a relative sense not many people who want to come."[21]

These forecasts could not have been more wrong. They seem oblivious to the possibility that a group of persons previously prevented from immigration, such as the Asians, could use the few skill visas available to establish a beachhead and then use the family-reunification provisions to sponsor the entry of an increasing number of close and not-so-close relatives.[22] Moreover, they ignore the fact that, because immigration decisions are largely motivated by economic factors, differences in income levels between the United States and some source countries are likely to generate large migration flows (as long as immigration policy allows these flows to occur).

It is clear that the de-emphasis of skills in the awarding of entry permits and the wholesale redistribution of visas among source countries drastically altered the nature of the American offer in the immigration market. As a result, the economic impact of immigration has probably changed substantially in the past two or three decades.

Much of the debate over immigration policy in the 1980s focused on the issue of illegal immigration. The resulting legislation, the Immigration Reform and Control Act of 1986, addressed this problem and

32

did not change any important aspect of immigration policy for legal entrants. I discuss this statute, along with the problem of illegal immigration, in chapter 4.

U.S. Refugee Policy

Refugee policy is dominated by the question of who is a refugee. Is an immigrant fleeing political oppression or is he fleeing poor economic conditions?

To a great extent, the determination of refugee status and the allocation of refugee visas to applicants reflect the political environment of American foreign policy.[23] Prior to 1980, the United States defined a refugee as a person fleeing a Communist country, a Communist-dominated area, or the Middle East. The Refugee Act of 1980 redefined a refugee as someone who is residing outside his country of nationality and who is unable or unwilling to return because of a "well-founded fear of persecution on account of race, religion, nationality, membership in a particular social group, or political opinion."[24] To qualify for admission under refugee status, applicants must meet the definition of a refugee, must not be firmly resettled in any other country, and must otherwise be admissible under U.S. law.

The 1980 legislation sets an annual limit of 50,000 on the number of refugees granted admission. In fact, however, the actual number of authorized refugee entries (as well as the allocation among source regions) depends on political conditions in the source countries and in the United States and is determined each year by consultation between the President and Congress. In 1980, the influx of Southeast Asian refugees led to an authorized limit of 231,700; in 1983 to 90,000; and in 1987 to 70,000.[25]

More than 2 million permanent residents have entered the United States as refugees (or asylees) since 1946. The largest refugee flow originated in Cuba (473,000), and the second largest originated in Vietnam (411,000).[26] Refugee admissions have become increasingly important since the 1960s. The fraction of total immigration attributable to refugee admissions increased from 6 to 19 percent between the 1960s and the 1980s and is rapidly approaching the level reached immediately after World War II (25 percent), when a large flow of displaced persons entered the United States.

Admission under refugee status has certain advantages. Persons who do not have relatives in the country and who do not qualify for any of the few skill-based visas find that entering as a refugee is about the only way in which legal immigration is possible. An interesting example of this loophole in the law occurred in 1988. In recent years, more than 90 percent of the Soviet Jews leaving the USSR, upon reaching Vienna (their traditional port of entry into the West), would approach the American embassy and request asylum, a request that was ordinarily granted. This practice greatly disturbed Israeli officials, who are well aware of their country's disadvantaged position in the immigration market. As Israeli minister Ezer Weizmann puts it: "Israel is not an attractive enough country . . . so that Soviet Jews will decide to come here."[27]

To ensure "that Soviet Jews who request exit visas for Israel do in fact arrive directly in Israel," the Israeli cabinet attempted to alter the terms of its offer in the immigration market.[28] In particular, the Israeli cabinet wanted the official invitation allowing Soviet Jews to leave the USSR to stipulate that they travel to Romania, pick up the exit visa at the Israeli embassy in Bucharest, and first migrate to Israel. If these individuals wished to remigrate to the United States, they would have to approach the American embassy in Israel. Because they were already "firmly resettled" in another country and are Israeli citizens under Israel's Law of Return, the applicants could no longer claim to be refugees and would have to qualify for entry under the restrictions imposed by the 1965 amendments.

The Israeli cabinet's attempt to "encourage" Soviet Jews to migrate to Israel was not successful. Because Israel does not have diplomatic relations with the Soviet Union, the Netherlands represents Israel's interests in the USSR, and it is the Dutch embassy that issues the official exit invitations to emigrating Soviet Jews. The Dutch government was unwilling to implement the Israeli cabinet's decision and continued to issue invitations that ignored the cabinet's ruling. Emigrating Soviet Jews, therefore, still exercise their option of applying for refugee status in an American embassy, and continue to accept the American offer in the immigration market in overwhelming numbers.[29]

A second advantage of refugee status is that refugees are immediately entitled to a vast array of social services unavailable to other immigrants.[30] These services are costly. For instance, between 1981 and

1987, about $600 million per year (in 1988 dollars) were appropriated for the assistance of refugees, roughly $7,000 per refugee admitted during the period.[31] These expenditures funded the provision of cash and medical assistance, as well as English-language training and employment-related services.

U.S. Emigration Policy

The United States participates in the immigration market not only through its entry restrictions but also through its exit policies. Because no laws restrict the movement of persons trying to leave the United States, statistics on the number of emigrants are extremely hard to come by.[32]

Both U.S.-born and foreign-born persons currently residing in the United States make up the population of emigrants. There are large communities of Americans in such countries as Canada, France, Germany, and the United Kingdom. The United States competed for these individuals in the immigration market, but they perceived foreign opportunities to be better than domestic opportunities.

More relevant for this book is the fact that not every person who immigrates to the United States remains here. The emigration rate of the foreign-born is remarkably large. Recent studies suggest that 18 percent of immigrants leave the United States within a decade after their arrival and that at least 30 percent of the immigrants eventually leave.[33]

It is unlikely that these emigrants are representative members of the foreign-born population in the United States. For instance, the emigrant group may be composed mostly of persons who failed in the U.S. labor market. Alternatively, they may be persons who succeeded in the United States, who accumulated substantial wealth and capital, and who chose to "retire" in their home countries. Little is known about the socioeconomic characteristics of the emigrant population. Nevertheless, the fact that they are not typical immigrants has important implications for the assessment of the economic impact of immigration and will be discussed at length in subsequent chapters.

Changes in the National Origin of Immigrants

The redistribution of visas among source countries that was initiated by the 1965 amendments—and by changes in economic and political conditions in the source countries—led to a substantial shift in the national-origin mix of the immigrant flow entering the United States. As table 2.2 illustrates, during the Great Depression, a period in which the size of the immigration flow was at a record low, nearly two-thirds of the immigrants originated in Europe, and the remainder originated in the Western Hemisphere. By the 1950s, the fraction of persons originating in Europe had declined to about half, the percentage originating in the Americas had increased to about 40 percent, and the size of the Asian immigrant flow was no longer trivial (6 percent of the immigrants). During the 1980s, the share of Europeans declined further to 11 percent, the share of Western Hemisphere immigrants was 38 percent, and Asian countries accounted for almost half of the immigrant flow.

The dramatic change in the national origin of immigrants is perhaps best illustrated by the fact that even though German immigrants were the largest national-origin group in each decade between 1930 and 1960, by the 1970s German immigration was not sufficiently large to place it among the "top ten" flows of national-origin groups. By contrast, six of the countries in the top ten in the 1970s (the Philippines,

TABLE 2.2

Origin of Legal Immigration Flows, 1931–1986

Period	Percent of Immigrant Flow Originating in:			
	Africa	Asia	America	Europe
1931–1940	.3	3.0	30.3	65.8
1941–1950	.7	3.1	34.3	60.0
1951–1960	.6	6.1	39.6	52.7
1961–1970	.9	12.9	51.6	33.8
1971–1980	1.8	35.3	44.1	17.8
1981–1986	2.7	47.4	38.1	11.1

SOURCE: U.S. Immigration and Naturalization Service, *Statistical Yearbook of the Immigration and Naturalization Service, 1986* (Washington, D.C.: Government Printing Office, 1987), pp. 2–5; and U.S. Bureau of the Census, *Statistical Abstract of the United States, 1988* (Washington, D.C.: Government Printing Office, 1987), p. 10. The rows do not add up to 100 percent because some immigrants originated in Oceania and because the national origin of a small number of immigrants is unknown.

Korea, Vietnam, India, the Dominican Republic, and Jamaica) were not important source countries as recently as the 1950s.[34]

It is incorrect to attribute this shift in the national-origin mix of the immigrant flow solely to changes in U.S. immigration policy. Obviously, the lifting of the restrictions on immigration from Asia is responsible for *allowing* Asian migration to occur, and the cutback in the number of visas allocated to Western European countries clearly reduces the potential size of the immigrant flow from those countries. Even if visas are freely available, however, potential migrants cannot be forced to come to the United States unless they gain from the move.

For instance, even prior to the 1965 amendments, quotas allocated to some European countries went unfilled. During the first half of the 1960s, the United Kingdom was allocated more than 65,000 quota visas per year, but the annual flow averaged fewer than 28,000 persons.[35] Visas were freely available to British citizens, but there were few takers. Obviously, economic and political conditions in the countries participating in the immigration market also affect the size and national-origin mix of the immigrant flow.

The number of immigrants entering the United States is sometimes quite large relative to the population of the source countries. In other words, immigration has an important impact not only on demographic change and economic conditions in the United States, but also on demographic change and economic conditions in the source countries. As table 2.3 shows, the emigration rate, the fraction of the source country's population that migrated to the United States between 1951 and 1980, ranges from the trivially small (.03 percent for India) to the

TABLE 2.3

Rate of Emigration to the United States
Size of Immigrant Flow to the United States in 1951–1980 as a Percent of
the 1980 Population in the Country of Origin

Europe		Asia		Americas	
Germany	1.0	China	1.9	Canada	2.8
Greece	2.4	India	.03	Cuba	6.3
Italy	.9	Japan	.1	Dominican Republic	4.3
Poland	.7	Korea	.8	Jamaica	10.3
United Kingdom	1.0	Philippines	.9	Mexico	2.0

SOURCE: George J. Borjas, "Self-Selection and the Earnings of Immigrants," *American Economic Review* 77 (September 1987): 541.

37

amazingly large (10.3 percent for Jamaica).[36] A huge fraction of the population of some source countries is residing in the United States!

What factors account for these differences in the propensity of national-origin groups to migrate to the United States? Recent studies document that, to a large extent, the rate of emigration depends on the benefits and costs associated with the move.[37] In particular, countries that have relatively low per-capita incomes and that are geographically near the United States have higher emigration rates. Thus, immigration is more likely if the benefits to the move are substantial, which will be the case if the source country is relatively poor. Similarly, emigration rates are higher if the costs of immigration are small, which is more likely for nearby countries because short distances imply lower transportation costs and more reliable information about conditions in the United States.

Experience shows that government policies often do not work out the way they are intended. Immigration policy is yet another example of this proposition. After all, the 1965 amendments make it extremely difficult to obtain visas if the applicant does not already have relatives residing in this country. It would seem that the national-origin composition of the post-1965 immigrants must resemble that of the pre-1965 population.

Instead, the post-1965 period has seen a major increase in legal immigration from such countries as Mexico, Korea, and the Philippines. The framers of the 1965 amendments did not realize that we are not the only player in the immigration market. American immigration policy may set entry requirements, but persons who have better opportunities elsewhere simply will not migrate to the United States.

The improvement in economic conditions in Western Europe has clearly reduced the immigration incentives of Western Europeans, and, as we have seen, even free visas cannot convince prosperous Europeans to come here. Asians, by contrast, took advantage of the opportunity offered by the amendments. The backlog in the demand for family-reunification visas by Asians already residing in the United States, the availability of a few skill-based visas, and the economic incentives provided by the relatively low income levels of most Asian countries generated the right conditions for the immigration market to initiate the flow of large numbers of Asian immigrants soon after the 1965 amendments. After the settlement of these early immigrants, chain migrations, whereby the early migrants sponsor the migration of their relatives, began and accelerated.

The data thus indicate a dramatic shift in the nature of the U.S. offer in the immigration market. Changes in immigration policy, along with changes in economic conditions in the source countries and in the United States, have altered the competitiveness of our offer relative to the offers made by the source countries and by other host countries. Prior to 1965, because of entry costs imposed by U.S. immigration policy, immigrants in Asia, for instance, found it difficult to migrate. After 1965, as these entry costs were reduced, the number of Asian immigrants rose rapidly, and as the benefits from immigration shrank for Western Europeans, the number of these immigrants declined correspondingly.

Immigration policy is consciously used by policy makers as a way of picking and choosing among potential applicants. By raising entry costs for some classes of persons and lowering entry costs for others, the United States ensures that only certain types of persons are "recruited." Despite the best efforts of policy makers, however, the existence of other players in the immigration market implies that there is no guarantee that the actual effects of policy are the anticipated ones.

CHAPTER 3

A Statistical Portrait
of Immigrants

Because the immigration market generates a nonrandom sorting of persons among countries, the foreign-born population in the United States is likely to differ from the native-born in systematic ways. Just how different are they? Are they more or less skilled than natives? Older or younger? More or less likely to be unemployed? More or less likely to receive welfare?

This chapter uses the 1980 Census to sketch a statistical portrait of the demographic and economic characteristics of the typical immigrant in the United States and to contrast this portrait to that of natives.[1] These profiles reveal the existence of important differences and similarities in many socioeconomic characteristics between the typical immigrant and the typical native.

The data also indicate, however, that focusing solely on the average differentials between immigrants and natives obscures an important aspect of the sorting generated by the immigration market. Immigrant groups differ from each other as much as, if not more than, they differ from natives. There is substantial variation in demographic and economic characteristics among immigrants who arrived in the United States at different times and who originated in different countries. It seems that the immigration market allocates very diverse groups of people into the immigrant flow, and the distinctions among them are frequently overlooked in studies of the subject. The aggregation of immigrants over the various waves and national-origin groups that make up the total immigrant population generates a misleading portrayal of the immigrant experience.

Immigrants and Natives: A Statistical Profile

Who comes to the United States, and how do they compare to natives? The 1980 Census data reveal a number of striking differences and similarities in the socioeconomic characteristics of immigrants and natives. As table 3.1 indicates, the typical immigrant is much older than the typical native. Only 11 percent of natives are sixty-five years of age or older, but the percentage of senior citizens in the immigrant population is twice as high. Because migration decisions are made by adults, it is not surprising that immigrants tend to be older than natives. To the extent that an aging population makes more extensive use of

TABLE 3.1

Native and Immigrant Populations in 1980

	Natives	Immigrants
Personal Characteristics (Expressed in Percentage)		
Male	48.5	46.6
Aged 0–16	27.3	11.2
Aged 65 +	10.6	21.2
Educational Attainment (Percentage)		
8 years or less	14.2	33.3
16 years or more	14.5	14.5
Region of Residence (Percentage)		
East	21.3	31.8
North-central	27.1	14.8
South	34.6	20.5
West	17.0	32.9
Participation in Income-Transfer Programs (Percentage)		
On Welfare	8.0	9.1
On Social Security	25.7	31.8
Labor Force Characteristics of Men		
Percent in labor force	89.2	89.9
Percent unemployed	4.9	5.2
Percent white-collar	49.1	51.4
Percent in manufacturing	26.7	29.5
Annual hours worked	1,934	1,810
Hourly Wage rate	$9.53	$9.41

SOURCE: Author's tabulations from the 1980 Public Use Sample of the U.S. Census. The schooling data refer to the population of persons who are at least eighteen years of age. The data on participation in income-transfer programs refer to the population of households whose head is at least eighteen years old. The labor force characteristics refer to men aged twenty-five to sixty-four. All other characteristics refer to the entire populations of natives and immigrants.

social services and is more likely to receive social-insurance payments (such as Social Security), the skewed age distribution of the immigrant population could play an important role in any assessment of the long-run economic consequences of immigration.[2]

One of the central tasks of the immigration market is to sort persons of different skill levels among competing countries. The 1980 Census indicates that approximately 15 percent of both the immigrant and the native populations are college graduates. Many more immigrants, however, never even entered high school: even though only 14 percent of natives have fewer than nine years of schooling, one-third of the immigrants fall into this category.

The comparison of the schooling distributions of immigrants and natives suggests a significant bifurcation in the skills of the immigrant population.[3] The United States draws both highly educated persons and immigrants with little formal schooling. It seems that America's offer in the immigration market is profitable to these two extremes in the educational distribution. As I will show subsequently, this situation occurs because economic opportunities in the United States are attractive to college graduates originating in some source countries and to less educated workers originating in others.

Once in the United States, immigrants and natives reside in different geographic regions. While 38 percent of natives live either in the East or in the West, nearly two-thirds of immigrants live in these two regions. In fact, the degree of geographic concentration among immigrants is even more pronounced because immigrants tend to reside in a very small number of states. Even though the six states of California, New York, Texas, Florida, Illinois, and New Jersey contain only 37 percent of the U.S. population, they account for two-thirds of the immigrant population. Similarly, the twenty-five largest metropolitan areas contain only 39 percent of U.S. residents, but more than three-quarters of the immigrants.[4]

Therefore, immigrants live with other immigrants. This geographic concentration is often cited as a potential source of social conflict and economic problems. For instance, the crowding of immigrants into ethnic ghettos or enclaves may create a splintered society because immigrants have few incentives and opportunities for fully assimilating into the American economy or culture. After all, immigrants have little

42

to gain from assimilation if they work for other immigrants within the enclave or if they seldom interact economically, culturally, and socially with the American mainstream.[5]

Some observers also resent the "Third-Worldization" of many American cities. For example, Richard Lamm and Gary Imhoff observe, "The Cuban migration to Miami has created within the United States a major city that many Americans experience as culturally and socially foreign."[6] In this view, nothing less than our national identity is in jeopardy as major cities are overrun by foreigners.

The fact that immigrants reside in a relatively small number of localities also magnifies the group's impact on the native labor market. Due to their extreme geographic concentration, a 10-percent increase in the size of the immigrant flow amounts to a doubling of the immigrant population in a small number of cities. This major increase in the number of foreign workers entering the local labor market could have a significant adverse effect on the earnings and employment opportunities of natives. Moreover, the geographic concentration of immigrants may cause significant strains in the provision of social services and bloat the welfare budgets of affected areas. This is particularly true of large and unexpected refugee flows into certain metropolitan areas, such as the 1980 Mariel boatlift into Miami or the even larger influx of Southeast Asian refugees into a few California cities. For example, a study of settlement patterns of Indo-Chinese refugees reported that "more than ninety percent of refugees initially resettled into San Diego and San Francisco have been applying for public assistance within weeks after their arrival in the U.S."[7]

The 1980 Census provides information on immigrant participation in two types of income-transfer programs, public-assistance programs and the Social Security system. Public assistance includes cash receipts in such programs as Aid to Families with Dependent Children (AFDC) and Supplemental Security Income (SSI). The welfare participation rate, defined as the fraction of households that have at least one member receiving public assistance, is only slightly higher for immigrant households than for native households, 9 percent versus 8 percent. The typical immigrant household, therefore, has about as much chance of being on welfare as the typical native household. Immigrant households, however, are much more likely to have a family member participating in the Social Security system. This result is not unexpected because, as noted above, the fraction of persons aged sixty-five or over is substantially higher in the immigrant population.

Perhaps the most surprising insight provided by the statistical profile is that the labor market characteristics of immigrant men are often similar to those of native men. Both groups generally have the same labor force participation and unemployment rates, though immigrant men work about 120 fewer hours per year than natives. In addition, roughly the same numbers of immigrants and natives are employed in white-collar jobs and in manufacturing. Even more remarkable, the hourly wage rate of immigrants is $9.41 while that of natives is $9.53, a difference of only 1 percent. With the exception of hours of work, the statistical profile suggests that the study of differences between the labor market characteristics of immigrant and native men is hardly worth the effort.

The statistical profile presented here (along with the discussion throughout the book) focuses on the labor market experiences of immigrant and native men. A similar contrast can be made between immigrant and native women. This comparison would reveal that immigrant women are less likely to be in the labor force and are slightly more likely to be unemployed than native women. But it is well known that female labor supply is strongly affected by the family's fertility decisions.[8] Men tend to stay in the labor force throughout their entire working lives. Many women, by contrast, are likely to withdraw temporarily from the labor force when they reach their child-raising years. Therefore, it is difficult to infer anything from the differentials in the labor market experiences of immigrant and native women without conducting a companion study of immigrant fertility behavior, a topic that would carry the discussion far beyond the purview of this book.[9]

Differences Among Immigrant Waves

Although it is common to think of immigrants as if they were members of a homogeneous community, the immigrant population in the United States consists of many different groups. In fact, the very existence of an immigration market suggests that the immigrant population will not be a single, monolithic unit. After all, the attractiveness of the U.S. offer fluctuates over time, as changes occur in political and economic conditions here and abroad. Moreover, the offer will not seem equally lucrative to potential migrants in all source countries. The types of persons who find the offer attractive in one country differ from those who find it attractive in another. Therefore, there will exist substantial differences in skills and demographic characteristics among the various waves or cohorts and among the national-origin groups that make up the immigrant population.

The aggregation of immigrants over these groups can lead to a misleading statistical portrait because the aggregation smooths out differences within the immigrant population and obscures potentially important distinguishing features among many immigrant groups and natives. For example, the result that immigrant and native men have essentially the same wage rate may be nothing but a statistical fiction in the data. It is possible that some immigrant groups earn much more than natives, while others earn much less. By coincidence, the pooling of high-wage and low-wage immigrant groups may lead to an average wage similar to that of natives.

As shown in table 3.2, one major source of variation within the immigrant population is that immigrants enter the United States at different points in time. In the 1980 Census cross-section, a snapshot of the United States as of 1980, the various immigrant cohorts differ substantially in their demographic and economic characteristics. For instance, recent immigrant waves contain more college graduates but also contain more persons who never entered high school. The bifurcation of the schooling distribution of the immigrant population is becoming more pronounced over time.

The increase in the number of less educated immigrants is unexpected because there has been an upward drift in education levels among successive generations. That is, persons born in the 1950s have more schooling than persons born in the 1940s, who in turn have more schooling than persons born in the 1930s. This "inflation" in educational attainment among generations should presumably lead to the most recent (and younger) immigrant cohorts reporting higher schooling levels than earlier cohorts. The fact that the 1980 data do not support this conjecture indicates that, at least in terms of educational

TABLE 3.2

Differences Among Immigrant Waves as of 1980

	Year of Immigration		
	1950–1959	1965–1969	1975–1979
Personal Characteristics (Expressed in Percentage)			
Male	45.4	46.5	51.0
Aged 0–16	0	11.1	27.8
Aged 65+	12.3	5.3	3.1
Educational Attainment (Percentage)			
8 years or less	25.0	29.5	29.4
16 years or more	15.7	16.6	18.3
Region of Residence (Percentage)			
East	31.7	34.0	22.6
North-central	19.1	11.6	13.2
South	18.7	22.8	22.3
West	30.4	37.1	42.0
Labor Force Characteristics of Men			
Percent in labor force	92.2	93.9	83.5
Percent unemployed	4.3	4.9	6.7
Annual hours worked	1,912	1,862	1,614
Hourly wage rate	$10.33	$9.36	$7.87

SOURCE: Author's tabulations from the 1980 Public Use Sample of the U.S. Census. The schooling data refer to the population of persons who are at least eighteen years of age. The labor force characteristics refer to men aged twenty-five to sixty-four. All other characteristics refer to the entire population of immigrants.

attainment, recent immigrant waves are quite different from earlier waves. In particular, the new immigration is relatively less educated than the old. This finding hints at one of the major results of this book: changes in the immigration market have led to a steady deterioration in the skill composition of successive immigrant waves in recent years. Put differently, the U.S. offer in the immigration market has become increasingly attractive to more unskilled workers in the past two or three decades.

Once in the United States, recent immigrants make different residential choices from those of earlier immigrants. Recent immigrants are more likely to reside in the West and less likely to reside in the East. This shift in the residential location of immigrant cohorts is largely due to the changing national-origin mix of the immigrant flow. Immigrants from Mexico and Asia (who tend to dominate the recent flow) are more likely to settle in the Southwest or in California than in the northeastern states, which were the traditional destinations of earlier immigrant waves.

Finally, the 1980 Census documents dramatic differences in the labor market experiences of immigrants among the various waves. Recently arrived immigrant men have lower labor force participation rates, have higher unemployment rates, work fewer hours, and have lower wage rates than earlier immigrants.

The differences in the labor market characteristics of the various immigrant cohorts are sizable. The typical immigrant man in the 1975–1979 cohort earns almost eight dollars per hour, while his counterpart in the 1965–1969 cohort earns more than nine dollars per hour. This wage differential, along with the fact that the earlier cohort works 250 more hours per year than the more recent one, leads to a $5,000 differential in annual earnings. Recall that, as reported in table 3.1, the average immigrant man has a wage that is similar to that of the average native. The disaggregation by immigrant cohort clearly shows that this similarity is extremely misleading. In fact, the labor market experiences of many immigrant groups differ markedly from those of natives.

There are two reasons why, in the 1980 Census cross-section, the labor market characteristics of persons who immigrated in the late 1970s differ from those of immigrants who arrived earlier. The first is that productivity growth and some assimilation into the American labor market unavoidably take place as a cohort ages, as its members learn about the United States and the way the American labor market works, and as ties to the "old country" are weakened.[10] This process of labor market assimilation or adaptation implies that earlier immigrant waves are more likely to be in the labor force, are less likely to be unemployed, and are more likely to have higher wages.

An alternative reason is that the types of persons who chose to migrate to the United States in the 1950s are not necessarily the same, in terms of the relevant demographic and skill characteristics, as the types of persons who chose to immigrate in the late 1970s.[11] In other words, the skill sorting of persons among countries implied by conditions in the immigration market in the 1950s does not have to be the same as that implied by conditions in the late 1970s. Recent immigrant waves originate in different source countries, are admitted under different immigration policies, and choose from a different set of options.

47

Because the attractiveness of America's offer in the immigration market changes over time, there is no reason to suspect that the skill composition of the immigrant flow remained constant over the postwar period. Therefore, the various immigrant cohorts probably differ in fundamental ways, and these differentials create substantial variation within the immigrant population.

Of course, both of these factors are likely to be empirically important. Because earlier cohorts are more likely to have assimilated, and because earlier cohorts are also likely to contain different kinds of persons, it is impossible to read across the columns in table 3.2 and determine which explanation best fits the data.[12] Why is it that recently arrived immigrants earn less than earlier immigrants? The assimilation story would say that the earlier cohort accumulated useful skills over time and hence was able to "move up the ladder." The story that stresses differences in the skill sorting among immigrant cohorts would say that, due to changes in America's offer in the immigration market, skilled persons were much more likely to immigrate in the 1950s than in the 1970s. The statistical profile summarized in table 3.2 says simply that different immigrant waves are different. The cross-section data do not say *why* they are different.

Trends in Immigrant Skills

The 1980 Census cross-section hints at the possibility that recent immigrant waves differ in fundamental ways from earlier waves. To what extent did changing conditions in the immigration market alter the skill composition of immigrants entering the United States? A historical overview of the trends in the skills and labor market experiences of successive immigrant flows over the past five decades reveals that the new immigrants differ substantially from the old.

The data underlying this conclusion are drawn from four of the five decennial censuses conducted between 1940 and 1980 (the 1950 Census does not contain the data needed to carry out the analysis). Each of the decennial censuses allows the comparison of the characteristics of natives with those of the most recent immigrant wave, persons who immigrated to the United States in the five-year period prior to the census. For example, the 1940 Census allows the comparison between natives and immigrants who arrived between 1935 and 1939, the 1960 Census allows the comparison between natives and immigrants who arrived between 1955 and 1959, and so on.

The contrast among successive immigrant waves illustrates the impact of changing conditions in the immigration market on the skills of immigrants attracted by the U.S. offer. Because all of these waves have been in the United States for the same length of time (less than five years), they are all at similar stages of the assimilation process. The comparison of the demographic and skill characteristics among these waves, unlike the comparison that uses a single census cross-section, is not contaminated by the assimilation process and documents how the various waves differed at the time they entered the United States.

Figure 3.1 summarizes the historical trends in educational attainment, labor force participation rates, unemployment rates, hours worked per year, and hourly wage rates for native men and for the successive waves of immigrant men. These trends provide an unambiguous and striking insight: the gap between the skills and labor market characteristics of immigrants and natives is growing over time.

In 1940, the typical immigrant who had just arrived in the United States had nearly one more year of schooling than the typical native. This educational advantage narrowed over time, so that by 1970 the typical immigrant who had just entered the United States had roughly the same schooling as natives. The decline in the relative schooling of immigrants accelerated during the 1970s: the most recent immigrant wave enumerated in the 1980 Census had nearly one year of schooling less than natives. Soon after the 1965 amendments, therefore, the educational attainment of the immigrant flow, relative to natives, began to drop precipitously.

Higher educational attainment is associated with higher earnings.[13] If an additional year of schooling increases earnings by about 5 to 10 percent, the growing education gap between immigrants and natives would alone lead to a 5- to 10-percent decline in the relative immigrant wage in the past twenty years.

As figure 3.1 also shows, trends in a number of labor market charac-

FIGURE 3.1

New Immigrants Versus Natives in the Labor Market, 1940–1980

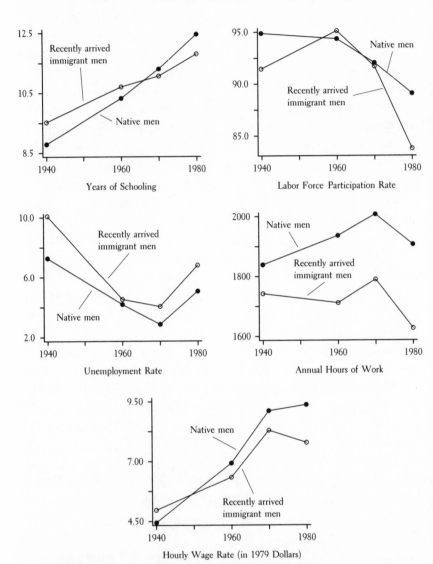

Hourly Wage Rate (in 1979 Dollars)

SOURCE: Author's tabulations from the Public Use Samples of the 1940, 1960, 1970, and 1980 U.S. Censuses. The statistics refer to the population of men aged twenty-five to sixty-four. The recent immigrant wave includes persons who migrated to the Unites States in the five-year period prior to the census. The unemployment rate is calculated in the sample of labor force participants, and the average hours of work and hourly wage rates are calculated in the sample of workers.

teristics reinforce the conclusion that the new immigrants are less skilled and less successful in the United States. For instance, the labor force participation rate of natives declined from about 95 percent in 1940 to about 89 percent in 1980.[14] The decline observed in the participation rate among successive immigrant waves is much larger. In 1940, toward the end of the Great Depression, recent immigrants had participation rates that were only 3 percentage points below those of natives. This differential vanishes in the 1960 Census (when recent immigrants actually had higher participation rates than natives) but reappears soon after the 1965 amendments. By 1980, the typical recent immigrant had a labor force participation rate that was 6 percentage points below that of natives.

Trends in the unemployment rate and annual hours of work tell the same story. In 1940, the unemployment rate of recent immigrants was about 3 percentage points higher than that of natives. The unemployment rate differential between the two groups vanishes by 1960 but again becomes sizable (almost two-thirds of the Great Depression differential) in 1980. Similarly, recent immigrants in 1940 worked about 100 fewer annual hours than natives, while recent immigrants in 1980 worked about 300 fewer hours.

The comparison of wage rates between natives and successive immigrant waves is perhaps the most revealing. In 1940, the most recent immigrant wave actually had about 13 percent *higher* wage rates than natives. By 1960, immigrants earned 8 percent less than natives. This wage disadvantage increased to about 10 percent in 1970 and to 17 percent in 1980.

These trends provide irrefutable evidence of a significant deterioration in the skill level and labor market performance of successive immigrant waves in the postwar period. Changing conditions in the immigration market over the past few decades, therefore, apparently led to a major decline in the skill level of the people who choose to immigrate to the United States. In short, the new immigrants are less skilled than the old.

Several questions of fundamental importance for U.S. immigration policy are raised by this finding. First, why did the decline in the skills of the immigrant flow occur? In other words, what changes in the parameters of America's offer in the immigration market are responsible for the deteriorating skills of immigrants? Second, are the declining skills among successive immigrant waves beneficial or harmful to the U.S. economy? Third, should the parameters of America's offer be changed to attract a more skilled immigrant flow, and if so, how? The subsequent chapters present a systematic analysis of these important questions.

Differences Among National-Origin Groups

There also exist substantial differences in demographic characteristics and labor market outcomes among the national-origin groups that make up the immigrant population. Such diverse factors as the source country's culture, political system, stage of economic development, and distance from the United States are likely to affect the potential migrant's perception of America's offer in the immigration market. Thus, it is not surprising that the United States is likely to attract different kinds of persons from different source countries. In table 3.3, I illustrate the extent of this variation for five selected countries: Canada, Korea, Mexico, the Philippines, and the United Kingdom. All of these countries were major sources of immigration in the postwar period, and they represent the various ethnic or racial groups that make up the bulk of the immigrant flow.

Not surprisingly, there is substantial variation in educational attainment among national-origin groups. Mexican immigrants have the lowest educational attainment: only 3 percent have a college diploma, and nearly two-thirds lack any high school education. Other national-origin groups, however, have much higher schooling levels than U.S. natives. For instance, even though only 15 percent of natives have a college diploma, more than one-third of the immigrants originating in the Philippines have one.

This result is particularly important because the native populations of Mexico and the Philippines have roughly the same educational attainment. The average schooling level in both of these countries is between six and eight years.[15] The persons who choose to migrate to the United States from these countries, therefore, are drawn from

TABLE 3.3
Demographic Characteristics of Different National-Origin Groups in 1980

	Country of Birth				
	United Kingdom	Korea	Philippines	Canada	Mexico
Personal Characteristics (Expressed in Percentage)					
Male	38.4	40.2	46.5	41.6	52.5
Aged 0–16	6.8	27.6	14.3	6.5	18.3
Aged 65+	29.3	2.8	11.0	29.2	7.5
Educational Attainment (Percentage)					
8 years or less	13.1	12.5	18.1	18.4	63.7
16 years or more	15.1	28.7	36.5	13.7	2.6
Region of Residence (Percentage)					
East	32.9	19.4	10.9	32.2	.8
North-central	16.6	17.6	11.3	18.5	10.0
South	21.0	19.0	11.1	16.2	24.3
West	29.6	44.0	66.6	33.1	64.9
Participation in Income-Transfer Programs (Percentage)					
On Welfare	5.4	6.3	10.3	6.2	12.7
On Social Security	41.0	5.3	20.2	41.5	15.1
Labor Force Characteristics of Men					
Percent in labor force	92.0	90.1	92.4	87.7	92.1
Percent unemployed	2.9	3.3	3.3	3.8	7.7
Annual hours worked	1,990	1,715	1,762	1,941	1,739
Hourly wage rate	$12.19	$12.81	$9.89	$11.18	$7.03

SOURCE: Author's tabulations from the 1980 Public Use Sample of the U.S. Census. The schooling data refer to the population of persons who are at least eighteen years of age. The data on participation in income-transfer programs refer to the population of households whose head is at least eighteen years old. The labor force characteristics refer to men aged twenty-five to sixty-four. All other characteristics refer to the entire population of immigrants of each national-origin group.

different parts of the educational distribution. It seems that the U.S. offer in the immigration market is particularly attractive to unskilled persons originating in Mexico, but at the same time is particularly attractive to highly educated persons originating in the Philippines. It will be seen later that differences in the returns to education among source countries, relative to the returns available in the U.S. labor market, are responsible for this difference in skill composition among national-origin groups.

The various national-origin groups generally live in different areas. For instance, Mexican and Filipino immigrants tend to reside in the West, while British and Canadian immigrants tend to reside in the

East. Immigrants are not only "crowded" into relatively small number of areas, but the national origin of immigrants differs markedly among these few localities.

Because the skill composition of the immigrant population is so different among national-origin groups, it is not surprising to find corresponding differences in the welfare participation rates of the groups. About 13 percent of Mexican and (despite their high educational attainment) 10 percent of Filipino immigrant households are on welfare; but only 5 or 6 percent of Canadian or British households receive public assistance. Immigrant households in some national-origin groups, therefore, are much more likely to be welfare recipients than native households.

There is also significant divergence among national-origin groups in their participation in the Social Security program. Immigrant households originating in Canada or the United Kingdom, which typically arrived in earlier waves and are therefore composed of older persons, are more likely to receive Social Security income than other national-origin groups, and than native households.

Finally, there is variation in labor market characteristics among national-origin groups. The labor force participation rates range from a low of 88 percent for immigrants originating in Canada to a high of 92.4 percent for immigrants originating in the Philippines. The unemployment rate ranges from 3 to 8 percent; annual hours of work range from 1,700 to nearly 2,000 hours; and the hourly wage rate ranges from seven dollars to thirteen. Clearly, an immigrant's experience in the U.S. labor market is strongly influenced by his national origin.

Because national-origin groups differ in their skills and labor market experiences, and because the national-origin mix of the immigrant flow has changed in the past two or three decades, there is an obvious link between the redistribution of entry visas among source countries and the changes in immigrant skills observed in recent years. The exact nature of this link—which is related to the fact that different national-origin groups perceive the profitability of America's offer in the immigration market differently—will be discussed at length in subsequent chapters.

Immigrants differ from natives and from one another. The statistical profiles summarized in this chapter reveal that there is no such thing as a "typical" immigrant. The demographic characteristics and economic well-being of immigrants vary widely among immigrant waves and national-origin groups. The immigration market, therefore, does not always lead to the same sorting of immigrants to the United States. Instead, it leads to the movement of flows that have very diverse skill and demographic characteristics.

CHAPTER 4

Illegal Aliens:
The Black Market
for Immigrants

THE DEBATE over immigration policy in the past decade has been dominated by questions about the size, composition, and economic impact of the illegal-alien population. The realization that the United States had lost control over its southern border led to the enactment of the Immigration Reform and Control Act of 1986 (IRCA). The main objective of this legislation is to stop the flow of illegal aliens. It is still too early to provide even a preliminary appraisal of the legislation's effectiveness. It is not too late, however, to review what we know about the illegal-alien population and to determine whether the intense concern devoted to this group of immigrants is justified.

How many illegal aliens are there, who are they, and what role do they play in the U.S. economy? The very nature of the illegal-alien population implies that the answers to all of these questions are elusive. Nevertheless, existing data portray a picture of the illegal-alien population quite different from the stereotype. The typical illegal alien is not a young, single Mexican man easily exploited by his agricultural employer. Instead, the typical illegal alien is about as likely to be non-Mexican as Mexican; about as likely to be a woman as a man. Most are permanently settled in the United States and reside with immediate family members; most are not employed in agriculture; and most face the same labor market opportunities as demographically comparable legal immigrants.

Participating in the Black Market

Whenever government regulations prevent individuals from voluntarily exchanging goods and services, incentives arise to create black markets for these goods and services. For instance, although the purchase of controlled substances or sex is illegal, consumer demand for these goods and services does not disappear simply because the government disapproves of such consumption activities. The demand persists and, if someone is willing to provide the goods and services at the right price, exchanges continue to take place in the black market.

Of course, governments often attempt to prevent such transactions, usually by punishing individuals caught conducting them. Such penalties as fines and incarceration increase the costs associated with black-market transactions for both buyers and sellers. As long as the costs associated with unlawful behavior are not prohibitively high, however, many individuals on both sides of the market find it worthwhile to incur the risk of detection, so they participate in the black market for the illegal goods and services.

The immigration market is no different. Immigration policy prohibits the entry of some classes of persons. Despite these restrictions, many persons in the affected groups still wish to migrate to the United States. Clearly, the entry restrictions increase immigration costs. Individuals may get caught crossing the border, or, even if they make it through, they may have to live like fugitives. There is always a possibility that the INS will catch up with them, disrupt their lives, make them lose their jobs, and deport them and their families. These costs clearly reduce the incentives of individuals to migrate illegally. But immigration will still occur as long as the economic benefits outweigh the costs. Legal or not, some potential migrants are still willing to offer their services, some employers are willing to hire these individuals, and exchanges are made.

The existence of a black market for immigrants and the size of this marketplace thus depend on the costs and benefits associated with unlawful behavior.[1] For instance, if economic opportunities are much better in the United States than in Mexico, many Mexicans perceive that there are substantial gains to be made by becoming illegal aliens and entering the black market. In 1984, the per capita gross national

57

product in the United States was eight times greater than per capita GNP in Mexico. In fact, even after netting out the costs associated with illegal immigration, such as transportation costs to the U.S. border and payments to "coyotes" (experienced guides who assist the illegal aliens across the border and lower the probability of detection), the wage differential between the two countries remains very high. It has been estimated that a person originating in a rural Mexican town can increase his income by 300 percent even after accounting for immigration costs.[2]

These significant economic incentives are reinforced by the relatively trivial penalties associated with illegal behavior both for illegal aliens and for firms hiring them. Until IRCA, firms participating in the black market for immigrants were not subject to penalties for their actions. Even though it was illegal for some persons to be in the United States and for these persons to work, firms were free to hire illegal aliens. Furthermore, deportation is the only penalty imposed on aliens caught participating in the black market, both before and after IRCA. The immigrant, of course, can attempt to reenter the United States whenever it is convenient and, if caught once more, try yet another time.

The existence and persistence of a black market for immigrants implies that *all* parties participating in these exchanges benefit from these voluntary transactions. Ineffective regulations, weak enforcement of existing laws, and sizable differentials in economic opportunities are all that is required for a black market to flourish.

Illegal Immigration from Mexico

Who is an illegal alien? Many illegal aliens are persons who lack the necessary documents for legal entry (a passport and visa) and who enter the United States by avoiding a border inspection. The INS refers to these individuals as EWIs, for "entry without inspection." Mexicans sneaking across the border in order to avoid detection by the Border Patrol are EWIs in action.

Persons who did have legal travel documents upon entry, but who remained in the United States after their visas expired, are a second major source of illegal immigration. These are "visa abusers" because they violated the conditions that permitted their initial entry. As it is much harder to swim across the Pacific or Atlantic than across the Rio Grande, persons originating in most source countries find it difficult to be EWIs. Instead, the typical illegal immigrant from these distant countries enters the United States by first obtaining a student or visitor's visa and then staying beyond the time permitted. The illegal immigrant flow, therefore, can originate in any country in the world, and in fact there is substantial evidence (presented below) that illegal immigration from other countries is almost as large as that from Mexico.

Nevertheless, the main focus of concern has been and remains illegal immigration from Mexico. Most of this chapter, therefore, reviews the available evidence describing the characteristics of the undocumented Mexican population. This focus is not meant to minimize the importance of illegal-immigrant flows originating in other parts of the world, but simply reflects the fact that more is known about Mexican illegal aliens than about other components of the illegal population.

The latest wave of illegal immigration from Mexico began in the late 1960s, after the discontinuation of the bracero program. This program was launched in 1942, when the U.S. and Mexican governments agreed to allow the temporary migration of agricultural workers from Mexico due to a labor shortage caused by World War II. In various guises, the program continued until 1964, when it was unilaterally ended by the United States. The main reason for the discontinuation was the undocumented presumption that the bracero program depressed the wages of native Americans in the agricultural industry.[3]

As figure 4.1 illustrates, there is a clear link between the end of the bracero program and the beginning of the illegal alien flow. The number of Mexican illegal aliens apprehended (an "apprehension" is defined as the arrest of a deportable alien by the Border Patrol) began to increase soon after the bracero program ended and peaked in 1986, when 1.7 million Mexican and 96,000 non-Mexican illegal aliens were apprehended. Data from the INS indicate that almost all of the Mexican-born immigrants who were apprehended were EWIs, but that only two-thirds of the non-Mexican aliens were EWIs (and most of them originated in Central America).[4]

What factors account for this major increase in the number of illegal

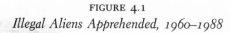

FIGURE 4.1

Illegal Aliens Apprehended, 1960–1988

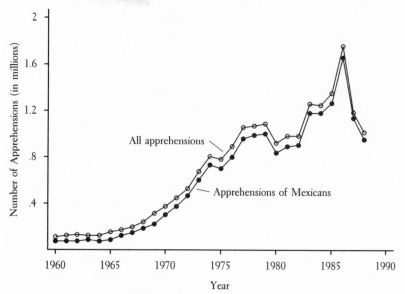

Source: U.S. Immigration and Naturalization Service, *Statistical Yearbook of the Immigration and Naturalization Service* (Washington, D.C.: Government Printing Office, annual).

aliens apprehended? It seems sensible to presume that the number of apprehensions reflects, to some extent, the size of the underlying pool of persons trying to enter the United States surreptitiously. In view of the upward trend in the number of apprehensions, this assumption suggests a large increase in the size of the illegal-alien flow since 1964. Even though it is clear that the end of the bracero program helped initiate the illegal flow, it cannot explain its continuing growth. After all, the bracero program was discontinued a quarter-century ago, yet the number of apprehensions rose rapidly during the 1980s and only began to decline in 1987, after the enactment of IRCA.

It turns out that the number of apprehensions is very sensitive to economic conditions in both the United States and Mexico.[5] Generally, fewer illegal aliens are apprehended when economic conditions in Mexico improve. In years in which the Mexican wage level is relatively high, or Mexico's unemployment rate is relatively low, the number of apprehensions drops, which presumably implies that fewer Mexicans attempted to enter the United States unlawfully in those years. Alternatively, when conditions in the U.S. economy improve, the number of apprehensions rises: increases in the U.S. wage level and decreases in the U.S. unemployment rate increase the number of illegal aliens apprehended. Further, the number of apprehensions is very sensitive to the prices of agricultural products in Mexico and in the United States. More illegal aliens are apprehended when conditions in the U.S. agricultural sector improve relative to those in Mexico. Thus, the flow of farm workers goes to whichever agricultural region offers relatively better economic opportunities. The evidence, therefore, implies that fluctuations in the number of apprehensions, which is presumably a proxy for the size of the illegal flow, partly reflect differences in economic opportunities between the two countries.

Of course, the number of apprehensions also depends on the effort made by the Border Patrol to detect the trespassers. It has been estimated that a doubling of the Border Patrol's budget doubles the number of apprehensions.[6] Not surprisingly, the more effort that is put into enforcing the law, in terms of more manpower and better equipment, the higher the number of illegal aliens caught crossing the border.

How Many Illegal Aliens Are There?

A very troubling aspect of the apprehensions data is simply the enormously large number of apprehensions carried out by the Border Patrol. In 1986, for instance, the Border Patrol apprehended a record 1.8 million persons attempting to enter the United States illegally. This amounts to 4,842 apprehensions per day, 202 apprehensions per hour, and more than 3 apprehensions per minute.

The sheer size of these numbers leads many observers to conclude that the United States is being overrun by hordes of illegal aliens. The argument usually is as follows. Suppose that for every person apprehended, a certain number of illegals actually make it through. The size of the illegal-alien population in the United States is then directly related to the number of apprehensions. For example, if one of every two illegal entrants is apprehended, 1 million apprehensions implies that 1 million persons avoided detection. After a decade of flows of this magnitude, the illegal-alien population would contain about 10 million persons.[7]

These huge magnitudes triggered much of the concern over illegal immigration in the 1970s and 1980s. It is shocking that estimates of the size of the illegal-alien population were reached in ways not much more thoughtful, and often less thoughtful, than the arbitrary procedure illustrated in the previous paragraph. For example, INS Commissioner Leonard Chapman once testified that there were 4 to 5 million illegal aliens in the United States. When asked how he had reached that conclusion, he replied: "It is just a mid-point between the two extremes. I have heard one or two million at one end of the scale and eight or ten million at the other. So, I am selecting a mid-point—just a guess, that is all."[8]

Because it responds to variations in economic opportunities, the number of apprehensions certainly reflects the size of the pool of persons attempting to enter the United States. But the use of apprehension statistics can lead to seriously misleading estimates of the size of the illegal-alien population for several reasons. First, there is probably a lot of double-counting in the data. Persons trying to cross the border from Mexico are caught and deported. Nothing prevents them from trying the same thing the next day, getting caught again, and getting deported again. The number of apprehensions keeps mounting, while the size of the potential illegal-alien flow remains unchanged.

Further, the number of apprehensions is strongly related to the level of expenditures made by the Border Patrol. Increases in the Border Patrol's budget, which lead to more officers, more helicopters, and tighter controls of the border, increase the number of apprehensions. After adjusting for inflation, the Border Patrol's budget rose by 240 percent between 1967 and 1986. Because a doubling of the Border Patrol's budget leads to twice as many apprehensions, the increase in spending accounts for more than half of the increase in the number of apprehensions during the period.[9]

Finally, estimates of the size of the illegal-alien population based on apprehension data ignore the fact that the immigration of many illegal aliens may be temporary. Some illegal aliens return to Mexico after the harvest, or return because labor market conditions in the United States deteriorate relative to those in Mexico. Because of the transient nature of the immigration for many, the number of undocumented persons residing in the United States at any point in time may be substantially lower than the number of persons who illegally entered the country prior to that time.

These caveats do not imply that apprehension data are a completely useless proxy for the size of the illegal-alien flow. The two are obviously related, but there are many other factors that influence the apprehension statistics and that must be taken into account when using these data for estimating the size of the illegal-alien population. Because it is difficult to account for these other factors, most estimates of the number of illegal aliens rely on other data sources.[10] These alternative data sources, however, are themselves not free of problems and require their own sets of assumptions in order to estimate the size of the illegal-alien population.

The best attempt to provide such an estimate is the analysis of the 1980 Census data by INS statistician Robert Warren and Bureau of the Census statistician Jeffrey Passel.[11] Their study, the results of which are summarized in table 4.1, indicates that the 1980 Census enumerated approximately 2.1 million illegal immigrants, of which slightly more than half, or 1.1 million, were born in Mexico. The significant presence of the illegal-alien population in the 1980 Census is not surprising because the Bureau of the Census made a particular effort to count persons who were missed in the 1970 census.[12]

The idea behind the Warren–Passel approach is quite simple. First of all, determine how many foreign-born persons were enumerated by

TABLE 4.1
Illegal Aliens in the 1980 Census

	Foreign-Born Persons Enumerated in the 1980 Census (in Thousands)		
	Born in Mexico	Born Elsewhere	Total
Total Census Count	2,531	11,610	14,141
Naturalized Citizens	205	5,913	6,118
Legal Aliens	1,195	4,771	5,966
Residual: Illegal Aliens	1,131	926	2,057

SOURCE: Adapted from Robert Warren and Jeffrey S. Passel, "A Count of the Uncountable: Estimates of Undocumented Aliens Counted in the 1980 United States Census," *Demography* 24 (August 1987): 377, 382.

the 1980 Census. Use INS data on the number of naturalizations and the number of legal aliens present in the country and, after adjusting these numbers for mortality and emigration of the foreign-born, estimate the number of legal aliens who should have been physically present in the United States on census day (April 1, 1980). The difference between the number of foreign-born persons actually enumerated by the census and the number who should have been counted is the number of illegal aliens.[13]

The Warren–Passel study reveals that the illegal-alien population counted by the census is not predominantly Mexican. Nearly half of the illegals originate in countries other than Mexico, with practically all of the countries that contribute to the legal immigrant flow also contributing to the illegal flow.[14] Because of the myopic concern over the illegal-alien flow originating in Mexico, therefore, the problems raised by the entry of large numbers of illegal aliens originating in other countries were neglected.

A major problem with the Warren–Passel methodology is that it only gives a count of the illegals who were enumerated by the census. The Bureau of the Census clearly missed some people, both legal and illegal residents, and the Warren–Passel estimates provide a lower bound for the size of the illegal-alien population. Nobody knows exactly what the undercount rate for this elusive population was. Thus, the number of illegal aliens residing in the United States may be much higher than the 2.1 million revealed by the 1980 Census.

Available data, however, suggest that the number of Mexican-born illegals missed by the census is relatively small. One piece of evidence is the mortality experience of Mexicans in the United States. These data indicate that 14,038 Mexican-born persons died in the United States in 1984 (the first year for which mortality data for Mexican-born persons by age is available). If the mortality rate of the Mexican-born population at every age is the same as that of the entire U.S. population, it is easy to calculate what the size of the Mexican-born population must have been in order to generate the observed number of deaths. It turns out that a population of 3 million Mexican-born persons leads to the observed number of deaths.[15] Of course, if the mortality rate of Mexicans in the United States is higher than that of Americans, a Mexican-born population of fewer than 3 million persons would account for the 14,038 deaths observed in 1984.

The Warren–Passel study indicates that the 1980 Census enumerated approximately 2.5 million Mexican-born persons residing in the United States (both legal and illegal). Even if no additional legal Mexican immigrants entered between 1980 and 1984, the census undercount of illegal aliens would have been at most half a million persons. In fact, more than 250,000 additional Mexicans entered the United States legally between 1981 and 1984, so the census undercount of the illegal-alien population is even smaller. At most, therefore, the census missed about one-half of the illegal Mexican population.

Moreover, the population counts provided by the Mexican census confirm these orders of magnitude. The study of these counts is based on the idea that if illegal immigration of men, particularly young men, to the United States is sizable, the Mexican census should reveal the presence of too few men in Mexico.[16] In other words, illegal immigration alters the sex ratio in the Mexican population (the ratio of the number of men to women at particular age groups). Because birth, mortality, and legal immigration statistics allow the estimation of what the true sex ratio should be, it is possible to determine how many persons are "missing" from the Mexican census counts. This type of analysis suggests that the number of missing persons is between 1.5 and 3.9 million.[17] It is very likely, however, that the Mexican census systematically undercounted some population groups: these missing persons may have been residing in Mexico, but simply were not enumerated by the Mexican government. Hence these estimates of the illegal-alien population are probably too high.

Therefore, there is a growing consensus among demographers that the number of illegal aliens in the United States is nowhere near the 5 to 10 million persons widely reported in the late 1970s, but is more on the order of 3 to 4 million.[18] I do not wish to suggest that the size of this population is "small": 3 or 4 million illegal aliens is not a trivial number. These numbers, however, are much lower than those carelessly thrown around in discussions of ways in which the United States should get a handle on the illegal-immigration problem.

Even though the focus of the debate over immigration policy (and of this book) is the impact of immigration on the United States, it is important to remember that the size of the illegal-migration flow must have a major impact on Mexico. In a study of the migration patterns of a small rural Mexican community, sociologists Josh Reichert and

Douglas Massey find that illegal immigration has a pervasive influence on that village.[19] Nearly 80 percent of the households in the community depend in one way or another on the fact that some family members earn wages in the United States. Because of the close political and economic ties between the two countries, it is clear that illegal immigration plays a much broader role and its impact has many more ramifications than those which dominate the American debate over immigration policy.

A Statistical Portrait of Illegal Aliens

Because large numbers of illegal aliens were enumerated in the 1980 Census, these data can be used to construct a statistical profile of the illegal-alien population. This profile reveals that illegal aliens enumerated in the 1980 Census, whether born in Mexico or elsewhere, are of relatively recent vintage. Between 40 and 50 percent of illegal aliens moved to the United States in the five-year period prior to the census, and another 25 to 30 percent arrived in the first half of the 1970s.[20]

Illegal aliens, like their legal counterparts, tend to reside in a small number of states. Half of the illegal aliens live in a single state, California, and more than 80 percent live in five states: California, New York, Texas, Illinois, and Florida. The geographic concentration of Mexican illegal aliens is even more pronounced: California has 75 percent of all Mexican illegal aliens, and Texas and Illinois each have 10 percent more.[21]

As I have mentioned before, the illegal-alien population is not predominantly male, and it is not dominated by a particular age group. Among Mexican illegal aliens, for instance, only 55 percent of the illegals are men, and only 34 percent are between the ages of fifteen and twenty-four. Similarly, among non-Mexican illegal aliens, 51 percent of the population is male and only 26 percent are between the ages of fifteen and twenty-four. Therefore, there is little evidence to suggest that the illegal-alien population, whether Mexican or otherwise, is dominated by young men.[22]

Perhaps the most surprising fact about the Mexican-born immigrant population is that it is not composed of single individuals living on their own or with unrelated persons. Most Mexican immigrants enumerated in the 1980 Census live in households with immediate relatives, where an immediate relative includes a spouse, a child, or a parent. Nearly 75 percent of all Mexican noncitizens, 73 percent of the recently arrived noncitizens, and even 65 percent of recently arrived noncitizen men are living with their immediate families.[23] Because a large fraction of these populations consists of illegal aliens, these results imply that most Mexican illegal aliens enumerated in the 1980 Census reside with their families. To the extent that immigrants living with their families should be viewed as relatively permanent migrants, the evidence suggests that most Mexican illegal aliens had settled in the United States even prior to the amnesty program initiated by IRCA.

Finally, Mexican immigrants are not predominantly employed in agriculture. For instance, only 15 percent of the Mexican noncitizen men enumerated in the 1980 Census and only 16 percent of the recently arrived noncitizens work in the agricultural industry.[24] Because these populations presumably contain a relatively large number of undocumented workers, the evidence suggests that the Mexican illegal-alien population is much more integrated into the U.S. economy than is commonly thought.

Data on the characteristics of the illegal population are also available from a number of studies that document the migration experiences of persons residing in selected rural villages in Mexico. Using a recent survey of four such communities, Douglas Massey compares the demographic and labor market characteristics of persons who had, at some point in the past, migrated to the U.S. legally with those of illegal aliens.[25] As table 4.2 indicates, the characteristics of legal and illegal immigrants originating in these rural communities are far from similar. The average U.S. hourly wage of an illegal alien was $5.98, while that of a legal immigrant was $9.54. Illegal aliens, moreover, are younger, are less proficient in English, and have much less experience on their U.S. job than legal immigrants. It is also interesting to note that both legal and illegal aliens have strong family links with U.S. residents. In both populations, more than 60 percent of the migrants had a family member residing in the United States. Finally, the survey shows that

TABLE 4.2
Legal and Illegal Mexican Immigrants
Originating in Four Rural Communities, 1982–1983

	Legal Migrants	Illegal Migrants
Average U.S. wage rate	$ 9.54	$ 5.98
Average age	32.9	28.7
Percent with family ties in U.S.	60	63
Percent that understands English	46	24
Percent with at least six years of schooling	32	40
Percent farm workers	53	60
Average years on U.S. job	4.5	1.4

SOURCE: Douglas S. Massey, "Do Undocumented Migrants Earn Lower Wages than Legal Immigrants? New Evidence from Mexico," *International Migration Review* 21 (Summer 1987): 255. The sample contains 323 observations, of which 72 percent are illegal immigrants.

even among immigrants originating in these rural communities, between 40 and 50 percent of the immigrants did not work in agricultural jobs.[26]

Other surveys of the Mexican population compare the illegal aliens not to legal Mexican immigrants or native Americans, but to Mexican residents who decide not to migrate. This comparison is crucial because it indicates the type of self-selection that generates the illegal flow.

A recent study by economist J. Edward Taylor presents such an analysis.[27] Using a survey of approximately 400 persons residing in a rural Mexican town, Taylor determined that approximately 14 percent of the individuals in the sample had been to the United States illegally in the previous calendar year (and then returned to Mexico). His data indicated that a few demographic characteristics differentiated which villagers became illegal aliens and which decided to remain in Mexico. The most important of these characteristics was whether the individual had family ties with U.S. residents. The presence of a family member in the United States increased the probability of an individual becoming an illegal alien by 50 percent. In addition, if the individual had been in the United States previously, the probability of migrating illegally increased by an additional 7 percent. In short, familiarity with the United States either through family or through personal experience, is a key determinant in the decision to become an illegal alien.

Taylor's study also found that illegal aliens typically belonged to households that were not relatively successful in the Mexican economy. The illegal flow, at least from this small rural village, was composed *not* of the most successful persons in the Mexican labor market, but of the least successful. To the extent that this result can be generalized to the entire Mexican illegal population, it suggests that illegal aliens are unskilled not only relative to the native U.S. population, but also relative to the Mexican population.

As noted earlier, the sorting generated by the immigration market need not lead to the United States attracting the most skilled and most productive workers in the source country. Instead, the skill composition of the immigrant flow depends on which country, the source country or the United States, pays higher prices for skills. If the Mexican economy offers a higher reward for skills than the U.S. economy, the immigrant flow originating in Mexico will be composed mostly of unskilled workers. After all, these workers are the ones who find America's offer in the immigration market most attractive.

Skilled Mexicans, who are better able to afford the transportation costs to the border and the smuggling costs paid to coyotes, should find it just as easy as unskilled workers to become illegal aliens. Yet they choose not to. In the end, the skill composition of the immigrant flow is not determined by whether the migration is legal, but by the differential rewards to skills offered by countries competing in the immigration market. This point has important implications for U.S. immigration policy: legislation that raises the cost of illegal immigration, such as IRCA, can do little about the skill composition of the illegal flow. Only those persons who gain from immigrating to the United States will do so. Although IRCA makes illegal immigration more costly, it does not alter the fundamental economic incentives that motivate the immigration in the first place.

It is clear, therefore, that the typical illegal alien is not randomly drawn from the Mexican population. He tends to have personal familiarity with the United States or family ties with U.S. residents, and he tends to be relatively unsuccessful in the Mexican economy. But these comparisons, based on small samples of individuals surveyed in rural Mexican villages, may provide a very misleading view of the illegal-immigrant experience for two important reasons. First, it is unknown whether illegal aliens who originate in other villages or in urban areas share these characteristics. Second—and perhaps most important— these small surveys can only "catch" migrants who returned to Mexico. The U.S. census data suggest that a large number of illegal aliens are permanently settled in the United States, reside with immediate relatives, and presumably have little intention of returning to Mexico (even prior to the amnesty program). It is reasonable to suspect that these permanent immigrants differ substantially from the transitory illegals who returned to Mexico. Unfortunately, nothing is known about ways in which the temporary migrants differ from the permanent settlers.

Who Hires Illegal Aliens?

The other major players in the black market for immigrants are the firms that hire illegal aliens. If penalties are absent (which was the case prior to IRCA), firms have no incentive to differentiate by legal status in their hiring decision. As long as workers are equally productive and are willing to work for the going wage (or lower), firms will hire whoever applies for a job. Which firms hire illegal aliens? What kinds of products do they produce? What kinds of services do they perform?

Every time an illegal alien is apprehended, the INS fills out a Record of Deportable Alien form. This form contains demographic characteristics of the alien (such as age, sex, and national origin), as well as the name and address of the alien's employer. This information was recently used by economist Barry Chiswick to conduct a survey of employers known to hire illegal aliens in the Chicago area (as these firms had been identified by the apprehended illegals).[28] He then contrasted the characteristics of these employers to those of a randomly chosen sample of Chicago firms.

Chiswick's analysis indicates that firms hiring illegal aliens tend to be larger, are more likely to be in the restaurant industry, and are more likely to be in industries with patterns of seasonal employment. It seems that certain types of employers demand the kinds of skills that illegal aliens have and are willing to offer. Hence a good match between illegal aliens looking for work and employers willing to hire them is struck in the black market. All of the participants in the transactions gain from participating in this marketplace.

An interesting aspect of the Chiswick study is that employers who hired illegal aliens were interviewed by the research team under the pretense that the survey would analyze "the hiring needs and practices of employers in different types of industries, and that the employers had been randomly selected."[29] In other words, employers did not have a clue that they had been included in the survey because the INS had apprehended one of their employees. During the interview, employers were asked if they thought it was legal to hire someone without a documented visa. More than 70 percent of the employers who hired illegal aliens thought it was illegal "knowingly [to] hire an immigrant who does not have a visa permitting him or her to work," even though it was perfectly legal to do so at the time.[30] Prior to IRCA, therefore, many employers already thought that hiring undocumented workers was illegal. Unfortunately, the survey does not indicate whether employers knew they were hiring illegal aliens, but it does raise serious doubts about IRCA's potential effectiveness in stopping the illegal flow.

This type of research, important as it is, uses a nonrandom sample of illegal aliens and firms. Employers are detected only if illegal aliens are apprehended. Which types of aliens are apprehended? It is likely that the illegals apprehended in a city like Chicago, which is far away from any problem border area, differ substantially from the many illegal immigrants living in Chicago who avoid detection. Unfortunately, nothing is known about ways in which the apprehended illegal aliens differ from those who consistently manage to evade the authorities.

Do American Employers Exploit Illegal Aliens?

There are many reasons why the illegal flow is considered to be a bad thing for the United States. One is the often heard claim that American employers exploit illegal aliens. Because undocumented workers are obviously concerned about being detected, they lack access to the regulatory institutions that protect the rights of workers. Firms take advantage of this situation and pay illegal aliens lower wages than they would pay equally qualified workers with legal work permits. The point is forcefully made by economist Vernon Briggs:

The alien workers are also frequently victimised by employers who know of their vulnerability to detection. Accounts of alien workers receiving less than the federal minimum wage; not having their social security deductions reported; being turned-in to the authorities by employers just prior to pay day;

not receiving overtime premiums; and being personally abused are legion. For as one government official who decried the exploitation of alien workers exclaimed: "Nobody gives a damn, since aliens are nobody's constituents."[31]

In view of the scarcity of data on the number of illegal aliens, let alone on their employment opportunities, it is difficult to know exactly what evidence leads to these sweeping conclusions. In addition, the economic and social implications of the alleged exploitation of illegal aliens are unclear. After all, these persons are in the United States voluntarily. They willingly entered the black market for immigrants, and they obviously benefit from being in the United States, for otherwise they would simply return to their country of origin where they could avoid the exploitation and stigma attached to illegal status.

Moreover, the empirical evidence, limited as it is, provides little support to the proposition that American employers take advantage of illegal aliens. As noted above, a study by Douglas Massey compares the earnings of legal and illegal aliens and reports that, on average, illegal aliens have about 37 percent lower earnings than legal immigrants.[32] But illegal aliens are also younger, less proficient in English, and more likely to work on a farm, and they have much less experience with their American employers than do their legal counterparts. All of these factors imply that, even apart from legal status, illegal aliens will earn somewhat less than legal immigrants.

In fact, after controlling for these differences in observed demographic characteristics, illegal aliens have essentially the same wage rate as legal immigrants.[33] In other words, if one compares two persons who are demographically similar (in terms of education, age, English proficiency, years on the job, and so on), legal status has no direct impact on the wage rate.

Therefore, despite the frequent claims of exploitation, the available (though limited) evidence suggests that the U.S. labor market prior to IRCA operated in a way that did not penalize illegal aliens. Generally, the same factors that determine the legal immigrant's wage also determine the illegal alien's wage. Persons with higher education, persons who are older, and persons who have been on the job longer earn more, regardless of whether they are legal.[34] Illegal aliens in the United States have lower wages than legal immigrants not because they are illegal, but because they are less skilled.

The Immigration Reform and Control Act of 1986

The Immigration Reform and Control Act did not change any of the statutes regulating the legal immigration process and summarized in chapter 2. Its goal, instead, was to get control of the problem of illegal immigration, particularly that from Mexico. The Act has four main provisions.[35] First, amnesty is granted to aliens who have been in the country illegally and "continuously" since before January 1, 1982, and who applied for amnesty in the year ending May 4, 1988. The restriction that individuals must have resided illegally in the United States throughout the entire period prevents foreign students who remained in the country after their visa expired from sneaking in through the amnesty program. The requirement of continuous U.S. residence has been interpreted to allow for "brief" or "casual" periodic trips outside the United States. If aliens qualify for amnesty under this provision, they become temporary resident aliens for eighteen months. They then have a twelve-month period in which to satisfy minimal English-language requirements and apply for permanent resident-alien status.

Second, amnesty is also given to agricultural workers through the Special Agricultural Workers (SAW) program if the illegal alien worked in perishable-crop agriculture in the United States for at least ninety days in the year ending May 1, 1986.

Third, IRCA defines a new category of agricultural workers through the Replenishment Agricultural Workers (RAW) program. Beginning in 1990 (and ending in 1993), replenishment workers may be admitted if there is a shortage of workers in perishable-crop agriculture. These workers, after working in perishable-crop agriculture for at least ninety days in each of three consecutive years, qualify for permanent resident-alien status. The number of replenishment workers allowed entry will be determined annually by the Department of Agriculture but is limited to the number of workers participating in the SAW program. Observers have called the RAW provision a form of "large scale agricultural guest-worker program."[36]

Fourth, beginning in 1988, it is unlawful for employers knowingly to hire an illegal alien. New employees must provide proof that they are either U.S. citizens, or permanent legal residents, or have visas

73

permitting them to work in the United States. Employers must then complete forms for each new employee hired certifying that the relevant documents establishing legal status were reviewed. Employers who disobey the law are liable for fines that, for first-time offenders, range from $250 to $2,000 per illegal alien hired. Criminal penalties can be imposed on repeated violators. These penalties include a fine of $3,000 per illegal alien and up to six months in prison.[37]

It is too early to assess IRCA's impact on the U.S. economy or on the size of the illegal-alien flow. Approximately 1.8 million persons applied for amnesty under the regular program, and an additional 1.3 million applied under the SAW program.[38] About 57 percent of the regular amnesty applicants (but 82 percent of the SAW applicants) are male, and about half of the applicants are over the age of thirty. Further, 70 percent of the regular amnesty applicants (but 81 percent of the SAW applicants) are of Mexican origin. Finally, nearly half of all applicants are married.[39]

The early impact of IRCA on the number of illegal aliens apprehended is mixed. Even though the number of apprehensions dropped from the record high of 1.8 million in 1986 to about 1 million in both 1987 and 1988, it is already clear that the legislation did not stop the flow of illegal aliens into the United States.[40] There are as many apprehensions now as there were in the late 1970s. Although no one knows what will eventually happen to the size of the illegal-alien flow as a result of IRCA, there are good reasons to be skeptical about the law's long-run effectiveness.

For instance, the only penalty imposed on apprehended illegal aliens is deportation. Even though the Border Patrol's manpower will be increased by 50 percent, once an alien is apprehended and deported he is free to attempt to reenter the United States whenever it is convenient. As deportation is unlikely to be a strong deterrent, a persistent illegal alien is likely to make it through after a number of tries. Therefore, employer sanctions may be the only provision in the law that could significantly raise the costs of participating in the black market. Through its fines and criminal penalties on employers, IRCA raises the cost of hiring illegal aliens. As a result, employers' demand for this type of labor will decrease, which reduces the attractiveness of the U.S. offer to potential illegal aliens. Effective employer sanctions could significantly shrink the size of the black market for immigrants.

But this provision of the law will be difficult to enforce. The INS and the Department of Labor's wages and hours division (which is already in charge of enforcing the Federal Labor Standards Act, including the minimum-wage and the overtime-pay provisions) are jointly responsible for enforcing the employer-sanctions provisions. As of January 31, 1989, only 16,000 employers (or .2 percent of the nation's 7 million employers) had been visited by the INS to inspect the forms that employers are now required to fill out when hiring new employees, and 12,000 of these visits were made as the result of tips.[41]

Moreover, a major loophole in the legislation is that employers need only certify that they reviewed the documents verifying the legal status of job applicants. The employer is not required to keep copies of these documents for inspection. Thus, the probability of detecting employers who decide to hire illegal aliens after "verifying" the documents provided by willing conspirators is small.[42]

In the end, the Immigration Reform and Control Act is unlikely to stop the flow of illegal aliens simply because the legislation did not alter some fundamental facts about the immigration market: the economic benefits associated with immigration to the United States remain sufficiently great to encourage the illegal migration of large flow of persons. Similarly, for some employers, the economic benefits associated with hiring illegal aliens may be substantial and provide incentives to continue the practice. A minor detail such as the legality of entry or of hiring will not deter the immigration of many individuals in the source countries or of employers hiring illegal aliens, as long as the costs associated with entering the black market are small relative to the benefits. In view of the difficulty of enforcing the employer-sanctions provisions in the legislation and of the absence of effective penalties on apprehended illegal aliens, it seems that America's offer in the black market for immigrants remains almost as attractive today as it was before IRCA.

While the worry over the illegal-alien flow dominated the political discussion between 1970 and 1986, more than 8 million legal immigrants entered the country. In retrospect, therefore, the excessive attention devoted to the illegal-alien population masked the fact that the larger flow of legal immigrants, along with changes in the legal immigration market, may have more serious repercussions on the U.S. economy.

PART II

THE ECONOMIC IMPACT OF IMMIGRATION

CHAPTER 5

The Impact of Immigrants
on Native Earnings
and Employment

THE FIRST four chapters introduced the conceptual framework that motivates and guides the analysis and presented an overview of the main trends that have characterized the immigration market in the past few decades. This section of the book turns to a detailed analysis of how the sorting generated by the immigration market affects the American economy.

Some of the most important and most emotional questions in the debate over immigration policy are the following: What is the impact of the immigrant flow on the earnings and employment opportunities of natives? Do immigrants truly have an adverse effect on these opportunities? If so, how large is the loss in the economic welfare of natives? Finally, are all native groups equally affected by the entry of immigrants into the labor market?

The fear that "immigrant hordes" displace natives from their jobs and reduce the earnings of those lucky enough still to have jobs has a long (and not so honorable) history in the policy debate. The presumption that immigrants have an adverse impact on the labor market continues to be the main justification for policies designed to restrict the size and composition of immigrant flows into the United States.

In addition, it is often argued that the labor market competition between immigrants and natives, particularly minorities, increases the likelihood of conflict among the groups and exacerbates the serious social problems afflicting many American cities. For example, in her perceptive account of the racial tensions that simmered in Miami through the 1970s and that erupted into violent riots in 1980, Joan Didion writes,

Desegregation had not just come hard and late to South Florida but it had also coincided, as it had not in other parts of the South, with another disruption of the local status quo, the major Cuban influx, which meant that jobs and services which might have helped awaken an inchoate black community went instead to Cubans, who tended to be overtrained but willing. Havana bankers took jobs as inventory clerks at forty-five dollars a week. Havana newspaper publishers drove taxis. That these were the men in black ties who now danced with the women in the Chanel and Valentino evening dresses . . . was an irony lost in its precise detail, although not in its broad outline, on the sons of the men who did not get jobs as inventory clerks or taxi drivers.[2]

Remarkably, until very recently little was known about the impact that immigrants have on the native labor market. When economists Michael Greenwood and John McDowell surveyed the literature in 1986 they concluded, "substantive empirical evidence regarding the effects of immigration is generally scarce. . . . Little direct evidence is available on immigration's impact on the employment opportunities and wages of domestic workers."[3] Put bluntly, measurements of the presumed effect that immigrants have on the U.S. labor market simply did not exist. Discussions of whether immigrants reduced the earnings and employment opportunities of natives were typically conducted in a factual vacuum, without any supporting evidence to buttress the arguments.

The absence of systematic empirical analysis did not reflect a consensus that the issues were uninteresting or unimportant. After all, the question of how immigrants and natives interact in the labor market is fundamental to any assessment of the benefits and costs of immigration. Instead, it reflected the unavailability of the data required to analyze this problem and the fact that, even if data existed, social scientists did not know how to go about measuring the labor market impact of an increase in the number of immigrants.[4] This situation has changed rapidly in the past few years, as a number of data sets became available to researchers and econometric methodologies were developed that allow a straightforward analysis of this important question.

Remarkably, economists have quickly reached a consensus on the direction and magnitude of the labor market impacts of immigration. The conclusion suggested by the empirical evidence is likely to be

The Impact of Immigrants on Native Earnings and Employment

controversial: the methodological arsenal of modern econometrics cannot detect a single shred of evidence that immigrants have a sizable adverse impact on the earnings and employment opportunities of natives in the United States.

The Alternative Hypotheses

There are two opposing views about the ways that immigrants affect the native labor market.[5] Some observers assert that immigrants take jobs away from natives: as immigrants enter the labor market, natives are displaced from their jobs. For instance, in his analysis of the economic consequences of illegal immigration, Vernon Briggs argues, "The bracero programme depressed domestic wage rates and retarded the normal market pressures that would have led to rising agricultural wages in the Southwest. Indeed their level, relative to wages in the nonagricultural sector, declined sharply. Since the end of the bracero programme, the illegal immigrants have had the same effect. The citizen workers who had hitherto been the mainstay of the regional labor force began an exodus."[6] At its most extreme, this hypothesis suggests that immigrants displace natives on a one-to-one basis. For every immigrant admitted into the United States, an American native worker inevitably loses his job.

Such assertions are typically not based on any empirical evidence. Instead, they follow from a set of assumptions about the way the U.S. labor market works and the types of immigrants allocated to the United States by the immigration market. Three assumptions are required to assert that immigrants displace natives on a one-to-one basis.

The first is that the number of jobs in the American economy is fixed. New labor market entrants compete with current workers for the limited number of jobs. Because no economic growth takes place as immigrants (or any other new workers) enter the labor market, this view of the labor market implies that for every person taking a job, some other worker must be displaced.

The second assumption is that the persons allocated into the immigrant flow by the immigration market are perfectly interchangeable with natives in the production process. After all, in order for an immigrant to be able to take over a job that was formerly held by a native, the immigrant must be qualified to take on that job. In the jargon of economics, immigrants and natives must be "perfect substitutes" in production.

It is still unclear why employers, when they could hire equally skilled immigrants or natives, prefer to hire immigrants. Why is it that immigrants displace natives, and why do employers not choose to keep the natives in their jobs and leave the immigrants unemployed? After all, firing old workers and hiring new workers is costly. Hence, a third assumption is required: immigrants are willing to work for lower wages than equally productive natives. Because immigrants offer cost-conscious employers a certain set of skills at a lower price, it necessarily follows that immigrants take jobs away from natives.

Viewed in terms of these three restrictive conjectures about the way the immigration and labor markets work, the proposition that immigrants displace native workers becomes less plausible. Obviously, the assertion that the U.S. economy has a fixed number of jobs is false. Increases in population, whether they occur through immigration or through natural fertility, boost the demand for goods and services. Employers will typically expand their workplaces to satisfy the additional demand, and more people will be employed.

Similarly, it is difficult to take seriously the conjecture that the typical Mexican illegal alien is perfectly interchangeable with the typical native in the labor force, or even with an unskilled young black residing in Watts or Harlem. After all, immigrants and natives differ in terms of their proficiency with the English language, their educational background, and their familiarity and experience with the American labor market. It is very unlikely that, on average, immigrants and natives are perfect substitutes in production.

Finally, there is no evidence suggesting that immigrant labor is cheaper than equally skilled native labor. Such a wage differential could arise if there were systematic labor market discrimination against foreign-born persons in the United States.[8] The available evidence, however, does not support the assertion that immigrants are systematically discriminated against.[9] Alternatively, it could be argued that illegal aliens, who are afraid of being reported to the immigration officials, are easy prey for exploitation and are paid less than the going wage by employers. As I noted in chapter 4, however, illegal aliens have the same wage as legal immigrants once differences in observable demographic characteristics are taken into account. Thus, there is no reason to believe that employers would prefer to hire immigrants over equally qualified natives. In sum, the presumption that immigrants must displace natives rests on a rather peculiar, and erroneous, view of how the immigration and labor markets operate.

Other observers of the immigrant experience in the U.S. labor market assert the opposite, that immigrants have no impact on the labor market opportunities of natives. Economist Michael Piore, for instance, believes that immigrants cause very little displacement of natives because immigrants "take on a distinct set of jobs, jobs that the native labor force refuses to accept."[10]

In this view of the world, the labor market is segmented into two sectors: a primary sector, which contains the "good" jobs, and a secondary sector, where the "bad" jobs are. Natives obviously prefer the better jobs available in the primary sector. Because of labor market discrimination against immigrants, or because some immigrant groups tend to be unskilled and have little knowledge of the English language or the way the U.S. labor market works, immigrants are crowded into the secondary sector and will hold jobs that natives refuse to take.

This approach to the labor market is flawed because it too depends on assumptions that are arbitrary, logically inconsistent, and without empirical support. First, the segmentation of the economy into two sectors, though appealing to people who prefer a "black-and-white" approach to the labor market, is an extremely simplistic view of the way labor markets operate and has been difficult to establish as empirically relevant.[11]

After all, if natives do not wish to work in secondary-sector jobs, it seems natural that a labor shortage for these jobs would quickly develop. Farmers would find their crops unpicked; consumers would find grocery shelves emptied of fresh fruits and vegetables; and householders would find their houses uncleaned and their lawns unmowed. In a market economy, the labor shortage in the secondary sector would increase competition for the workers willing to provide these services and lead to a bidding war among employers for the few persons willing to work in that sector. This would tend to equalize the rewards between the primary and secondary sectors. As wages rose in the secondary sector, even natives would be willing to work in the bad jobs.[12]

There is, therefore, no compelling theoretical rationale to support the assertion that natives refuse to work in certain types of jobs, and that immigrants are somehow crowded into these jobs. The conjecture that natives and immigrants do not interact in the labor market, like the one that immigrants displace natives from their jobs on a one-to-one basis, depends on arbitrary assumptions about the operations of the labor and immigration markets. Moreover, neither of these propositions is supported by any empirical evidence.

How then do immigrants and natives interact in the labor market? A more useful approach focuses on the question, what happens to a firm's incentives to hire native workers when the supply of immigrants increases?

It turns out that there is no definite answer to this question. It is certainly possible that immigrant and native workers are substitutes in production. That is, despite their differences, immigrants and natives tend to have somewhat similar skills and are suited for the same types of jobs. As immigrants enter the labor market, the supply of these skills increases, and there is more competition among the larger number of workers supplying the same human capital to employers. Because these skills are now relatively abundant, firms can attract workers, both immigrants and natives, at lower wage rates.

In addition, because of the lower wages now paid to native workers, the economic rewards to participating in the labor force decline. Hence some natives find it worthwhile to withdraw from the labor force, and the number of natives employed falls. This "displacement" will not occur on a one-to-one basis. The number of natives who quit their jobs depends on how many find it worthwhile to leave the labor market, which in turn depends on the value of the natives' alternatives (such as leisure or managing the household). In sum, when immigrants and natives are substitutes in production, an increase in the supply of immigrants increases the competition for jobs and leads to a reduction in the native wage, so that some natives find it worthwhile to drop out of the labor market, and native employment also falls.

It is possible, however, that immigrants and natives are not interchangeable types of workers, but that they complement each other in the production process. For instance, some immigrant groups may be relatively unskilled and have a comparative advantage in agricultural production. This frees the more skilled native work force to perform tasks that make better use of their human capital. The presence of immigrants increases native productivity because natives can now specialize in tasks in which they too have a comparative advantage.

If the two groups are complements in production, an increase in the number of immigrants raises the productivity of natives, which makes natives more valuable to employers and increases the demand for native labor. Because employers are now competing for native workers, native wages rise. Moreover, some natives who previously did not find it profitable to work see the higher wage rate as an additional incentive to enter the labor market, hence native employment also increases.

An important insight of this approach is that there exists a possibility that immigrants do not reduce the economic opportunities of natives. On the contrary, they may be quite beneficial. Conceptual discussions of the impact of immigrants on the native labor market typically make an assumption about the extent of substitutability or complementarity among the two groups.[13] There is, however, no compelling reason for assuming that immigrants are either "good" or "bad" for natives. This is an empirical question, and only a systematic look at the data can determine the way in which the earnings and employment opportunities of natives are affected by the entry of immigrants into the labor market.

Moreover, it need not be the case that *all* immigrants and *all* natives are related in the same way in the production process. Some immigrant groups may be close substitutes in production for some native groups but may complement the skills of others. In other words, various combinations of complementarity and substitutability among the many immigrant and native groups are possible. In fact, this ambiguity is implied by the way in which the immigration market allocates persons to host countries. As we have seen, the skills of immigrants vary greatly among the various cohorts and national-origin groups. Persons migrating under one set of economic and political conditions differ in significant ways from persons migrating under other circumstances and are, therefore, likely to have different impacts on the labor market.

85

Immigration and the U.S. Income Distribution

The Impact of Immigrants on Native Earnings

This conceptual approach suggests a simple way of determining empirically whether immigrants and natives are complements or substitutes in production. If immigrants and native are substitutes, the earnings and employment propensities of native workers should be relatively lower in labor markets in which immigrants are in abundant supply. By the same token, if immigrants and natives are complements, native earnings and employment should be relatively lower in labor markets in which few immigrants reside.

Practically all recent empirical research is based on this implication of the framework.[14] Using such data as the 1980 Census cross-section, the studies compare native earnings in labor markets or SMSAs (for Standard Metropolitan Statistical Areas) in which immigrants are a substantial fraction of the labor force (for example, Los Angeles or New York), with native earnings in labor markets in which immigrants are a relatively trivial fraction of the labor force (for example, Pittsburgh or Nashville).

Of course, native wages will vary among labor markets even if immigration does not exist. The validity of the analysis, therefore, hinges crucially on the extent to which one can control for all of the other factors that generate intercity dispersion in native wages. These factors include geographic differences in the skills of natives, regional wage differentials, and variations in the level of economic activity.

As the results of the empirical studies summarized in table 5.1 suggest, holding other factors constant, the average native wage is slightly smaller in labor markets in which immigrants tend to reside. That is, after controlling for geographic differences in the level of schooling, age, and other observable skills of natives and for differences in the level of economic activity among local labor markets, native earnings are slightly lower in markets with large numbers of immigrants.

But the decline in the native wage attributable to an increase in the supply of immigrants is numerically small. For instance, a 10-percent increase in the size of the immigrant population reduces native earn-

The Impact of Immigrants on Native Earnings and Employment

TABLE 5.1

The Impact of Immigrants on Native Earnings

Native Group	Change in Native Wage as a Result of a 10-Percent Increase in the Number of Immigrants (Expressed as Percentage)
1. All natives	−.2
2. White men	−.2 to −.1
3. Black men	−.3 to +.2
4. Women	+.2 to +.5
5. Young blacks	−.1
6. Young Hispanics	−.3 to +.2
7. Manufacturing workers	−.04

SOURCE: (1) Jean B. Grossman, "The Substitutability of Natives and Immigrants in Production," *Review of Economics and Statistics* 64 (November 1982): 596–603; (2) George J. Borjas, "The Sensitivity of Labor Demand Functions to Choice of Dependent Variable," *Review of Economics and Statistics* 68 (February 1986): 58–66; (3) George J. Borjas, "Immigrants, Minorities, and Labor Market Competition," *Industrial and Labor Relations Review* 40 (April 1987): 382–92; Thomas Muller and Thomas J. Espenshade, *The Fourth Wave* (Washington, D.C.: The Urban Institute, 1985); (4) Joseph Altonji and David Card, "The Effects of Immigration on the Labor Market Outcomes of Natives," in Richard B. Freeman and John M. Abowd, eds., *Immigration, Trade, and the Labor Market* (Chicago: University of Chicago Press, 1990); Borjas, "Sensitivity of Labor Demand Functions"; (5) Robert J. LaLonde and Robert H. Topel, "Labor Market Adjustments to Increased Immigration," in Richard B. Freeman and John M. Abowd, eds., *Immigration, Trade, and the Labor Market;* (6) LaLonde and Topel, "Labor Market Adjustments"; (7) Gregory DeFreitas and Adriana Marshall, "Immigration and Wage Growth in U.S. Manufacturing in the 1970s," in Barbara D. Dennis, ed., *Proceedings of the Thirty-Sixth Annual Meeting* (Madison, Wisc.: Industrial Relations Research Association, 1984), pp. 148–56.

ings by .2 percent. A doubling of the number of immigrants in the local labor market, therefore, reduces the native wage rate by only 2 percent. The overwhelming consensus of the literature seems to be that native and immigrant workers are, on average, weak substitutes in production. Despite all of the worry and discussion over the presumed large adverse impact of immigration on native earnings opportunities, careful empirical research suggests that this concern is not justified. The earnings of the typical native are barely affected by the entry of immigrants into the local labor market.

Moreover, the studies summarized in table 5.1 indicate that disaggregating the labor force by sex, age, race, and ethnicity does not alter this basic finding. Generally, immigrant groups tend to be weak complements with some native groups, and weak substitutes with others. Still, regardless of the particular permutation of groups being compared, the impact of an increase in the supply of immigrants on the wage of any native group remains numerically small.

It is often argued that blacks are the one group whose economic progress is most likely to be hampered by the entry of immigrants into

87

econometric research.

the United States. Perhaps the most surprising insight provided by the recent econometric evidence is that *no* study finds any evidence to support this claim. On the contrary, some studies report that blacks residing in cities with relatively large numbers of immigrants actually have slightly higher wages than blacks residing in other labor markets. In fact, a 10-percent increase in the number of immigrants increases the average black wage by about .2 percent. Moreover, a 10-percent increase in the number of Hispanic immigrants, who are presumably the source of much of the concern, reduces the black wage by less than .1 percent.[15] Finally, a 10-percent increase in the number of immigrants reduces the earnings of young blacks, a group that is particularly sensitive to changes in economic conditions, by only .1 percent.[16]

Recent econometric research, therefore, has not been able to establish a single instance in which the increase in the supply of immigrants had a significant adverse impact on the earnings of natives. This unexpected finding raises an important question: Why is the empirical evidence so at odds with the typical assumption in the political debate?

As noted above, economic theory provides little guidance in what to expect from a careful, objective analysis. Immigrants can be either complements or substitutes with natives, and the various immigrant and native groups are likely to interact differently. Many participants in the public debate have continuously, and without justification, assumed that immigrants and natives are strong substitutes in production.

Perhaps the most plausible reason for the absence of any sizable adverse effects is that immigration to the United States in the past two decades, though large and increasing in size, was a relatively small component of demographic change, particularly in terms of the immigrant contribution to the growth of the labor force.

At the same time that immigrants were entering the labor force in increasing numbers, two other and much larger groups of natives were also entering the labor force: women and the baby-boom cohort of young workers. The increase in the size of the labor force due to the entry of these two groups dwarfed the increase due to the entry of immigrants. In particular, the labor force participation rate of women increased from 38 percent in 1960 to 52 percent in 1980. This increase in female participation rates alone accounted for an additional 8.5 million women entering the labor market over the period.[17] Moreover,

Contemplate = gazing upon

The Impact of Immigrants on Native Earnings and Employment

an average of more than 4 million people were born annually in the United States during the baby-boom years (1945 to 1960). This cohort also entered the labor market in the late 1960s and 1970s.[18]

During the 1950s, immigration accounted for 17 percent of the growth in the labor force. During the 1970s, however, immigration accounted for perhaps as little as 11 percent, despite the large increase in the number of immigrants entering the country.[19] Therefore, the contribution of immigration to labor force growth was overshadowed by other, much more important demographic changes. Thus, it is not surprising that the labor market hardly reacted to the entry of immigrants and that native earnings opportunities were not greatly affected.

The Impact of Illegal Aliens on Native Earnings

It is often argued that illegal aliens, particularly those from Mexico, have a major adverse impact on the earnings and employment opportunities of natives, particularly those of unskilled natives and minorities. This concern was perhaps the main impetus behind the enactment of IRCA. For example, during the congressional debate, Congressman Shaw (D.-Fla.) claimed that "American workers . . . are being discriminated against, because they are losing jobs to illegal aliens who are coming to this country and working for less," while Congressman Burton (R.-Ind.) stated, "Part of the unemployment problem is that . . . illegal workers take jobs from Americans. There are nine million Americans looking for work. There are five to twenty million illegal aliens. These numbers suggest a solution to the unemployment problem."[20] Because the studies discussed in the previous section do not distinguish between the labor market impacts of legal immigrants and illegal aliens, they may be ignoring what many consider to be the most important aspect of the problem.

As I noted in chapter 4, the 1980 Census enumerated more than 1 million illegal aliens of Mexican origin. Using INS administrative data on the number of Mexican-born citizens and legal immigrants, it is possible to estimate how many illegal aliens resided in each of a large number of labor markets.[21] These data then allow the comparison of the earnings of natives who reside in labor markets with relatively few illegal aliens to the earnings of natives who reside amidst large illegal populations. This methodological approach was used in a recent study by sociologists Frank Bean, Lindsay Lowell, and Lowell Taylor.[22] They

adverse = opposed to ;
adversary
adversity = misfortune

contrast the earnings of natives among forty-seven cities in the southwestern United States and determine how these earnings are affected by the presence of Mexican illegal aliens in the locality.

The main lesson provided by these comparisons is that the entry of Mexican-born illegal aliens barely affects the earnings of natives. A 10-percent increase in the size of the Mexican illegal-alien population reduces the earnings of Mexican-American men by .1 percent; does not change the earnings of black men; reduces the earnings of other men by .1 percent; and increases the earnings of women by .2 percent.[23] There is no evidence, therefore, to suggest that illegal immigration had a significant adverse impact on the earnings opportunities of any native group, including blacks. It seems that much of the political debate over the enactment of IRCA was based on conjectures that had little basis in fact.

The Impact of New Immigrants on Immigrant Earnings

Immigrants may affect not only native earnings but also the earnings of the preexisting immigrant population. As new immigrants enter the local labor market, they change the productivity of foreign-born persons already residing there, and, as a result, employers adjust their demand for immigrant labor. As with natives, the exact direction of the adjustment depends on whether the new immigrants are complementary to the old or substitutable for them.

The empirical evidence indicates that immigrant earnings respond substantially to the entry of additional immigrants into the labor market. Immigrants are likely to have a much more adverse impact on their own earnings than on the earnings of natives.[24] A 10-percent increase in the number of immigrants decreases the earnings of other immigrants by at least 2 percent. In other words, immigrants are more substitutable for themselves than for natives.

This result is not surprising, because the demographic and skill characteristics of new immigrants are more likely to resemble those of other immigrants than they are to resemble those of natives. Groups that are more alike in economically relevant characteristics are more easily substitutable, and the evidence suggests that immigrants may be highly interchangeable with themselves. Thus, the labor market impact of immigration seems to be borne mostly by the immigrants themselves.

90

The Impact of Immigrants on Native Employment

Even though immigrants have only a minor impact on the wages of natives, they may have a significant effect on the number of natives employed and on the length of their work year. Focusing solely on immigration's impact on native wages and ignoring its impact on native employment may provide an incomplete, and perhaps misleading, picture of the role immigrants play in the U.S. labor market. It turns out, however, that the employment effects of immigration are as negligible as the wage effects.

Immigrants influence the employment experience of natives in a number of ways. For instance, through their impact on the native wage, immigrants affect the labor force participation decision of natives. If the entry of immigrants into the labor market lowered the native wage, natives would have fewer incentives to work because the attractiveness of entering the labor market, relative to other alternatives, would be reduced. In addition, due to increased labor market competition, natives might have difficulty in finding work and might have higher unemployment rates, or natives might be less willing to work long hours for the lower wages.

The methodology used to estimate the employment effects of immigration is the same as that used for measuring the wage effects. The employment outcomes experienced by natives are compared among different labor markets. If immigrants have a major displacement effect on native employment opportunities, natives should have lower labor force participation rates, higher unemployment rates, and work fewer hours in those areas of the country in which immigrants concentrate.

As table 5.2 shows, however, immigrants have a negligible impact on native employment opportunities. A 10-percent increase in the number of immigrants reduces the labor force participation rate of white natives by only .1 percentage point; reduces the number of weeks worked by .3 percent; and does not affect the native unemployment rate. The data also indicate that immigrants have little impact on the labor force participation rates or weeks worked of black native men.[25]

The weight of the empirical evidence, therefore, indicates that immigration has practically no impact on the earnings and employment opportunities of natives. Although the conjecture that immigrants take jobs away from natives has been a prime force behind efforts to make

The Economic Impact of Immigration

TABLE 5.2
The Impact of Immigrants on Native Employment

Native Group	Change in Native Employment as a Result of a 10-Percent Increase in the Number of Immigrants
1. Labor force participation rate of white men	—.1 percentage point
Labor force participation rate of black men	—.1 to +.4 percentage point
2. Weeks worked of white men	—.3 percent
Weeks worked of black men	—.1 percent
3. Unemployment rate of natives	0

SOURCE: (1) Joseph Altonji and David Card, "The Effects of Immigration on the Labor Market Outcomes of Natives," in Richard B. Freeman and John M. Abowd, eds., *Immigration, Trade, and the Labor Market* (Chicago: University of Chicago Press, 1990); George J. Borjas, "The Sensitivity of Labor Demand Functions to Choice of Dependent Variable," *Review of Economics and Statistics* 68 (February 1986): 58–66; (2) Altonji and Card, "Effects of Immigration"; (3) Julian L. Simon and Stephen Moore, "The Effect of Immigration Upon Unemployment: An Across City Estimation," mimeograph, 1984.

immigration policy more restrictive throughout American history, there is no empirical evidence documenting that the displacement effect is numerically important (at least in recent years). This conclusion does not imply that one should not be concerned about the economic impact of current immigration policy. As I show in subsequent chapters, immigrants play a much broader role in the American economy and impose a number of additional costs on the native population. It is this broader impact of immigration that suggests that perhaps the time has come for a reevaluation of U.S. immigration policy.

Objections to the Empirical Studies

The ideal way to measure how immigration affects native labor market opportunities would be to conduct a controlled experiment wherein the history of the past two or three decades would be relived, with the exception that the United States would prohibit immigration. This experiment simulates the type of scientific investigation that is possible in the physical sciences. The resulting labor market outcomes in this experimental world would then be compared to those which actually occurred, and the direction and magnitude of the impact of immigration would be precisely measured.

Obviously, such controlled experiments are impossible in the social sciences. Instead, the research findings discussed in this chapter are based on comparisons of native earnings and employment propensities among different labor markets. These comparisons are used to infer how the presence or absence of immigrants in the locality affects labor market conditions. As noted above, however, native wages and employment propensities vary among labor markets for many other reasons, including regional differences in the average skill level of the labor force, geographic variations in the level of economic activity, and cost-of-living differentials.

Therefore, in order to isolate the impact of immigration on native earnings and employment opportunities, it is important to control for other factors that generate differences in labor market conditions among localities. The econometric studies control for this extraneous variation in a number of ways. They compare individuals who have the same demographic characteristics; they compare labor markets that have similar unemployment rates, industrial structures, and levels of economic activity; and they deflate for regional wage differentials.

Nevertheless, there are many other factors that influence the earnings and employment opportunities of natives in a city, and no study can truly claim to have controlled for all variables. At a particular point in time, economic conditions in the local labor market depend on its history of economic growth and development, on the policies of state and local governments, on the quality of its educational system, and on a myriad of other parameters. It is difficult to quantify or even identify many of these factors. Further, some of them may be correlated with the presence or absence of particular types of individuals in the city's work force. Thus the findings presented in this chapter are potentially misleading because of the inability to control for many of the relevant factors that generate differences in labor market conditions among localities.

One possible way of avoiding the problem is to observe the earnings and employment opportunities available to natives in the *same* labor market prior to and after the immigrant flow. This "longitudinal" comparison holds constant all of the factors that are specific to the

93

locality because pre-immigration conditions are compared to post-immigration conditions in a particular labor market.

Some of the available studies indeed track the earnings and employment opportunities of natives in a number of labor markets between 1970 and 1980.[26] If immigrants have an adverse impact on the earnings and employment opportunities of natives, the tracking of native labor market conditions should reveal a substantial deterioration in those labor markets which experienced a large immigrant inflow. In fact, none of the studies suggests that this is the case. Instead, they confirm the general validity of the cross-section results summarized above. The tracking of local labor market conditions between 1970 and 1980 suggests that a 10-percent increase in the number of immigrants decreases the earnings of white men by .3 percent and increases the earnings of black men by .2 percent.[27] Therefore, there is no evidence that native labor market conditions worsened particularly in those labor markets which experienced immigrant inflows during the 1970s.

The finding that economic conditions in the local labor market are not responsive to the entry of even large immigrant flows is confirmed by economist David Card's careful study of the impact of the Mariel flow on Miami.[28] On April 20, 1980, President Fidel Castro declared that Cuban nationals wishing to emigrate to the United States could leave freely from the port of Mariel. By September 1980, about 125,000 Cubans had chosen to undertake the journey in a flotilla of rafts, pleasure boats, and fishing vessels. This immigrant flow was composed of relatively unskilled workers and contained a large number of career criminals who created substantial social havoc in southern Florida. Moreover, the numerical impact of the "Marielitos" on Miami's population and labor force was sizable. Almost overnight, Miami's labor force had grown by 7 percent.

Nevertheless, Card's systematic analysis of the available data clearly documents that the economic characteristics of the native labor force, *including* those of Miami's unskilled blacks, were barely affected by the Mariel flow. The economic changes experienced by Miami between 1980 and 1985, in terms of wage levels and unemployment rates, were similar to those experienced by other American cities (such as Los Angeles, Houston, and Atlanta), cities which did not experience the Mariel flow. The tracking of economic conditions in Miami in the post-Mariel period leads Card to conclude that there is "no indication of any short- or longer-term impact of the Mariel immigration on the wages and unemployment rates of non-Cubans in Miami."[29]

A second potential flaw with the empirical studies is that immigrants and natives choose in which labor markets to reside. If natives perceive that the entry of immigrants into the labor market leads to a deterioration of their earnings and employment opportunities, they will vote with their feet. They will move to cities that provide better opportunities and thus dampen the adverse effects of immigration. Nevertheless, accounting for the fact that both immigrants and natives migrate to localities that offer them the best economic opportunities does not change the central conclusion.[30] A 10-percent increase in the number of immigrants still leads to numerically negligible effects on native earnings and employment opportunities.

Finally, the empirical studies can be criticized because they focus on comparisons of native earnings and employment opportunities among labor markets or SMSAs and ignore other channels through which immigrants affect labor market conditions, such as the taking over of specific industries by some immigrant groups. An alternative approach to the problem, rare in economics but widely used in other social sciences, is the "case-study" method, whereby a descriptive history of an industry in a specific city (such as the apparel or restaurant industries in New York or Los Angeles) is traced as immigrants first enter the market and then presumably take over the jobs in the industry, displacing natives from their jobs.[31] Although these case studies are informative and make interesting reading, they do not address the fundamental question of what happens to the natives after they leave the industry. By focusing on a narrow set of jobs, these studies cannot track the native experience as the labor market adjusts to the entry of immigrants and as natives presumably move on to different jobs.

An alternative approach compares native earnings among industries within a local labor market. To the extent that the presence of immigrants in an industry depresses wage opportunities in that sector, the earnings of natives employed in "immigrant-intensive" industries should be lower than those of natives employed in "native-intensive" industries.

A recent study of the Los Angeles labor market indicates that Mexican immigrants indeed tend to concentrate in a specific group of industries.[32] Even though the apparel industry employs only 2.3 percent of all workers in that labor market, it employs almost 10 percent of Mexican immigrants. The comparison of earnings among industries in the Los Angeles area reveals that the typical native with a high school education is not greatly affected by the presence of immigrants in his industry. A 10-percent increase in the number of immigrants in an industry reduces the earnings of natives in that industry by .4 percent. Therefore, interindustry comparisons in native earnings confirm the results obtained by studies of intercity differences in native labor market conditions.[33]

CHAPTER 6

Assimilation and the Earnings of Immigrants

WHEN a newly arrived immigrant first enters the U.S. labor market, his wage is much lower than that of natives. Over time, the immigrant becomes proficient in the English language, learns about alternative job opportunities, and acquires skills that are valued by American employers. As immigrants adapt to the U.S. labor market, therefore, they become more and more like natives, and their wages begin to catch up to those of natives. How important is this process of labor market assimilation in the working lives of first-generation immigrants? In this chapter, I review existing empirical evidence to establish the extent of economic mobility among immigrants, to document whether immigrants eventually reach wage parity with natives, and to describe the channels through which assimilation takes place.

Because the immigration market allocates different types of persons into the immigrant flow, the extent of labor market assimilation may differ greatly among the various immigrant groups. This chapter also documents the variation in the rate of economic mobility among national-origin groups and identifies the factors responsible for generating these differences.

The Melting Pot

The assimilation of immigrants—whether in terms of their cultural integration into American society or in terms of their economic adaptation to the labor market—has always been an integral part of the debate over immigration policy. Today, the struggle continues between those who believe that the assimilation of immigrants is essential if the

United States is to preserve its economic health and national identity, and others who value the ethnic diversity of the various groups and who maintain that the process of Americanization robs individuals of their cultural backgrounds.[1]

The notion that, as time elapses, social, political, and economic differences between immigrants and natives fade is the essence of the assimilation hypothesis. Most of the historical, sociological, and economic studies in the immigration literature consist either of conceptual developments of this basic idea, or of presentations of evidence either supporting or disproving the melting-pot hypothesis.[2]

For many years, it was generally believed that the melting-pot metaphor correctly described important aspects of the immigrant experience. Immediately upon arrival, the immigrants would differ from natives in culture, language, voting habits, and many other characteristics. Over time, however, the immigrants assimilated; and the differences began to narrow, if not disappear, in one generation. Over the course of a few generations the American-born children of immigrants became indistinguishable from the native population. This romantic view of the immigrant experience was the basis of Israel Zangwill's 1909 play *The Melting Pot,* which dramatized the way that the historical enmity among European national-origin groups melted and was forged into a new American identity by their life in the United States.

Recent sociological and historical research rejects the notion that full assimilation is an unavoidable outcome of the immigrant experience.[3] These studies stress the fact that the United States remains a multicultural, pluralistic society and cite as evidence the deep-rooted attachment that some immigrant and ethnic groups have for their cultural heritage and language. In their classic study *Beyond the Melting Pot,* Nathan Glazer and Daniel Moynihan conclude, "The point about the melting pot . . . is that it did not happen. . . . This is nothing remarkable. On the contrary, the American ethos is nowhere better perceived than in the disinclination of the third and fourth generation of newcomers to blend into a standard, uniform national type."[4]

Studies of economic assimilation, which are the focus of this chapter, deal with a much narrower definition of the integration process. Economists are mainly concerned with ascertaining how immigrants perform in the U.S. labor market and specifically with the process that determines immigrant earnings. Most studies of the economic assimilation experience, therefore, focus on the question, what happens to the earnings of immigrants vis-à-vis the earnings of natives as the immigrants learn about and adapt to the American labor market? In this context, assimilation is defined as the rate at which immigrant earnings catch up with those of natives as both groups age in the United States.

As with cultural integration, the evidence from the historical literature is that economic assimilation was a relatively rare event among first-generation immigrants. A large number of studies analyzing such diverse groups as immigrants in Boston in the 1850s, the Irish in Poughkeepsie in the late 1800s, and Mexicans in Santa Barbara in the early 1900s find that only a small fraction of immigrants, perhaps fewer than 15 percent, were able to progress to a better occupation during their lifetimes.[5] In a review of the evidence provided by these studies, historian John Bodnar concludes, "Although most immigrants had no other direction to go but upward if they remained in the United States, the overall impression from historical mobility studies is that such movement was an unrealistic expectation in their lifetimes . . . significant occupational mobility was not normally part of the immigrant experience in industrial America."[6]

The research findings reported in this chapter summarize the conclusions of a new and rapidly growing econometric literature that provides precise measurements of the rate of economic mobility experienced by recent immigrant waves.[7] Although most of the recent studies focus on the process of economic assimilation, this emphasis does not imply that other aspects of the assimilation experience are unimportant.[8] Nevertheless, much of the debate over immigration policy emphasizes economic issues. The fear that unassimilated immigrants will form a permanent underclass and have a major detrimental impact on the economic health of the United States is a serious concern to many.

Cross-Section Comparisons of Immigrant and Native Earnings

To measure the extent of economic mobility among immigrants, most studies use cross-sectional data sources, such as the 1970 Census.[9]

These data allow the comparison of a typical immigrant's earnings to those of a "demographically comparable" native—a native who resembles the immigrant in education, age, sex, marital status, region of residence, health, hours of work, and many other observable demographic characteristics. By contrasting the earnings of immigrants to those of their native counterparts at every age, it is easy to ascertain whether the immigrant wage is catching up to that of comparable natives, and a rate of economic mobility or assimilation can be calculated.

The pioneering study was conducted by Barry Chiswick in 1978, when he measured the extent of economic assimilation experienced by immigrant men enumerated in the 1970 Census cross-section and employed in the wage and salary sector.[10] The results of Chiswick's influential study (see figure 6.1) indicate that at the time of entry into

FIGURE 6.1

Earnings of Immigrants and Comparable Natives over the Working Life in the 1970 Census Cross-Section

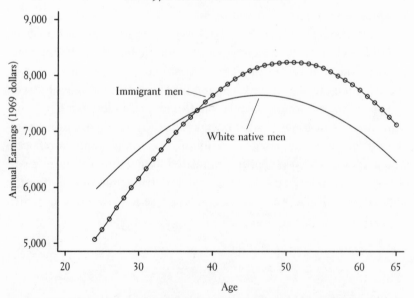

SOURCE: Adapted from Barry R. Chiswick, "The Effect of Americanization on the Earnings of Foreign-Born Men," *Journal of Political Economy* 86 (October 1978): table 3, column 1 of table 2. The predicted earnings profiles are based on a regression wherein the dependent variable is log annual earnings, and they are evaluated at the mean characteristics observed in the sample of immigrants. The demographic characteristics included in the regression are education, age, weeks worked, rural and southern residence, marital status, immigrant status, and years since migration. Predicted annual earnings are given by the antilogs of the regression predictions.

the United States, the annual earnings of immigrant men are 15 percent lower than the earnings of native men with the same schooling, age, number of weeks worked, and other demographic characteristics. The earnings of immigrants, however, grow at a much faster rate than the earnings of comparable natives. Earnings parity between the two groups is reached about fourteen years after arrival, and thereafter immigrants earn more than natives. After thirty years in the United States, the typical immigrant actually earns 10 percent more than a demographically comparable native. Not only is economic mobility an important aspect of the immigrant experience, it is also sufficiently strong to guarantee that for most of their working lives, first-generation immigrants outperform natives in the American labor market.

This remarkable finding was explained in terms of two hypotheses. When immigrants first arrive, they lack skills valued by American employers. These skills include not only language and educational credentials, but also more subtle forms of human capital such as knowing what the best-paying jobs are and where they are located, along with such intangibles as acceptable modes of behavior in the American workplace. As immigrants accumulate labor market experience in the United States, these skills are acquired and labor market assimilation occurs in the sense that immigrant earnings begin to catch up to the earnings of comparable natives.[11]

This argument explains why immigrants' earnings grow faster than those of natives, but it does not account for the fact that after fourteen years immigrants begin to earn more than demographically comparable natives. After all, why should immigrants end up accumulating more human capital than natives? It seems that the cross-sectional data are saying that immigrants not only assimilate, they assimilate "too well."

To explain the result that immigrant earnings eventually overtake the earnings of comparable natives, the cross-section studies resorted to a selection argument: immigrants are different from the rest of us. In particular, immigrants are "more able and more highly motivated" than natives, so that "for the same schooling, age, and other demographic characteristics immigrants to the United States have more innate ability or motivation relevant to the labor market than native-born persons."[12] In other words, immigrants are smarter and harder working, and it is not surprising that they eventually earn more than natives.

The Economic Impact of Immigration

The usual story justifying this assumption is roughly as follows: The nature of the sorting generated by the immigration market implies that immigrants to the United States are not randomly selected from the populations of the countries of origin. They are, therefore, likely to differ in significant ways from persons who do not migrate, from persons who migrate elsewhere, and from natives residing in the United States. The fact that immigrants eventually outperform comparable natives must imply that the sorting of persons among countries leads to highly productive persons migrating out of the source countries and into the United States. Presumably, this sorting occurs because only persons with exceptional ability, drive, and motivation would pack up everything they own, leave family and friends behind, and move to a foreign country to start life anew.

This story, however, begs a fundamental question. Why exactly are the persons with excessive drive and motivation the ones who choose to leave their home countries and come to the United States? After all, these persons could remain in their home countries and presumably also become very successful there. The conjecture that these are the persons who decide to migrate to the United States is really a claim that America's offer in the immigration market is particularly attractive to highly skilled workers. Is this, in fact, a key characteristic of our offer? In other words, do highly skilled persons in all source countries and at all times find that the United States rewards their skills more than their source countries do?

The 1970 cross-section results reported in the Chiswick analysis, along with the many studies that replicated these basic findings on a number of alternative cross-section data sources, were extremely influential in forming the current conventional wisdom that legal immigrants perform quite well in the U.S. economy.[13] The fact that these studies contradict the vast historical literature, which concludes that first-generation immigrants typically experience very little economic assimilation, was not addressed by the econometricians.

The conclusions implied by figure 6.1 have two policy implications of fundamental importance. First, the observation that newly arrived immigrants usually have very low wage rates is not a cause for concern. Within a decade or two, they will reach earnings parity with American natives, and thereafter they will earn more than natives. Therefore, immigrants are unlikely to become permanent public charges to the taxpayer. If anything, the American taxpayer should worry about his native neighbor who, in the long run, has lower earnings than the immigrants and presumably a higher probability of going on welfare. Second, to the extent that earnings reflect productivity, the immigrant contribution to American economic performance may be substantial because (for particular demographic characteristics) immigrants are more productive than natives. Immigration, therefore, is an important source of economic growth. If one is to take the cross-sectional studies seriously, economic growth is hampered not by immigrants but by the relatively unproductive native workers who make up the bulk of the labor force.

In retrospect, the notion that the earnings of the typical first-generation immigrant not only catch up to but surpass the earnings of comparable natives is preposterous. There is one fatal flaw in the statistical analysis summarized in figure 6.1, which invalidates the conventional interpretation of the cross-sectional evidence.[14]

The basic problem is that inferences about the growth of immigrant workers' earnings over time are drawn from a single snapshot of the immigrant population. In other words, the dynamic process of wage growth is inferred from a stationary data set, such as the 1970 Census cross-section.

In Chiswick's original study, estimates of immigrant wage growth come from a comparison of the 1969 earnings of newly arrived immigrants with the 1969 earnings of immigrants who arrived ten or twenty years earlier and who still reside in the country. As noted in chapter 3, this comparison among different immigrant waves need not imply anything about how the wage of a specific wave changes over time in the United States. Is the cross-section observation that earlier immigrants earn more than recent immigrants caused by labor market assimilation or by the possibility that recent immigrant waves are substantially different from earlier waves?

The fact that a large fraction of the immigrants eventually return to their countries of origin contaminates the cross-sectional comparisons of immigrant earnings. Studies of the emigration propensity of the foreign-born indicate that perhaps 30 percent of the immigrants will leave the United States within a decade or two of their arrival.[15] Little is known about which types of immigrants decide to return to their birthplaces (or migrate elsewhere), but almost certainly the typical emigrant is not a representative member of the foreign-born population.

For instance, some immigrants may find that things worked out much better than expected in the United States and that they can return home with a substantial amount of wealth and live comfortably for the rest of their lives. In a sense, these return migrants are the "successes." By contrast, other immigrants may find that things did not turn out as well as expected. These persons find that they hold worse jobs than the ones they had before immigration, that their earnings are relatively low, and that they are particularly prone to layoffs as a result of adverse economic conditions. The population of emigrants may be dominated by these labor market "failures."

Unfortunately, the United States keeps no records on the number, let alone the skill composition, of persons who leave the country permanently.[16] Regardless of who the emigrants are, however, the fact that return migration is an important phenomenon implies that cross-sectional comparisons of immigrant earnings are inherently misleading.

To illustrate, suppose that the so-called failures leave the United States. The most recent immigrant wave then contains many individuals who are not doing well in the labor market and who will eventually leave the country. The average earnings of the most recent wave, therefore, are pulled down by the presence of the eventual emigrants in the census survey. The earlier waves of immigrants, by contrast, have been "weeded out." These early cohorts are composed mainly of persons who have succeeded in the United States (because the failures have left the country and are not surveyed by the Bureau of the Census) and who have relatively high wage rates. In essence, the emigration of the failures leads to the more recent cohorts having lower average earnings than the earlier cohorts. Thus, the cross-sectional finding that immigrants who have been in the country for many years earn more than recent arrivals is obtained even if immigrants do not experience any labor market assimilation whatsoever.

A second problem with the cross-sectional comparisons is their implicit assumption that the skill composition or productivity level of successive immigrant waves is constant. This is unlikely to be the case, for conditions in the immigration market, which determine the skill composition of the immigrant flow, change frequently.

104

After all, it is probable that because of the 1965 amendments, the types of persons admitted to the United States in the 1970s differ from the types of persons admitted in the 1950s. For the sake of argument, suppose that due to changing conditions in the immigration market, pre-1965 immigrants were relatively skilled and productive, while post-1965 immigrants are less skilled. The decline in skills among successive waves implies that, in a cross-section, the earnings of the most recent immigrants will be relatively low, while the earnings of the earlier, more productive waves will be relatively high, even if immigrants do not experience any labor market assimilation.

So what do the cross-sectional data say about the extent of assimilation or economic mobility among first-generation immigrants? Nothing. The statistical evidence can be interpreted in a number of contradictory ways. In particular, the cross-sectional data are consistent with the hypothesis that immigrants assimilate in the labor market, but are also consistent with the hypothesis that they do not. Unfortunately, the strong influence that the cross-sectional studies had on the public's perception of the immigrant experience may have been based on an incorrect interpretation of the data.

The Tracking of Immigrant Cohorts

Because a single cross-section of data provides no information about the extent of labor market assimilation, more recent econometric studies track specific immigrant cohorts across the various censuses or study immigrant earnings by using longitudinal data sets, in which a single individual is surveyed at different times.[17] This approach estimates the rate of economic mobility because the earnings of a single immigrant or immigrant cohort is observed at several points in the working life. The wage growth experienced by immigrants can then be compared to that experienced by comparable natives.

To illustrate, the 1970 Census reports the 1969 hourly wage differential between a specific immigrant cohort (for example, immigrants who arrived between 1960 and 1964) and demographically comparable natives. The 1980 Census reports the 1979 wage differential between the same immigrant cohort and comparable natives, both groups now being ten years older. Thus, the tracking of each immigrant wave and of natives across censuses estimates the extent to which immigrant wages are responding to the assimilation experience.[18] Using the estimated rates of wage growth, it is then possible to predict how the wages of the various immigrant waves will change in the future, as immigrants accumulate experience in the U.S. labor market.

This type of statistical analysis, summarized in figure 6.2, indicates that, at the time of entry into the United States (at age twenty), men who migrated between 1975 and 1979 earned 21 percent less than comparable natives.[19] After twenty years the wage gap will narrow to

FIGURE 6.2

*The Impact of Assimilation on the Wage
of Two Immigrant Waves*

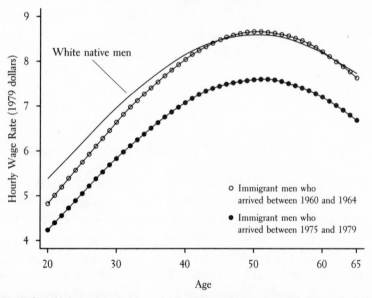

SOURCE: Author's tabulations from the 1970 and 1980 Public Use Samples of the U.S. Census. The predicted earnings profiles are based on log wage rate regressions estimated in the samples of immigrant and native white men aged twenty-five to sixty-four, where the estimated equations are evaluated at the mean value of the demographic characteristics observed in the immigrant population. The regressors include education, age, marital status, health status, an indicator of metropolitan residence, an indicator of whether the observation was drawn from the 1970 or the 1980 Census, the cohort of immigration, and years since migration. Predicted wage rates are given by the antilogs of the regression predictions. For technical details on the regression model used in the estimation, see George J. Borjas, "Immigration and Self-Selection," in Richard B. Freeman and John M. Abowd, eds., *Immigration, Trade, and the Labor Market* (Chicago: University of Chicago Press, 1990).

13 percent, but even after forty years in the United States the predicted wage differential will be 12 percent. The most recent immigrant cohort in census data, therefore, has a substantial wage disadvantage throughout its entire working life. There is some catching up, but the impact of labor market assimilation on the hourly wage is insufficient for the new immigrants ever to overcome the initial wage disadvantage. By contrast, immigrants who arrived in the United States between 1960 and 1964 entered the labor market with a wage disadvantage of 10 percent, and the wage gap disappeared after about two decades. Wage parity between this immigrant cohort and comparable natives remains until retirement age. Therefore, the tracking of specific immigrant cohorts across censuses reveals an important difference in the skill composition of the various immigrant waves. The labor market performance of the most recent immigrant wave is substantially poorer than that of the earlier cohort at any stage of the working life.

This finding has important policy implications. As suggested by the statistical profile presented in chapter 3, changes in the immigration market during the past two or three decades have led to a deterioration in the skill composition of the immigrant flow. The reasons for the changing nature of the U.S. offer, and for the resulting decline in the productivity of immigrant cohorts, are discussed in detail in the next chapter.

Contrary to the cross-sectional results, the impact of labor market assimilation on the hourly wage of immigrants is not sufficient for some immigrant cohorts to reach parity with comparable natives. The new waves of immigrants are unlikely to assimilate fully into the U.S. labor market during their lifetimes. Therefore, the optimistic picture of immigrant economic performance painted by the cross-section studies needs to be completely revised. The poor labor market performance of the new immigrants, in fact, implies that these groups are much more prone to be unemployed, more likely to lie below the poverty line, and more likely to qualify for public assistance than either natives or the earlier immigrants. The admission of unskilled immigrants is not costless in a welfare state. In view of this fact, it is important to determine whether the United States benefits from admitting large groups of relatively unskilled immigrants who find it difficult to assimilate into the U.S. economy.

Assimilation and National Origin

The data underlying the wage profiles of immigrants and natives in figure 6.2 can be used to calculate a measure of the rate of labor market assimilation, the rate at which the immigrant wage converges with that of comparable natives. Between ages twenty and fifty, the immigrant wage increased by 81 percent, or an annual growth rate of about 2.0 percent. Over the same period, the native wage increased by 61 percent, or a growth rate of 1.6 percent. The impact of assimilation on the immigrant wage, defined as the difference in the average rates of wage growth, is .4 percent. Although this rate of assimilation is not sufficient for recent immigrant waves to overcome their initial disadvantage, it is not numerically trivial. On average, labor market assimilation is an important feature of the immigrant experience in the United States.[20]

By tracking the earnings of different national-origin groups across censuses, the extent of labor market assimilation experienced by each of the groups can be estimated. As table 6.1 shows, assimilation rates differ greatly among the various groups. National origin plays a crucial role in determining the extent to which the earnings of immigrants catch up to the earnings of natives. For instance, immigrants originating in Germany or the Dominican Republic experience no labor market

TABLE 6.1

National-Origin Differentials in Assimilation Rates

Europe		Asia		Americas	
Germany	0	China	.8	Canada	.2
Greece	.4	India	.9	Cuba	1.2
Italy	0	Japan	1.1	Dominican Republic	0
Poland	.4	Korea	1.8	Jamaica	.4
United Kingdom	.3	Philippines	1.5	Mexico	.6

SOURCE: Adapted from George J. Borjas, "Self-Selection and the Earnings of Immigrants," *American Economic Review* 77 (September 1987): 542. The rate of assimilation is defined as the difference in the annual rate of growth (in percent) of immigrant and native wages between the ages of twenty and fifty. The calculations are based on log wage rate regressions estimated in the samples of immigrant and white native men aged twenty-five to sixty-four, using the 1970 and 1980 Public Use Samples of the U.S. Census. The dependent variable in these regressions was the logarithm of the hourly wage rate, and the regressors included education, age, marital status, health status, an indicator of metropolitan residence, an indicator of whether the observation was drawn from the 1970 or 1980 Census, the cohort of immigration, and the number of years since immigration. The three national-origin groups that report zero assimilation rates actually had slightly lower wage growth than comparable natives, but the differences between the two groups were statistically insignificant.

assimilation whatsoever. By contrast, the earnings of Chinese or Indian immigrants grow about .9 percent more per year than those of comparable natives; the earnings of Cuban immigrants about 1.2 percent more; and the earnings of Korean immigrants about 1.8 percent more.

It turns out that this variation in assimilation rates among the groups can be systematically understood in terms of underlying characteristics describing conditions in the immigration and labor markets.[21] In particular, the assimilation rate of an immigrant group depends on the group's incentives for adapting to the American labor market and on the similarity between the source country's economy and that of the United States.

The insight that persons who have the most to gain by adapting to the labor market invest the most in human capital is not new. In fact, this idea proved extremely useful in the analysis of the wage differential between men and women. An influential study by economists Jacob Mincer and Solomon Polachek argues that a person has more incentive to invest in human capital, the longer the period in which those skills will be used.[22] This hypothesis implies that women entering the labor market may have fewer incentives to accumulate marketable skills than men because women have a higher probability of quitting their jobs and engaging in child-raising activities, and this tendency partly accounts for the relatively lower female wage.

This hypothesis also suggests that immigrants have greater incentives to adapt when the possibility of return migration is small. If immigrants know that they are in the United States to stay, the investments made in skills valued by American employers have a longer expected payoff period and, thus, a higher potential return.[23] For example, immigrants who seek refuge from an oppressive political system typically find that return migration is very costly, so they have the most to gain by quickly deciding that they are here for good and might as well make the best of it.[24]

In fact, holding other factors constant, immigrants originating in countries that have just experienced Communist revolutions, or that have very unstable political regimes, have high labor market assimilation rates. By the same token, immigrants originating in politically stable democracies such as those in Western Europe have lower assimilation rates. The analysis of assimilation rates of forty-one national-

109

origin groups indicates that the earnings of refugees from Communist regimes grow at a rate of about 1 percent more per year than the earnings of immigrants originating in Western European countries.[25]

Immigrant adaptation to the U.S. labor market also depends on characteristics of the source country's economy. In particular, immigrants originating in countries with a high per capita GNP experience higher rates of assimilation. A doubling of the source country's per capita GNP increases the assimilation rate of the immigrant group by .2 percent. The swift assimilation of immigrants who originated in countries that resemble the United States suggests that persons who are more familiar with the types of jobs, industrial structure, and technological conditions prevailing in this country find it easier to adapt to the new economic environment.[26]

The main lesson provided by the differential rates of economic mobility among the national-origin groups is that assimilation is not an inevitable by-product of the immigrant experience. Some immigrants assimilate rather quickly, while others assimilate very slowly. The sorting generated by the immigration market allocates many types of persons into the population flow headed toward the United States. Because the various national-origin groups have different incentives and aptitudes for adapting to the United States, the immigration market not only determines who comes but also controls their long-run economic prospects.

Other Determinants of Immigrant Earnings

Many other factors besides assimilation generate differences between immigrant and native wage rates. As shown in chapter 3, immigrants differ from natives in their socioeconomic characteristics, such as education, English-language proficiency, and region of residence. These demographic characteristics are important determinants of earnings. Up to this point, in order to isolate the pure impact of labor market assimilation, the discussion has focused on the wage gap between immigrants and demographically comparable natives. The fact that large demographic differences exist between the two groups may

110

intensify or attenuate the wage differentials created by the assimilation process.

For instance, a major source of wage differentials between immigrant and native men is the difference in educational attainment between the two groups. In 1980, adult immigrant men had an average of 11.7 years of schooling, while white native men had 12.7 years. Moreover, American employers attach a higher value to schooling obtained in the United States. Apparently the types of skills taught in American schools are better suited for the U.S. labor market than the types of skills taught in the educational systems of other countries. In fact, the percentage increase in earnings associated with an additional year of school is at least 1 percentage point higher for natives than for immi-grants.[27] The combination of the immigrants' lower schooling levels and lower payoffs for foreign schooling implies that immigrants will earn substantially less than natives.

An additional factor that leads to significant wage differentials is the obvious difference in English-language proficiency between the groups. In a recent study, economists Walter McManus, Finis Welch, and William Gould document the importance of English-language acquisition in determining the U.S. wages of immigrants originating in Spanish-speaking countries.[28] Proficiency in the English language increases the earnings of Hispanic immigrant groups by a substantial amount: for a typical Hispanic, the lifetime dollar gain for becoming proficient in English is $79,000 (in 1988 dollars).[29]

English proficiency has a beneficial impact on immigrant earnings because bilingualism opens up many earnings and employment opportunities. A bilingual immigrant can choose from many more jobs in the labor market. These additional options increase the chances that the immigrant will find a better-paying job.

It could be argued, however, that most immigrants reside in ethnic enclaves, such as the Cubans in Miami's Little Havana, the Mexicans in East Los Angeles, or the Chinese in San Francisco's Chinatown. Immigrants residing in these enclaves, as long as they are of the "right" national origin, have little need for the English language, because they spend most of their working lives in an environment in which they can use the language and culture of the old country.[30] Furthermore, available evidence suggests that many immigrants living in ethnic enclaves work for employers of the same national origin. A survey of the Cuban enclave in Miami reveals that almost half of those who arrived in the Mariel boatlift in 1980 worked for Cuban employers in 1986.[31]

Nevertheless, living and working in an enclave does not eliminate the economic gains associated with English proficiency. Although the clustering of immigrants into ethnic ghettos reduces the need for bilingualism, it also restricts the set of economic opportunities available to them. Immigrants who lack familiarity with the English language and who work for their compatriots in the enclave are, in a sense, working in a one-company town. They can only offer their labor to a limited number of employers, which limits the extent of the market. Earnings and employment opportunities, therefore, are lower than they would be if they could speak English and trade with the outside world.

A final source of wage differentials between immigrants and natives is that the two groups live in different geographic regions. More than 75 percent of the immigrants live in the twenty-five largest smsas, but only 39 percent of natives reside in these areas. It is well known that persons living in metropolitan areas have substantially higher wages than persons living elsewhere. For instance, natives living in metropolitan areas earn about 21 percent more than their nonmetropolitan counterparts.

Because many more immigrants live in metropolitan locations, immigrant earnings should be significantly higher. But the typical immigrant residing in a metropolitan area earns only about 7 percent more than the immigrant who resides in a nonmetropolitan area.[32] The crowding of immigrants into a small number of labor markets leads to a relatively small payoff for metropolitan residence. The empirical evidence presented in chapter 5 implies that immigrant wages are sensitive to high concentrations of immigrants: the larger the number of immigrants in the local labor market, the lower the immigrant wage.

Presumably, as assimilation takes place, immigrants should learn that better job opportunities are available in other regions, and they should begin to disperse themselves over the country. In fact, the available evidence suggests that little geographic dispersion of this type takes place.[33] Immigrants arrive, take up residence in a small number of labor markets, and for the most part remain there for the rest of their lives. Therefore, there is no reason to suspect that internal migration within the United States is an important channel through which immigrants assimilate into the labor market.

112

The Actual Wage Gap Between Immigrants and Natives

The different demographic backgrounds of immigrants and natives implies that the comparison between immigrants and demographically comparable natives does not truly capture the differential in economic well-being between the two groups.[34] In particular, the actual wage gap between immigrants and natives may differ substantially from measures of the wage differential that standardize for differences in demographic characteristics. For instance, even though immigrants earn less than comparable natives, immigrants may have a more favorable demographic background, and the actual wage disadvantage experienced by the typical immigrant will be smaller than that indicated by the standardized wage gap. Alternatively, immigrants may have less favorable demographic characteristics than natives, and the standardized wage differential underestimates the actual wage gap between the two groups.

As figure 6.3 shows, the actual wage gap between the most recent immigrant wave and natives far exceeds the standardized gap. Men who migrated between 1975 and 1979 entered the labor market earning 26 percent less than natives, even though they only earned 21 percent less than comparable natives. Even after thirty years in the United States the actual wage disadvantage is estimated to remain a sizable 19 percent, while the standardized disadvantage at this time should be only 13 percent. Therefore, the fact that the 1975–1979 immigrant cohort has relatively unfavorable demographic characteristics increases their wage disadvantage relative to natives.

By contrast, the actual wage differential between immigrant men who arrived between 1960 and 1964 and natives does not differ all that much from the standardized differential. At the time of entry into the United States, these immigrants earned 11 percent less than natives, but earned only 10 percent less than comparable natives. After thirty years in the United States, the immigrants should earn about 2 percent less than natives, while having reached wage parity with comparable natives. Hence the demographic characteristics of this cohort are only slightly less favorable than those of natives, and the distinction between standardized and unstandardized wage differentials is not particularly significant.

113

FIGURE 6.3

*Actual Wage Gaps Between Immigrants and Natives
over the Working Life*

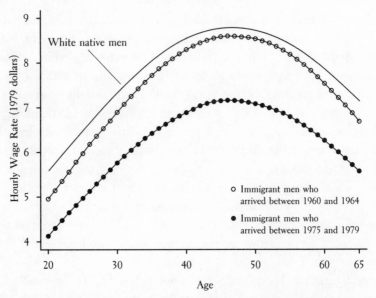

SOURCE: Author's tabulations from the 1970 and 1980 Public Use Samples of the U.S. Census. The predicted earnings profiles are based on log wage rate regressions estimated in the samples of immigrant and native white men aged twenty-five to sixty-four. The regressors include age, an indicator of whether the observation was drawn from the 1970 or the 1980 Census, the cohort of immigration, and years since migration. Predicted wage rates are given by the antilogs of the regression predictions. For technical details on the regression model used in the estimation, see George J. Borjas, "Immigration and Self-Selection," in Richard B. Freeman and John M. Abowd, eds., *Immigration, Trade, and the Labor Market* (Chicago: University of Chicago Press, 1990).

The striking contrast between figure 6.2 and figure 6.3 indicates that differences in demographic characteristics between immigrants and natives are playing an increasingly important role in the U.S. labor market. In particular, the demographic characteristics of immigrants have deteriorated significantly in the past two or three decades. Because of this decline, the actual wage of recent immigrants will remain far below that of natives throughout their entire working lives. The impact of assimilation on earnings is just too small to ensure that the new immigrants will ever reach wage parity with natives in the U.S. labor market.

CHAPTER 7

Why Are the New Immigrants Less Skilled Than the Old?

RECENT IMMIGRANT waves are not as successful in the U.S. labor market as earlier waves.[1] Entry wages for the typical person who migrated in the late 1970s were significantly lower than entry wages for the immigrant who arrived in the early 1960s. The fact that the productivity and skills of successive immigrant waves have declined during the past two or three decades has considerable policy significance. Why did this sizable decline in immigrant skills occur? Is the decline economically beneficial for the United States? Should the decline be slowed and perhaps even reversed in the future and, if so, how?

This chapter shows that changes in immigration policy and in economic and political conditions here and abroad have altered the nature of America's offer in the immigration market, have attracted a different type of immigrant, and have consequently led to the declining skills of immigrant flows entering the United States.

Lifetime Wealth of First-Generation Immigrants

Chapter 6 documented that many immigrant groups have lower wage rates than natives throughout much of their working lives. If one takes these wage rates, for any particular length of the work year (say 2,000 hours), one can easily predict potential annual earnings at each age.[2] By adding these annual earnings over the working life, and after discounting future earnings at a 5-percent rate of interest, it is possible to estimate the present value of the earnings stream for each of the groups.[3] This present value measures the potential lifetime earnings or wealth that can be accumulated in the American labor market by each of the immigrant waves and by natives.

As table 7.1 shows, the potential lifetime earnings of the typical white native man has a present value of a little more than $277,000 (in 1979 dollars). The typical person who immigrated between 1975 and 1979 can expect lifetime earnings of approximately $218,000, about 21 percent less than natives. In contrast, the typical immigrant in the 1950–1959 cohort, who migrated prior to the 1965 amendments, has lifetime earnings of $273,000. Members of this immigrant cohort experienced only a 2-percent lifetime earnings disadvantage relative to natives. The decline in potential lifetime earnings that has occurred among successive immigrant waves, therefore, is substantial. The actual earnings differential between immigrants and natives is

TABLE 7.1

Potential Lifetime Earnings of Immigrant Versus Native Men

| | | Percentage Difference in Potential Lifetime Earnings Between Immigrant Men and: | |
Group	Present Value of Earnings Stream (in 1979 Dollars)	White Natives	Comparable White Natives
White native men	$277,458	—	—
Immigrant men			
1950–1959 cohort	272,996	−1.6	−2.0
1960–1964 cohort	262,162	−5.5	−3.7
1965–1969 cohort	248,502	−10.4	−6.1
1970–1974 cohort	230,074	−17.1	−10.0
1975–1979 cohort	218,013	−21.4	−15.5

SOURCE: Author's tabulations from the 1970 and 1980 Public Use Samples of the U.S. Census. The calculations are based on log wage rate regressions estimated in the samples of immigrant men and white native men aged twenty-five to sixty-four. The dependent variable in these regressions is the logarithm of the hourly wage rate, and the regressors include age, an indicator of whether the observation was drawn from the 1970 or the 1980 Census, the cohort of immigration, and the number of years since immigration. In the calculation of the differential between immigrants and comparable natives, the regression also includes education, marital status, health status, and an indicator of metropolitan residence. The wage rates are converted into potential annual earnings by taking antilogs of the predictions and by assuming a 2,000-hour work year throughout the life cycle for all groups. The present value calculations use a 5-percent rate of discount. For technical details on the econometric methodology and the data, see George J. Borjas, "Self-Selection and Immigration," in Richard B. Freeman and John M. Abowd, eds., *Immigration, Trade, and the Labor Market* (Chicago: University of Chicago Press, 1990).

116

often much larger than the standardized one. As noted in the previous chapter, controlling for differences between the two groups in such demographic characteristics as education, health, and residential location generally increases the earnings of immigrants relative to those of natives, particularly for the most recent immigrant cohorts. For example, men who migrated between 1975 and 1979 will earn an average of 16 percent less than a demographically comparable native over their working lives, but will earn 21 percent less than the typical native. These figures indicate that immigrants who arrived in the late 1970s have a less favorable socioeconomic background than the typical native.

By contrast, immigrants who came in the 1950s have potential lifetime earnings that are only 2 percent lower than those of natives, regardless of whether demographic characteristics among the groups are held constant. Earlier immigrant waves, therefore, have demographic characteristics that are, on average, quite similar to those of natives, and standardization for differences in these characteristics barely affects the magnitude of the earnings gap.

In short, there has been a significant and steady decline in skills and earnings potential among the successive immigrant waves that entered the United States between 1950 and 1980. Immigrants who arrived in the 1950s have about 25 percent higher lifetime earnings than immigrants who arrived in the late 1970s. Moreover, even if demographic characteristics are held constant between the groups, immigrants who arrived in the 1950s still have about 16 percent higher lifetime earnings than immigrants who arrived in the late 1970s. This deterioration in the skill composition of the immigrant flow over the past two or three decades is the most important single feature of postwar immigration to the United States.

Although these results document that many immigrant cohorts, particularly the most recent ones, perform poorly in the U.S. labor market, they do not imply that immigrants lose by coming to the United States. Just because immigrants do not earn as much as natives does not suggest that immigration was a poor investment. After all, despite their poor labor market performance, most immigrants choose to remain in the country. The implication is that they still gain relative to opportunities available elsewhere.

National Origin and Economic Performance

There is substantial variation in potential lifetime earnings among national-origin groups.[4] As shown in table 7.2, immigrants originating in Western European countries or in advanced economies (such as Germany, Canada, and Japan) tend to have higher lifetime earnings, relative to natives, than immigrants originating in the less developed South American or Asian countries. The typical British immigrant who came in the late 1970s has about 21 percent higher lifetime earnings than natives, while immigrants originating in China or Mexico have a very large lifetime earnings disadvantage, earning at least 30 percent less than natives.

Because of changing economic conditions in the United States and abroad and because of shifts in immigration policy, the source countries responsible for immigration to the United States have changed drasti-

TABLE 7.2
Potential Lifetime Earnings of the 1975–1979 Cohort

Immigrant Men's Country of Origin	Percentage Difference in Potential Lifetime Earnings Between Immigrant Men and:	
	White Native Men	Comparable White Native Men
Europe		
Germany	18.2	7.6
Greece	−18.0	−10.1
Italy	−6.2	5.1
Poland	−18.9	−17.5
United Kingdom	20.6	11.1
Asia		
China	−30.9	−30.7
India	−6.8	−28.6
Japan	20.4	7.7
Korea	−8.1	−16.8
Philippines	−13.2	−17.2
Americas		
Canada	20.5	15.5
Cuba	−29.2	−23.7
Dominican Republic	−49.3	−14.5
Jamaica	−32.6	−25.6
Mexico	−38.0	−14.5

SOURCE: Adapted from George J. Borjas, "Immigration and Self-Selection," in Richard B. Freeman and John M. Abowd, eds., *Immigration, Trade, and the Labor Market* (Chicago: University of Chicago Press, 1990), tables 3 and 6. The methodological details are the same as for table 7.1.

cally in the past two or three decades. Whereas seven of the ten countries with the largest immigration flows in the 1950s were in Europe, only one country in the top ten was European in the 1970s. European countries accounted for more than half of the immigrants in the 1950s, for one-third of the immigrants in the 1960s, and for fewer than 20 percent of the immigrants in the 1970s. By contrast, Asian and Latin American countries accounted for about 40 percent of the immigrants in the 1950s, but for more than 80 percent of the immigrants in the 1970s.[5]

The sizable earnings differentials among the various nationalities suggest that the shift in the national-origin mix of the immigrant flow may be largely responsible for the decline in immigrant skills since the 1950s. In fact, during the 1950s, the national-origin groups that accounted for most of the immigrant flow also tended to be the most successful in the United States. Such groups as the British, Germans, and Canadians, which accounted for a large fraction of the immigrant flow, usually have higher lifetime earnings than natives. In other words, there was a positive correlation between the fraction of the immigrant flow originating in a particular source country and the U.S. earnings of that national-origin group.

The sign of this correlation has changed in recent years. Today, the national-origin groups that account for most of the immigrant flow, such as Mexicans, Filipinos, and Koreans, typically have much lower lifetime earnings than natives. Therefore, there is now a negative correlation between the fraction of the flow originating in the source country and the labor market performance of that group.[6] The changing correlation indicates the existence of a strong link between the declining skills of immigrant waves and the concurrent change in the national-origin mix of the immigrant flow.

It is tempting to conjecture that perhaps most of the decline in skills is due to the entry of large numbers of unskilled illegal Mexicans during the 1970s and that the "problem" would be solved once this flow is stopped. But this is not the case. As figure 7.1 shows, the decline in potential lifetime earnings among successive immigrant waves is as pronounced among non-Mexican immigrants as it is among the entire immigrant pool, including the Mexican flow.

It is certainly true that the entry of unskilled Mexicans substantially lowers the average earnings observed in the immigrant population. For

119

FIGURE 7.1

*The Impact of Mexican and Indo-Chinese Immigration on the Lifetime
Earnings Disadvantage of Immigrant Waves*

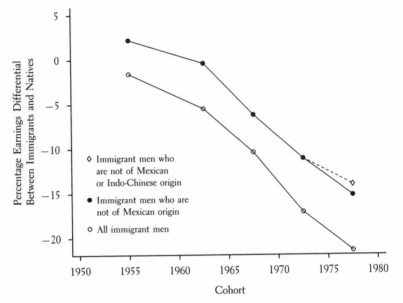

SOURCE: Author's tabulations from the 1970 and 1980 Public Use Samples of the U.S. Census. The results are obtained from log wage regressions in which the samples of Mexican or Indo-Chinese immigrants are deleted from the immigrant population. The methodological details are the same as for table 7.1

instance, the average lifetime earnings disadvantage between immigrants who came in the late 1970s and white natives is 21 percent if Mexicans are included in the calculations and 15 percent if they are not. Hence the Mexican flow is by itself responsible for one-third of the wage disadvantage between recent immigrants and natives.

Even if Mexicans had not migrated to the United States, however, the recent immigrant waves would have substantially lower lifetime earnings than earlier waves. In particular, the typical non-Mexican who migrated in the late 1970s is predicted to have about 17 percent lower lifetime earnings than the typical non-Mexican who migrated in the 1950s. If the Mexican population is included in these comparisons, the magnitude of the decline in lifetime earnings is slightly larger, about 20 percent.

It is also tempting to attribute the poor economic performance of the immigrant wave that entered in the late 1970s to the large number of Indo-Chinese refugees present in that wave. These refugees, originating in Cambodia, Laos, and Vietnam, may have had exceptional difficulties in the U.S. labor market because they were uprooted from their home countries in a relatively short period of time and with little advance planning. The poor performance of this sizable immigrant flow would then account for the relatively low earnings of the immigrant wave that arrived between 1975 and 1979. This conjecture, however, is incorrect. As figure 7.1 also shows, the decline in lifetime earnings among successive immigrant waves would have been observed, and would have been almost as steep, even if the Indo-Chinese refugee flow had never reached the United States.

Therefore, the entry of large numbers of Mexican illegal aliens and the arrival of Indo-Chinese refugees during the 1970s are not the main factors responsible for the overall decline in average skills among successive immigrant waves. Rather, that decline reflects a much more fundamental shift in the national-origin mix of the immigrant flow. This insight, however, does not really provide an answer to the questions why such a decline in immigrant skills took place and why immigrants from some countries tend to be less skilled than immigrants from other countries. What factors account for the poor labor market performance of immigrants who originate in the countries that make up the bulk of immigration today?

The Deteriorating Socioeconomic Background of Immigrants

As noted above, recent immigrant waves have less favorable demographic characteristics than earlier waves. Perhaps the most visible manifestation of this trend is the precipitous decline in the educational attainment of successive immigrant waves (relative to natives). The evidence presented in chapter 3 indicated that the typical immigrant who arrived in the United States in the late 1950s had .3 years more schooling than natives, while the typical immigrant who arrived in the late 1970s had .7 years fewer schooling.

The reason for the relative decline in educational attainment among successive immigrant waves lies in the changing national-origin mix of the immigrant flow. The populations of the source countries responsible for the bulk of immigration today tend to have relatively little schooling. In Mexico, the average schooling level is only six years, and in the Philippines it is eight years. By contrast, persons who migrated in the 1950s or early 1960s tended to originate in countries with relatively well-educated populations. The typical person living in Germany or the United Kingdom has about eleven years of schooling.[7] Even if the immigration market randomly allocated persons in each source country to the immigrant flow, it is likely that the new immigrants would have less schooling and lower earnings than the old.

But persons are not randomly allocated into the immigrant flow. Highly educated persons in the country of origin choose to migrate only if the American labor market rewards their education more than the source country does. Alternatively, the United States will attract less-educated workers if schooling is better rewarded in the source country.

The average rate of return to schooling in the countries responsible for the immigrant flow in the 1970s is about 10 to 15 percent higher than in the countries responsible for the flow in the 1950s.[8] This change implies that highly educated workers have less incentive to migrate to the United States now than before.

Because the populations of the source countries responsible for the new immigration have relatively little schooling, and because these source countries tend to offer a higher payoff to schooling, the new immigrants are likely to have less education than the old. In fact, these two factors are responsible for a decline of about half a year in the average educational attainment of immigrants (relative to natives).[9] If a year of schooling increases lifetime earnings by about 10 percent, the increasing gap between immigrant and native educational attainment is responsible for a 5-percent drop in the relative earnings of immigrants.

Therefore, much of the decline in the schooling level of successive immigrant waves is attributable to the changing nature of America's offer in the immigration market. Nonetheless, the data indicate that the drop in immigrant earnings cannot be entirely explained in terms of changes in education or in other socioeconomic characteristics. Immigrant earnings declined even after controlling for the differences in demographic characteristics among successive immigrant waves. The following discussion addresses the factors responsible for this sizable decline.

Economic Development in the Source Countries

National origin influences the labor market performance of immigrants in the United States because source countries differ dramatically in their level of industrialization and economic development. Clearly, the kinds of skills workers acquire in highly developed economies are not the same as those acquired in the less developed countries.

After all, the industrial structure of advanced economies and the types of skills rewarded by those labor markets greatly resemble the industrial structure of the United States and the types of skills rewarded by American employers. It is likely, therefore, that skills acquired in advanced economies are highly transferable to the U.S. labor market. Immigrants originating in such countries can carry their skills with them and will generally find U.S. employers who attach a high value to that human capital.

In contrast, the industrial structures and labor markets of less developed countries require skills that are much less useful in the American labor market. The human capital embodied in residents of the less developed countries is, to some extent, specific to those countries and is unlikely to be easily transferable to the American economy. Persons originating in less developed countries are likely to lack many of the skills valued by U.S. employers and will probably be relatively unsuccessful in the labor market.[10]

In fact, even after controlling for differences in demographic characteristics among immigrants, there is a strong positive correlation between immigrant earnings and the level of economic development in the country of origin, as measured by the country's per capita GNP. Immigrants who originate in high-income countries have higher lifetime earnings than otherwise similar immigrants who originate in less developed countries: doubling the source country's per capita GNP increases the lifetime earnings of immigrants in the United States by 5 percent.[11]

This positive correlation partly explains why the new immigrants have lower lifetime earnings than the old. The typical person who immigrated in the 1970s originated in a country with a 1980 per capita GNP of $3,500 (in 1980 dollars), while the typical immigrant in the 1950s originated in a country with a per capita GNP of $7,600. The shift in the national-origin mix of the immigrant flow cut by half the per capita GNP of the country represented by the typical immigrant during this period. As a result, immigrants who arrived in the 1970s will earn about 5 percent less than demographically comparable immigrants who arrived in the 1950s.

The Rewards for Skills in the Source Countries

The nonrandom sorting of persons among countries generated by the immigration market implies that immigrants are not representative members of the populations of their countries of origin. The skills of foreign-born persons residing in the United States differ from the skills of persons who decide to remain in their home countries, from the skills of persons who migrate elsewhere, and from the skills of U.S. natives.

Individuals in any country are on the lookout for the best place to live. The home country provides a specific set of economic and political opportunities, and a few potential host countries provide alternative opportunities. In addition, both the source country and the potential host countries have migration policies that affect the costs of moving across international boundaries. Bearing in mind the constraints imposed by entry and exit policies and by other immigration costs, individuals compare the various options and choose the country that appears to offer the most promise.

Some persons find it best to migrate to the United States; others find that host countries such as Australia or Canada provide better opportunities; and most simply perceive that the costs of immigration far exceed the benefits and decide to remain in their birthplace. In the immigration market, a nonrandom subset of persons chooses to migrate to the United States.

A central question is raised by this approach. Which types of persons are the ones most likely to be attracted by the United States? In particular, are they the most or the least skilled persons from the population of the source country? As we have seen, the nature of the skill sorting generated by the immigration market depends on which country pays the highest prices for the skills that individuals have to offer.

Education is only one of a variety of skills and abilities that determine a person's earnings, and a summary measure of the prices of skills is needed to assess whether a favorable or an unfavorable skill sorting takes place overall. Such a summary measure is given by the amount of inequality in a country's income distribution.

For instance, an economy with an egalitarian income distribution pays relatively low returns to skills. In such an economy, highly skilled workers do not earn much more than the unskilled. Returns to skills, therefore, are higher in the United States than in countries with egalitarian income distributions. Because persons migrate to countries that provide the best economic opportunities, the immigrant flow originating in source countries with less income inequality than the United States will have above-average skills or productivities. The skill composition of this immigrant flow resembles a classic "brain drain," in which the typical immigrant is more skilled than the average person in the population.[12]

Alternatively, the returns to skills are higher in source countries that have more income inequality than the United States. Highly skilled persons then face relatively better economic opportunities in their country of origin and have little incentive to migrate to the United States. The immigrant flow from those countries, therefore, is likely to contain a large number of unskilled workers.

Like goods, skills flow to countries that value them the most. The nonrandom sorting generated by the immigration market suggests that the United States is likely to attract highly skilled workers from some countries and unskilled workers from others. Moreover, the nature of the selection that characterizes the immigrant flow should depend on the extent of income inequality in the source country relative to that in the United States. In fact, if demographic characteristics are held constant, there exists a negative correlation between the potential lifetime earnings of immigrant groups in the United States and the amount of income inequality in the source country. The typical immigrant originating in a country with a level of income inequality like that of Mexico earns about 4 percent less than an immigrant originating in a country with a level of inequality like that of the United Kingdom, *even if* the two source countries had exactly the same per capita GNP.[13] The data clearly indicate that differences in income inequality among source countries—or, more precisely, differences in the prices of skills—lead to very different types of persons choosing to become immigrants.

In a recent study, J. Edward Taylor examined the migration histories of persons originating in a rural Mexican village, and his results provide strong complementary evidence.[14] His data suggest that persons who migrated to the United States had incomes below the town average prior to migration. Immigrants originating in this Mexican village, therefore, were relatively unsuccessful in the Mexican labor market.

This type of sorting occurs because the economic returns to skill are higher in Mexico than in the United States.[15] Thus it is the least skilled Mexicans who have the most to gain from immigration.

The fact that the amount of dispersion in the source country's income distribution determines the type of person who finds it profitable to migrate provides an additional explanation for the old immigrants being more skilled, on average, than the new. Not only did the typical 1950s immigrant originate in a more advanced economy (and have more transferable skills), he also originated in a country that has less income inequality than did the typical 1970s immigrant.

In fact, the changing national-origin mix of the immigrant flow increased by 50 percent the amount of income inequality characterizing the typical immigrant's source country.[16] This increase is responsible for a 2-percent decline in the lifetime earnings of immigrant waves over the period.[17] Therefore, the shift that occurred in the national-origin mix of the immigrant flow since 1950 led to a deterioration in the nature of the skill sorting generated by the immigration market.

The decrease in the level of economic development in the countries responsible for immigration to the United States and the increase in the extent of income inequality characterizing these source countries together account for a 7-percent decline in the lifetime earnings of immigrants. The deteriorating educational attainment among successive immigrant waves is responsible for a further 5-percent drop. These factors alone, therefore, explain about 60 percent of the decline in immigrant earnings between the wave of the 1950s and that of the 1970s.

Economic Conditions in the United States

The sorting generated by the immigration market depends not only on economic conditions in the source countries, but also on economic conditions in the United States. Obviously, the size of the immigrant flow is affected by fluctuations in this country's business cycle. It is no coincidence that during the 1930s only 528,000 persons came to the

United States, the smallest immigrant flow of any decade since the 1820s.

The skill composition of the immigrant flow is also affected by cyclical fluctuations. There is a positive correlation between the lifetime earnings of immigrants and the U.S. unemployment rate at the time of immigration: persons who come to the United States during periods of high unemployment tend to be more skilled. In fact, a 1 percentage point increase in the U.S. unemployment rate leads to the migration of persons who have about 3-percent higher potential lifetime earnings.[18]

It is well known that high unemployment rates have a particularly adverse effect on the earnings and employment opportunities of unskilled workers.[19] During recessions, not only are the unskilled the first to be laid off, they are also the ones whose real wages fall the most. When the U.S. unemployment rate is high, the attractiveness of the U.S. offer declines for all potential migrants in the source countries, so that fewer persons immigrate. But because of the disproportionate effect of unemployment on unskilled workers, the migration incentives are reduced most for these workers, and the average skill level of the smaller immigrant flow increases.

Political Conditions in the Source Countries

Immigrant flows arise not only as a result of international differences in economic opportunities, but also in response to political upheavals in source countries. Between 1946 and 1987, more than 2 million persons migrated to the United States as refugees or asylees. Who are the refugees? Why do they come to the United States? How do they perform in the U.S. labor market?

It is traditional to think of refugees as "noneconomic" immigrants. In their quest for freedom at any price, refugees presumably are blind to the economic consequences of their immigration decision.[20] A more practical approach allows for the possibility that immigration is not necessarily a life-or-death decision for all refugees. Many indeed have

127

the luxury of comparing economic opportunities among potential countries of residence, and many take into account the economic consequences of their decision.

The immigration incentives of "economic" refugees are clearly illustrated by the kinds of persons who seek refuge soon after a Communist takeover. Prior to the political upheaval, the market economy in the source country ensured that highly skilled individuals, who possess certain abilities or entrepreneurship, were relatively successful. A Communist revolution (at least in the first few years) subverts this relationship between skills and earnings. Typically, one of the first actions of the Communist regime is to confiscate financial and entrepreneurial assets, redistributing these assets to persons who were not successful in the market system that existed prior to the revolution. Persons who used to do well in the market economy see their assets confiscated, and their economic position worsens. Persons who did not do well in the market economy are now heavily subsidized, and many probably gain substantially from the political upheaval.

It is not surprising, therefore, that skilled persons are the ones with the largest economic incentive to leave the Communist system behind, while unskilled workers, who may be better off in the new political structure, have the least incentive to migrate because they gain the most from the revolution and because they lack the skills and abilities needed to succeed in the U.S. economy. In this view, therefore, refugee flows are determined by the same comparisons of earnings and employment opportunities among countries that determine the flows of other immigrants. Of course, it may well be the case that political oppression is also an important factor motivating the immigration decision. But it is not the only factor.

Recent research suggests that the skills of immigrant flows change as a result of political upheavals in the source country.[21] In particular, immigrants leaving a source country soon after a Communist takeover have higher earnings potential than immigrants who left that country prior to the political turmoil. The labor market experiences of different waves of Cuban immigrants in the United States illustrate this result. Cubans who immigrated in the 1950s, prior to the 1959 Communist revolution, have potential lifetime earnings that are 15 percent lower than the earnings of natives. The first wave of refugees, who arrived in the United States between 1960 and 1964, are estimated to earn about 2 percent less than natives over their working lives. As the political changes in Cuba became permanent, and the pool of skilled workers shrank, the earnings potential of the subsequent waves of Cuban immigrants returned to its prerevolutionary level. Cubans who immigrated in the late 1960s, for instance, have 17 percent lower earnings than natives, while those who immigrated in the late 1970s have 29 percent lower earnings than natives.[22]

Discrimination Against Immigrants

Some readers are undoubtedly surprised by the fact that I have scarcely mentioned the possibility that labor market discrimination against immigrants might be responsible for much of their wage disadvantage. Ever since the path-breaking work of economist Gary Becker in 1957, the literature on discrimination by race, sex, or ethnic origin has grown substantially.[23] A frequent empirical result in this literature is that blacks earn less than demographically comparable whites. This fact is typically interpreted as evidence of employment discrimination against blacks.[24]

The data indicate that many immigrants have lower earnings than demographically comparable white natives. I have attempted to explain these earnings differentials in terms of underlying skill and productivity differences, not in terms of discriminatory behavior by American employers against specific national-origin groups. It would seem that a much simpler approach would be to follow the lead of the employment-discrimination literature and simply conclude, based on the empirical evidence, that immigrants who are not white, northwestern Europeans tend to be discriminated against.

There are several reasons, however, why such an inference would be incorrect. First, the earnings differentials between the various national-origin groups and natives can be understood in terms of economic and political characteristics of the source countries and of the United States; in other words, the parameters of the U.S. offer in the immigration market determine much of the wage gap between immigrants and natives. For example, unless it is argued that American firms arbitrarily

The Economic Impact of Immigration

discriminate against persons who happen to originate in countries with large levels of income inequality, the discrimination hypothesis is unable to explain the poor labor market performance of these immigrant groups. But this result is clearly implied by the sorting generated in an immigration market in which no employer discriminates on the basis of national origin.

In addition, several recent studies provide strong evidence that systematic discrimination against Hispanics or Asians (the two dominant groups in recent immigrant waves) is not an important aspect of the American labor market.[25] For instance, native men of Mexican ancestry earn about the same as demographically comparable white non-Hispanic natives.[26] In other words, the U.S. labor market does not tax Hispanics because of their ethnicity. Thus, the low wage of Hispanic immigrants cannot be attributed to their Hispanic background because natives of Hispanic origin perform as well in the labor market as comparable non-Hispanic natives. And it cannot be attributed to the fact that they are immigrants, because non-Hispanic immigrants often outperform them in the labor market.

Similarly, Asian natives (persons of Asian background, but born in the U.S.) are quite successful in the United States. In fact, these workers earn about 3 percent more than white natives.[27] Again, it is difficult to explain the fact that many Asian immigrants have lower earnings than comparable white natives in terms of labor market discrimination against Asians, for the American labor market does not seem to discriminate against Asian natives.

Objections to the Empirical Analysis

The empirical finding that recent immigrant waves have substantially lower potential lifetime earnings than earlier waves is based on the contrast of immigrant labor market performance between the 1970 and 1980 Censuses. These wage comparisons are clearly influenced by the deterioration in aggregate labor market conditions during the decade. The unemployment rate in 1970 was only 4.8 percent, but it had increased to 7.0 percent by 1980. It is possible that part of the observed change in the immigrant wage across the censuses reflects a much greater sensitivity to cyclical fluctuations in the immigrant population.

If the economic opportunities of immigrants decline much faster than those of natives when a cyclical downturn occurs, the earnings of an immigrant cohort would not grow much between 1970 and 1980, which would be interpreted as evidence of little economic assimilation. Moreover, the earnings of newly arrived immigrants in the 1980 Census would be relatively lower than the earnings of newly arrived immigrants in the 1970 Census, which would be taken as evidence that the most recent wave is less skilled than the earlier wave. Therefore, the differential impact of cyclical fluctuations on immigrants and natives, or, as demographers call them, "period effects," may be responsible for the substantive findings discussed in this chapter.

The research studies summarized above make an explicit assumption about the impact of the business cycle on immigrant and native earnings. In particular, changes in aggregate economic conditions have the same percentage effect on the earnings of immigrants as on the earnings of natives.[28] If this assumption is true, the calculation of immigrant wage growth relative to native wage growth accounts for the worsening economic conditions, and the conclusions drawn in this chapter immediately follow.

It is possible, however, that immigrant earnings respond to the business cycle in a different way. The earnings of immigrant men may be as sensitive as those of young native men, a group known to be greatly affected by changes in economic conditions. It can be argued that, in some sense, newly arrived immigrants resemble young persons entering the labor market for the first time, so that the impact of the business cycle on labor market conditions may be quite similar for the two groups.

As table 7.3 shows, the lifetime earnings differential between immigrants and comparable natives remains large even if immigrant earnings are assumed to be as sensitive to the business cycle as the earnings of young natives are. For the group of persons who immigrated in the late 1970s, the lifetime wage disadvantage drops from the previously reported 16 percent to 12 percent.

Alternatively, immigrant earnings may be as sensitive to cyclical fluctuations as are the earnings of disadvantaged native minorities, such

131

TABLE 7.3

The Business Cycle and the Lifetime Earnings of Immigrants

Group	White Native Men	Young Native Men	Black Native Men	Mexican-American Men
	Percentage Difference in Lifetime Earnings Between Immigrant and Comparable White Native Men if the Immigrant Wage Is as Responsive to Cyclical Fluctuations as the Wage of:			
1950–1959 cohort	−2.0	−.5	4.5	2.3
1960–1964 cohort	−3.7	−1.6	−.5	−1.0
1965–1969 cohort	−6.1	−3.4	−5.5	−4.7
1970–1974 cohort	−10.0	−6.8	−11.8	−9.7
1975–1979 cohort	−15.5	−11.8	−20.1	−16.7

SOURCE: Author's tabulations from the 1970 and 1980 Public Use Samples of the U.S. Census. The sample of young native men includes persons aged eighteen to twenty-four. The methodological details are the same as for table 7.1.

as blacks or Mexican-Americans. During the 1970s, however, the earnings of black men increased much more than the earnings of white men, due perhaps to the impact of affirmative action programs.[29] Hence black earnings were actually less sensitive to the worsening economic conditions than were the earnings of other groups. If the immigrant wage were as responsive to business cycle fluctuations as the black wage, the lifetime earnings disadvantage of the most recent immigrant wave would actually increase to 20 percent, while if it were as responsive as the wage of Mexican-Americans, the lifetime earnings disadvantage would increase to 17 percent.

Therefore, relaxing the assumption that the effect of business cycle fluctuations on the immigrant wage resembles the effect experienced by the typical white native does not alter the results. In fact, the estimated lifetime earnings disadvantage may be larger than that reported in this chapter and almost certainly will not be much smaller.

Additional problems with the statistical analysis arise because of data limitations inherent in the decennial censuses. For instance, the finding of declining immigrant skills may be the result of changes in census-enumeration procedures: it can be argued that many more unskilled immigrants were "found" in recent waves in 1980 than in 1970. The finding can also be explained in terms of the selective emigration of the foreign-born. It is certainly possible that only highly skilled workers from the immigrant waves arriving in the 1960s found it worthwhile to remain in the United States until the time of the 1970 Census, while only the relatively unskilled from the waves arriving in the 1970s remained until the time of the 1980 Census. The comparison of immigrant earnings across censuses would suggest declining immigrant skills even if the skill composition of the immigrant flow, prior to emigration, had not changed over time. Unfortunately, there is no way to determine the practical importance of these problems with currently available data. Nevertheless, as shown in chapter 3, the deteriorating skills of successive immigrant waves documented in this chapter are part of a long-run trend extending back to the mid-1930s. It is therefore unlikely that the findings result solely from changes in enumeration procedures across censuses or from arbitrary changes in the nature of the emigration process over time.

The argument that the new immigrants are less skilled than the old recurs throughout American history. In 1919, economist Paul Douglas (who went on to become a U.S. Senator from Illinois) wrote, "it is the custom of each generation to view the immigrants of its day as inferior to the stock that once came over."[30]

The empirical evidence presented here resurrects the debate yet another time. The facts are clear: the skills and earnings of recent immigrant waves are substantially below the skills and earnings of earlier waves.

CHAPTER 8

Employment and Poverty
in the Immigrant Population

THE PREVIOUS two chapters documented the magnitude and source of the substantial differences in wage rates both between immigrants and natives and within the immigrant population. The economic well-being of immigrants, however, depends on total labor earnings (as well as on returns to other assets), not simply on the wage rate per unit of time worked. An immigrant's labor market earnings in any particular year are affected by his labor force participation decision, by his success in finding and holding a job, and by the number of hours he works when employed.

Therefore, a comprehensive assessment of the economic welfare of immigrants requires a complementary analysis of their employment experience. How strongly are immigrants attached to the U.S. labor market? How does this level of attachment differ from that of natives? And how much variation is there in the employment experiences of different immigrant groups?

These questions play a central role in the debate over the economic impact of immigration. Because of their low hourly wages, recent immigrant waves are already likely to have a relatively high incidence of poverty. This propensity will surely increase if these immigrant waves also have a relatively weak attachment to the labor market or if they have a difficult time getting a job and remaining employed.

The "crowding" of unskilled immigrants into unemployment and poverty may have major social and economic costs. After all, the creation and growth of an immigrant underclass can only compound many of the serious problems that afflict modern American society. In addition, immigrants may be responsible for substantial cost increases in the many income-transfer programs that make up the welfare state. For instance, it has been claimed that illegal aliens alone cost American

134

taxpayers about $25 billion a year because of their frequent participation in these programs.[1]

This chapter describes three aspects of the employment experience of immigrants: the labor force participation rate, the unemployment rate, and the number of hours worked per year.[2] The empirical evidence is striking. More recent immigrant waves have lower participation rates, have higher unemployment rates, and work fewer hours per year than earlier waves. Because the recent cohorts are also less skilled, the differentials in employment propensities among successive immigrant waves suggest a much steeper decline in the economic well-being of immigrants than the decline in hourly wages documented in the previous two chapters. In fact, the empirical evidence suggests that the deterioration in the labor market performance of immigrants may be responsible for a sizable decline in national income.

The overall impact of all these trends on the incidence of poverty in the immigrant population is sizable and disturbing. Recent immigrant waves, and some immigrant national-origin groups, have poverty rates that exceed those of black natives.

Immigrant Labor Supply

The Bureau of Labor Statistics defines a labor force participant as a person who is either working or actively looking for work. Many people find it worthwhile to be in the labor force, but many other people do not. Each person makes his labor force participation decision by comparing the gains to be made from being employed with the gains to be made from staying at home and engaging either in leisure or in "household-production" activities, such as raising children.

Therefore, a person enters the labor force when the job more than compensates for the value he attaches to his nonmarket time. In other words, he works when the wage rate is higher than the value of his time in the household.[3] This hypothesis implies that, for instance, women with preschool children are less likely to participate in the labor force and that persons with higher wage rates are relatively more likely to work.

Because hourly wage rates vary substantially within the immigrant population, work incentives are likely to vary significantly among immigrant groups.[4] Immigrants who have relatively high wage rates have more to gain by entering the labor force. Thus, the differences in participation rates between immigrants and natives, as well as among national-origin groups, should mirror the variation in wage rates and skills documented earlier, so the dispersion in economic well-being among the groups is intensified by the labor supply decision. Skilled immigrant groups, who have relatively high wage rates, are more likely to work, and they will have substantial incomes entering the household. In contrast, relatively unskilled immigrants command lower wage rates and are less likely to work, so incomes in these groups will typically be quite low.

The weaker work incentive of low-wage or unskilled immigrant groups does not imply that these groups lack the "work ethic" that natives and other immigrants presumably have. Differences in labor supply among the groups may have little to do with variations in the tastes for leisure. Instead, they can be completely due to differences in the economic returns to working (as measured by the hourly wage rate) among the various groups.

When unskilled immigrants enter the labor force, they are likely to have difficulty finding and holding on to a job. Adverse conditions in the American economy are particularly detrimental to the employment opportunities of persons with little schooling and with few marketable skills.[5] Unskilled immigrants, therefore, are less likely to find a job quickly, and if they do have a job, they are more likely to be laid off when a cyclical downturn occurs. Hence low-wage or unskilled immigrant groups will have relatively high unemployment rates.

Labor force participants must also decide how many hours to work. Workers with relatively high wage rates find that time is money and that it is quite expensive to take time off for leisure activities. The earnings foregone when these persons take on jobs with short work-weeks, such as part-time work, may be substantial, and these types of individuals will work long hours. At the same time, high-wage persons are the ones who can afford to have short workweeks. The results summarized below indicate that more skilled immigrant groups work significantly more hours, so that the differences in hours of work further intensify the differentials in economic well-being among the groups.

136

Finally, immigrant labor supply is likely to be affected by the process of labor market assimilation. A new immigrant is likely to spend considerable time searching for better job opportunities during his first few years in the United States. As he learns about the American labor market, the immigrant becomes aware of crucial aspects of the wage structure, such as the extent of regional, industry, and occupational wage differentials. The search for better economic conditions probably entails a substantial amount of job shopping and job changing as the immigrant discovers and tries out alternative employment opportunities. Over time, the immigrant's labor force participation propensity and hours of work are likely to increase, and the unemployment rate is likely to decrease, for presumably the immigrant will find the "right" job after a few years.

As we have seen, the assimilation process also increases the immigrant's marketable skills. The resulting increase in the immigrant wage leads to even greater incentives for the immigrant to participate in the labor force. Labor market assimilation, therefore, should involve not only an increase in the immigrant's wage as he accumulates experience in the American labor market, but also an increase in his labor supply and a decrease in his unemployment propensity.

By tracking the employment experience of immigrant waves between the 1970 and 1980 Censuses, it is possible to determine the extent to which the labor supply differential between immigrants and natives narrows as assimilation occurs. As table 8.1 indicates, immigrant men who arrived between 1975 and 1979 have a labor force participation rate that is 8 percentage points below that of white native men at the time of entry into the country.[6] This is a remarkably large difference in employment propensities. After all, the differential in labor force participation rates between black and white natives, which is the focus of so much concern, is only 7 percentage points.[7]

Earlier immigrant waves were not as disadvantaged (in terms of their labor force participation) at the time they entered the country. For instance, the immigrant wave that arrived between 1965 and 1969 had a labor force participation rate that was only about 4 percentage points lower than that of natives at the time of entry. The most recent immigrant wave, therefore, differs from its predecessors in the underlying economic and demographic characteristics that lead to high levels of labor force participation.

TABLE 8.1
Employment Propensities of Immigrant Versus White Native Men

Immigrant Cohort	Difference in Labor Force Participation Rate		Difference in Unemployment Rate		Percentage Difference in Annual Hours Worked	
	At Time of Entry	Thirty Years After Entry	At Time of Entry	Thirty Years After Entry	At Time of Entry	Thirty Years After Entry
1950–1959	−5.7	3.6	1.1	0	−12.2	−1.2
1965–1969	−3.5	5.8	1.4	.3	−13.0	−2.0
1975–1979	−8.3	1.0	2.4	1.3	−20.0	−9.0

SOURCE: Author's tabulations from the 1970 and 1980 Public Use Samples of the U.S. Census. The calculations are based on regressions of the labor force participation and unemployment propensities (using the linear probability model) and of the logarithm of annual hours worked, estimated in the sample of immigrant and white native men aged twenty-five to sixty-four. The labor force participation and unemployment data refer to the individual's labor market activity in the census week, while annual hours of work refer to the calendar year prior to the census. The unemployment regression is estimated in the subsample of labor force participants, and the hours-of-work regression is estimated in the subsample of workers. The regressors included age, an indicator of whether the observation was drawn from the 1970 or the 1980 Census, the cohort of immigration, and the number of years since immigration. The percentage differentials in annual hours of work are calculated from the antilogs of the predictions from the log hours regression.

Over time, the assimilation process not only narrows but often reverses these differentials. After thirty years in the United States, the labor force participation rate of immigrants is as high as, if not higher than, that of natives. In fact, the impact of assimilation is so strong that immigrants in earlier waves eventually have labor force participation rates that are 4 to 6 percentage points higher than those of natives.

In the long run, therefore, many immigrants (particularly those who migrated prior to the 1970s) do have a stronger labor force attachment than natives, at least as measured by the labor force participation rate. This difference is probably due to the fact that immigration is a costly investment. Work activity is one of the few ways in which immigrants can collect returns on their investment. Immigrants who do not work cannot take advantage of the economic opportunities that motivated the migration in the first place, and they have no way of recouping their migration costs. Therefore, most immigrants are likely to have additional incentives, beyond those provided by the wage rate, for participating in the labor force.

The differences in labor market outcomes among immigrant waves are also evident in their unemployment propensities. At the time of entry, the typical immigrant in the 1975–1979 cohort had an unemployment rate that was about 2 percentage points higher than that of natives. Because newly arrived immigrants have limited information about the availability and location of particular types of jobs in the U.S. labor market, and because they tend to be relatively unskilled, it is not surprising that they have difficulty finding and retaining a job. Nevertheless, the unemployment disadvantage experienced by immigrants in the 1975–1979 cohort is greater than the disadvantage experienced by earlier waves. Thus, the new immigrants have a higher propensity for unemployment than the old.

Similarly, men who immigrated in the late 1970s work about 20 percent fewer hours than natives at the time of entry.[8] The existence of this large differential in labor supply is not surprising because much of that first year is probably spent looking for work, switching across jobs, and generally trying out the American labor market. What is surprising is that the length of the work year at the time of entry was much higher for earlier waves. For instance, men who immigrated in the late 1960s worked only 13 percent fewer hours than natives when they first entered the United States.

The empirical evidence thus shows that the various immigrant waves differ in more than just their earnings potential. Persons who immigrated in the late 1970s have substantially lower participation rates, have higher unemployment rates, and work fewer hours than persons who immigrated in the 1950s or 1960s. In fact, these differences in employment propensities remain even after standardization for differences in demographic characteristics among the various cohorts. Therefore, changing conditions in the immigration market generated a skill sorting wherein the more recent waves are less successful in all of the dimensions of labor market outcomes that are crucial determinants of economic well-being.[9]

There are, of course, sizable differences in the labor supply and unemployment propensities of immigrants among different national-origin groups. Among the fifteen countries listed in table 8.2, the labor force participation rate of adult men ranges from 88 percent to 96 percent; the unemployment rate ranges from 2 percent to 9 percent; and the number of hours worked per year ranges from 1,700 to 2,000. Immigrants originating in some Asian or Latin American countries tend to have relatively low labor force participation rates, high unemployment rates, and short work years. For instance, British or German

TABLE 8.2

*National-Origin Differentials in the Labor Market Attachment of
Immigrants in 1980*

Country of Origin	Labor Force Participation Rate	Unemployment Rate	Annual Hours Worked
Europe			
Germany	93.4	3.0	2,006
Greece	91.6	4.4	1,850
Italy	89.9	5.8	1,846
Poland	89.0	4.5	1,910
United Kingdom	92.0	2.9	1,990
Asia			
China	90.2	2.5	1,848
India	95.5	3.2	1,876
Japan	90.4	2.1	1,880
Korea	90.1	3.3	1,715
Philippines	92.4	3.3	1,762
Americas			
Canada	87.7	3.8	1,941
Cuba	92.0	4.0	1,878
Dominican Republic	88.6	9.0	1,679
Jamaica	91.2	6.9	1,693
Mexico	92.1	7.7	1,739

SOURCE: Author's tabulations from the 1980 Public Use Sample of the U.S. Census.

immigrants work about 15 percent more hours per year than Mexican
immigrants and about 19 percent more hours than immigrants originating in Jamaica or the Dominican Republic.

Are the source countries responsible for immigrant flows that have
relatively high wage rates also responsible for flows that have high levels
of labor supply? The answer is an unqualified yes. There is a positive
correlation between the national-origin group's labor supply and its
wage rate, even after demographic differences are held constant among
the various groups.[10] This correlation is not surprising, because the
wage rate plays a crucial role in determining whether the individual
decides to work. Immigrant groups with the highest wage rates, and
hence the most incentive to work, tend to have the strongest attachment to the labor market.

This correlation suggests that, to a large extent, the same factors
responsible for the decline in immigrant skills are also responsible for
the decline in labor force attachment. The changing parameters of the
U.S. offer in the immigration market generated not only a less skilled

immigrant flow, but also an immigrant flow with poorer employment prospects.

Implications for Labor Market Earnings

The differentials in potential lifetime earnings reported in the previous chapter captured only the variation in hourly wage rates between immigrants and natives. They ignored an important determinant of the economic well-being of immigrants: recent immigrant waves not only have a lower wage rate, they also work fewer hours than earlier waves. Moreover, the strong impact of labor market assimilation on labor supply implies that many immigrant groups quickly reach parity with natives in terms of their employment experience. What is the impact of this variation in hours of work over time and among cohorts on the actual lifetime earnings (as opposed to the potential earnings) of immigrants and natives?

As table 8.3 shows, the lifetime earnings disadvantage of immigrants increases when the calculations take into account the fact that immigrants and natives do not work the same number of hours.[11] For instance, the potential lifetime earnings of persons who immigrated in the late 1970s are about 21 percent lower than those of natives (assum-

TABLE 8.3
Lifetime Earnings of Immigrant Men

Group	Percentage Difference in Lifetime Earnings Between Immigrant Men and White Native Men if:	
	Both Groups Work Full-Time	Differences in Hours of Work Are Taken into Account
1950–1959 cohort	−1.6	−7.7
1960–1964 cohort	−5.5	−11.1
1965–1969 cohort	−10.4	−16.4
1970–1974 cohort	−17.1	−22.4
1975–1979 cohort	−21.4	−31.6

SOURCE: Author's tabulations from the 1970 and 1980 Public Use Samples of the U.S. Census. The differentials in lifetime earnings that hold labor supply constant are based on log hourly wage rate regressions, while the differentials that allow for differences in hours of work are based on log annual earnings regressions estimated in the samples of immigrant men and white native men aged twenty-five to sixty-four. The regressors include age, an indicator of whether the observation was drawn from the 1970 or the 1980 Census, the cohort of immigration, and the number of years since immigration. The wage rates are converted into potential annual earnings for the first column by taking antilogs of the predictions and by assuming a 2,000-hour work year throughout the life cycle for all groups. For technical details on the econometric methodology and the data see George J. Borjas, "Self-Selection and Immigration," in Richard B. Freeman and John M. Abowd, eds., *Immigration, Trade, and the Labor Market* (Chicago: University of Chicago Press, 1990).

141

ing that the two groups worked full-time throughout the life cycle). Because of the differences in hours of work, however, the actual lifetime earnings disadvantage experienced by this immigrant cohort will be 32 percent. Moreover, the decline in lifetime earnings among successive immigrant waves is greatly intensified by the concurrent decline in labor supply. Immigrants in the 1975–1979 wave have about 17 percent lower potential earnings than persons who migrated in the early 1960s. But because of the weaker labor force attachment of the recent wave, they will actually earn about 23 percent less. Therefore, the precipitous decline in the skills, productivity, and labor market attachment of immigrants led to a significant deterioration in the economic prospects of the most recent immigrant waves.

National Income and Declining Immigrant Skills

After accounting for the lower skills and shorter work year of recent immigrant waves, the empirical evidence indicates that the present value of lifetime earnings is $183,000 for the typical man who immigrated between 1975 and 1979 and $238,000 for the typical man who immigrated in the early 1960s. Due to the differences in skills and hours worked between these two waves, therefore, lifetime earnings for the typical immigrant dropped by $55,000 over the period, or by $90,000 (in 1988 dollars) after adjusting for inflation. In present-value terms, this decline is equivalent to the typical new immigrant earning $5,000 less than an old immigrant every single year of his working life.[12]

In fact, about 1.7 million men immigrated to the United States legally and illegally between 1975 and 1979.[13] Thus, the foregone national income associated with the entry of unskilled immigrant men in the late 1970s is approximately $8.5 billion per year during the cohort's working life ($5,000 times 1.7 million immigrants). Put differently, had the skill composition of male immigrant flows remained constant between 1960 and 1980, annual national income would have been $8.5 billion higher.

This estimate needs to be adjusted for three important factors. First, perhaps 30 percent of the immigrants return to their home country or migrate elsewhere. If these emigrants are randomly chosen and if they leave soon after immigration, the loss in national income is reduced to about $6 billion. Emigrants are unlikely to be randomly selected, however. Hence the actual adjustment will be somewhat different and will depend on whether it is the "failures" or the "successes" who leave the United States. Unfortunately, little is known about the skill composition of this population.

Second, 1.7 million women also entered the United States legally and illegally between 1975 and 1979, and they too have different productivities and skills than earlier waves.[14] Because many women do not work continuously over the life cycle, the calculation of the present value of female lifetime earnings and the assessment of their contribution to national income is much more complex and requires a systematic study of fertility behavior in immigrant families. Nonetheless, even if the decline in skills exhibited by female immigrants is but a small fraction of the decline exhibited by their male counterparts, the total "reduction" in national income attributable to the 1975–1979 immigrant cohort probably exceeds $6 billion.

Finally, immigrants are likely to have an impact on native incomes. Therefore, the calculations must take into account not only that unskilled persons add less to the GNP than do skilled workers, but also that native incomes may be affected differently by the immigration of different types of workers. The empirical evidence presented in chapter 5 indicated that immigrants have little impact on the earnings and employment of natives, regardless of the particular permutation of immigrant and native groups being analyzed. This conclusion implies that the estimated reduction in national income need hardly be adjusted to account for the impact that these immigrants have on native labor market opportunities.[15]

Yet there are other ways in which immigration affects the real incomes of natives. For instance, it is likely that the immigration of unskilled workers benefits natives because these immigrants are better suited to work in specific industries (such as agriculture). The comparative advantage that immigrants have in these jobs allows the cheaper production of some goods, and natives benefit because they can purchase these goods at a lower price. For instance, if unskilled immigrants specialize in the planting and harvesting of crops, natives will find

143

agricultural produce to be relatively abundant and inexpensive in the marketplace and will experience an increase in real incomes.

Similarly, the immigration of skilled workers could also lead to an increase in natives' real incomes. After all, skilled immigrants may have a comparative advantage in the production of other goods and will specialize in alternative industries and occupations (such as the development of computer hardware and electronic equipment). Natives' real incomes then increase because of the favorable impact that skilled immigration has on the price of these other consumer goods.

Natives clearly gain from admitting immigrants who have a comparative advantage in certain types of work activities. It is impossible to determine, at a conceptual level, which type of immigrants natives would prefer: skilled, unskilled, or some mix of the two. Each skill sorting has a different economic impact, and the optimal sorting can only be determined by measuring the effects of alternative types of immigration on natives' real incomes. Unfortunately, such estimates do not exist.

The existing evidence only indicates that the entry of relatively unskilled workers in the late 1970s (as compared to the early 1960s) led to a direct reduction of at least $6 billion in national income and to an indeterminate change in the real incomes of natives. As the discussion indicates, however, it is far from clear that the immigration of relatively unskilled workers is more beneficial for natives than the immigration of relatively more skilled workers. In fact, if natives' real incomes respond more favorably to the immigration of skilled persons, then the estimated losses reported here are too low.

It is certainly the case that in terms of the total U.S. economy, the $6 billion reduction in national income is only a drop in the bucket. In 1986, national income attributable to wages and salaries and to the incomes of proprietors amounted to $2.8 trillion.[16] The entry of relatively unskilled immigrants reduced potential national income by only .2 percent.

Nevertheless, an annual decline in national income of $6 billion is not something to be ignored. For example, the admission of unskilled immigrants has a nontrivial impact on tax revenues. If we assume a 25-percent tax rate, the entry of the relatively unskilled immigrant wave during the late 1970s reduced annual tax revenues by $1.5 billion. Moreover, these losses are incurred by the United States in every single year of the cohort's working life. In fact, the present value of the reduction in national income over the cohort's lifetime is approximately $110 billion, with a $27.5 billion corresponding loss in tax revenues.

In addition, these estimates only measure the losses associated with the entry of the relatively unskilled 1975–1979 immigrant wave. If the immigrants who entered the United States between 1980 and 1984 are as unskilled as their predecessors, the losses to national income today would be twice as high as those reported above. Thus, the entry of wave after wave of unskilled immigrants is responsible for a substantial reduction in national income today and for many years to come. The deterioration in the employment and earnings opportunities of the immigrant flow, therefore, is far more than just an intellectual curiosity.

Of course, these calculations address only one side of the fiscal balance sheet associated with unskilled immigration. After all, the lower taxes paid by unskilled immigrants could be offset by fiscal savings if these immigrants used fewer government services. If the programs of the U.S. government mainly benefited higher income groups, the admission of unskilled immigrants would lead not only to lower tax revenues, but also to lower levels of government expenditures. Then it would be unclear if the United States gains from the admission of a more skilled immigrant flow.

Careful studies by the Tax Foundation of the redistributive aspects of U.S. government spending, however, conclude that the "spending activities of governments favor the lower income groups," mainly because, on the whole, government programs are designed to benefit the poor.[17] It is therefore reasonable to infer that unskilled immigration is not only associated with lower tax revenues, but also with higher levels of government spending. One particular and controversial form of these expenditures—the costs of immigrant participation in welfare programs—will be discussed in detail in the next chapter.

I should also note that although these calculations are instructive, there is a sense in which they are misleading. The conceptual experiment compares actual national income with that which would have been observed if the new immigrants had been as skilled as the old. It is doubtful that the United States in the late 1970s, even if it had not changed its immigration policies, could have attracted the types of persons who came here in the early 1960s. Changes in political and economic conditions in many source countries may have reduced the attractiveness of the American offer to skilled workers and would have led to a decline in this type of immigration regardless of American policy. The calculations presented here, therefore, simply provide a rough illustration of the way that changes in the composition of the immigrant flow strongly influence aggregate economic conditions in the United States.

If nothing else, the calculations indicate that not all types of immigration are equally beneficial. There is a lot of variation in the economic impact of different American offers in the immigration market. For example, if the U.S. offer is particularly attractive to unskilled workers, natives benefit because they can buy the goods produced by these immigrants at a lower price. But this type of immigration also imposes substantial costs on American society: unskilled workers contribute less to national income and reduce tax revenues. Further, as will be seen below, the migration of these unskilled workers increases the incidence of poverty in the immigrant population and the propensity of immigrants to enter the welfare rolls. The fundamental problem facing American immigration policy today, therefore, is to ascertain the exact economic and political nature of these tradeoffs and to determine which of the alternative offers that the United States could make in the immigration market would be most beneficial for the country.

Immigrant Poverty

An unavoidable consequence of the deterioration in immigrant skills in the past two or three decades is an increase in the poverty rate of the immigrant population. The poverty rate is defined as the fraction of the population whose household income is below the officially defined poverty line, with the poverty line dependent on family size, family income, and household composition.[18] The poverty rate summarizes the influence of all of these factors on the economic welfare of native and immigrant families, thus it is a much more encompassing measure of the economic well-being of these populations than the measures of labor supply and wages that are the focus of the research studies summarized above.

As table 8.4 indicates, the poverty rates of natives, even of natives belonging to minority groups, decreased slightly between 1970 and 1980.[19] Overall, the native poverty rate declined from 13 to 12 percent, that of black natives from 33 to 29 percent, and that of Hispanic natives (persons of Hispanic ancestry born in the United States) from 25 to 24 percent. In contrast, the poverty rates of immigrants bucked the national trend. They increased slightly over the same period, from 14 to 15 percent.

The source of the increasing incidence of poverty in the immigrant population is evident when one compares the poverty rate of the various immigrant cohorts between the two censuses. Soon after arrival, persons who immigrated between 1965 and 1969 had a poverty rate of only 18 percent. By contrast, persons who immigrated in the late 1970s had a poverty rate of 29 percent soon after arrival. The changing skill composition of the immigrant flow, therefore, resulted in an 11 percentage point increase in the incidence of poverty between these two immigrant waves.

It is remarkable that this huge increase in poverty rates among successive immigrant waves occurred at a time that the incidence of poverty in the native population was declining slightly. This suggests

TABLE 8.4
Poverty in the Immigrant and Native Populations, 1970 and 1980

Group	Fraction of Individuals Below the Poverty Line	
	1970	1980
All Natives	13.3	11.7
White natives	10.1	8.5
Black natives	33.4	29.0
Hispanic natives	25.1	23.7
All Immigrants	13.7	15.2
1950–1959 cohort	10.5	9.4
1960–1964 cohort	11.4	12.9
1965–1969 cohort	18.4	14.2
1970–1974 cohort	—	17.2
1975–1979 cohort	—	29.4

SOURCE: Author's tabulations from the 1970 and 1980 Public Use Samples of the U.S. Census.

147

The Economic Impact of Immigration

that the deteriorating economic performance of recent immigrant waves cannot be blamed solely on the possibility that immigrants are particularly sensitive to adverse economic conditions, such as those which characterized the economy in 1980. After all, these adverse economic conditions did not lead to an increase in the poverty rate of any native group, including disadvantaged minorities such as blacks and Hispanics.

The reason for the increasing incidence of poverty in the immigrant population lies elsewhere. It lies in the fundamental changes that have occurred in the immigration market during the past two or three decades and in the changing attractiveness of the U.S. offer to potential migrants. These changes altered the nature of the skill sorting characterizing the immigrant flow and led to recent immigrant waves having the same poverty rate as black natives.

The link between the changing composition of the immigrant flow and the increase in immigrant poverty is clearly illustrated by the sizable variation that exists in poverty rates among national-origin groups. Poverty rates tend to be lowest for immigrants originating in European countries and highest for immigrants originating in South American countries (see table 8.5). For instance, while British immigrants have a poverty rate of only 7 percent, the poverty rate of Korean immigrants is 14 percent, that of Mexican immigrants is 26 percent, and that of persons originating in the Dominican Republic is 34 percent. Changes in the national-origin composition of the immigrant flow, along with the impact of these changes on skills and on the labor market attachment of immigrants, are largely responsible for the increasing incidence of poverty exhibited by successive immigrant waves.

TABLE 8.5
Poverty Rate Differences Among National-Origin Groups in 1980

Fraction of Individuals Below the Poverty Line					
Europe		Asia		Americas	
Germany	8.2	China	12.5	Canada	7.7
Greece	10.4	India	6.0	Cuba	12.2
Italy	8.2	Japan	13.0	Dominican Republic	33.7
Poland	8.1	Korea	13.5	Jamaica	14.4
United Kingdom	7.2	Philippines	5.8	Mexico	26.0

SOURCE: Author's tabulations from the 1980 Public Use Sample of the U.S. Census.

148

Employment and Poverty in the Immigrant Population

Few issues facing the United States are as important, and as difficult to resolve, as the persistent problem of poverty in our midst. Despite the best of intentions, a quarter-century of government programs, and billions of taxpayer dollars, the problem of poverty remains, as intractable as ever.

The empirical evidence presented here suggests that immigration is exacerbating this problem. Changes in America's offer in the immigration market led to the migration of relatively unskilled persons, who have relatively low levels of labor force attachment and who are quite likely to be poor (as this concept is officially defined). Therefore, changes in the skill sorting generated by the immigration market in the past two or three decades are bound to have a major impact on the social and economic well-being of the immigrant and native populations in the United States for many years to come.

CHAPTER 9

Immigration and
the Welfare State

THE SHIFT toward a more unskilled immigrant flow imposes many
social and economic costs on the United States. One important component of these costs is the potential increase in the expenditures associated with maintaining a welfare state.[1]

Are immigrants more likely to be on welfare than natives? Is the
welfare participation rate of recent immigrant waves substantially
higher than that of earlier waves? Does the process of assimilation
eventually reduce the immigrant's propensity for welfare participation?

This chapter documents the extent to which immigrants participate
in the welfare system.[2] To put it bluntly, the evidence is worrisome.
Immigrant welfare participation is on the rise. In some national-origin
groups, more than 30 percent of the female-headed households are on
welfare! Not only are the new immigrants more likely to be welfare
recipients than the old, but also the welfare participation rate of a
particular cohort increases the longer the cohort has been in the United
States. Evidently, the assimilation process improves income "opportunities" in the welfare sector as well as in the labor market.

Welfare and the Immigration Market

The conflict between immigration and the existence of a welfare
state raises questions of fundamental importance for social policy. Yet,
until recently, little was actually known about the extent to which
immigrants participated in the welfare system.[3] For instance, a 1978
congressional report reviewed the available evidence and concluded
that "Immigrants undoubtedly have an effect on the cost of providing
a whole range of public services. . . . Few of these effects, however, have

150

received more than cursory attention by immigration researchers or by the administrators of these public services."⁴

Despite the absence of systematic empirical evidence describing the participation of immigrants in the welfare system, there is a widespread, and seemingly unshakable, perception that some "immigrants have a penchant for welfare" and that "illegal aliens are not the chief cause of the rise in welfare costs in America, but they do constitute a significant part of the cost of welfare in many areas and states."⁵

Underlying this view are two related concerns. First, unskilled immigrants are more likely to qualify for the various entitlement programs, so the immigration of unskilled workers, such as illegal aliens, imposes substantial costs on American taxpayers. In addition, a relatively generous welfare system increases the attractiveness of America's offer in the immigration market particularly for those potential migrants most likely to qualify for public assistance. In other words, the types of persons who would migrate to the United States in the absence of any public assistance programs are likely to be quite different from the types of persons attracted to the country today. As Richard Lamm and Gary Imhoff passionately argue in their assessment of immigration's impact on the United States, "America of the 1980s is vastly different from America of the 1880s. Now we have social service and welfare programs that are easy to deceive and exploit. We have a cash-wage economy with high unemployment, vastly different from the empty frontier that greeted previous immigrants. And we have a new social phenomenon wherein all groups can "demand" almost instant entry into the American middle class, not as a result of hard work but as a matter of entitlement."⁶ In this view, the welfare state fundamentally alters the parameters of the U.S. offer in the immigration market. This offer not only describes the labor market opportunities but also incorporates the income levels promised by the welfare system.

In practice, the welfare system provides an income floor that insures immigrants and natives against poor labor market outcomes.⁷ This income floor is the safety net below which incomes, consumption, and living standards are not allowed to fall. Because of the large differences in living standards among countries, this floor is likely to be an important feature of the American offer in the immigration market for many potential migrants. Thus, the existence of a wide array of welfare programs in the United States alters the immigration incentives of persons residing in many source countries. Unless otherwise prohibited, some people may immigrate simply to take advantage of the income opportunities available in the welfare sector.

After all, the income opportunities available through the U.S. welfare system are sometimes better than the typical income opportunities available in many source countries. For instance, in 1980, the per capita GNP in the Philippines was under $700, and in Mexico it was $1,900, as compared with the average income of $2,800 for an immigrant welfare household in the United States.[8] Therefore, many potential migrants surely conclude that the worst possible outcome if they were to migrate to the United States is probably better than the typical economic opportunities they face in the country of origin.

Obviously, the welfare system is unlikely to be a motivating factor for the immigration of highly skilled persons, simply because they can do much better by participating in the labor market.[9] Immigration incentives, however, are clearly altered for the unskilled, because the economic insurance provided by the welfare state makes the U.S. a more attractive destination for these workers.

The perception that America's offer in the immigration market may seem particularly attractive to persons who are welfare-prone has had a pronounced impact on policy makers in recent years. In particular, Congress has shown an increasing willingness to enact legislation (discussed below) that explicitly restricts immigrant participation in the welfare system and that limits the entitlements available to the foreign-born.

Welfare Use in the Immigrant Population

Before proceeding to a discussion of the empirical evidence on immigrant participation in the welfare system, it is useful to describe exactly what is meant by "welfare." A household is on welfare if at least one family member participates in such cash programs as Aid to Families with Dependent Children (AFDC), old-age assistance, general assistance, and Supplemental Security Income (SSI).[10] This definition of welfare specifically excludes any receipts of "social insurance" such as

Social Security income, permanent-disability insurance payments, Medicare payments, and unemployment-insurance benefits, as well as any receipts of noncash payments such as food stamps or Medicaid. This definition is used simply because data on this type of welfare participation are readily available in the decennial censuses, not because other forms of immigrant participation in the welfare system are less important.[11]

As table 9.1 shows, immigrant households are only slightly more likely to receive welfare than native households; 9 percent of immigrant households are on welfare, as compared to 8 percent of native households.[12] Among both immigrants and natives, female-headed households are two to three times more likely to receive public assistance than male-headed households.[13] This fact is not surprising, for pro-

TABLE 9.1

Immigrant Participation in the Welfare System in 1980

Group	Fraction of Households with at Least One Member Receiving Public Assistance		
	All Households	Female-Headed Households	Male-Headed Households
Natives	8.0	16.1	4.8
All Immigrants	9.1	14.7	6.9
Immigrants Born in Europe			
Germany	4.6	7.5	3.0
Greece	6.4	12.9	4.9
Italy	7.1	12.1	5.2
Poland	6.3	9.1	4.9
United Kingdom	5.3	9.2	3.1
Immigrants Born in Asia			
China	8.4	15.0	7.2
India	2.8	6.5	2.5
Japan	5.7	9.0	4.0
Korea	6.3	8.7	5.7
Philippines	10.3	12.2	9.8
Immigrants Born in the Americas			
Canada	6.2	11.1	3.7
Cuba	17.3	31.7	13.1
Dominican Republic	25.9	41.0	12.9
Jamaica	7.4	12.1	3.9
Mexico	12.7	29.3	9.0

Source: George J. Borjas and Stephen J. Trejo, "Immigrant Participation in the Welfare System," mimeograph, University of California, Santa Barbara, September 1988, table 2. These statistics refer to the population of households in which the head is at least eighteen years of age. The statistics are tabulated from the Public Use Sample of the 1980 Census.

153

grams like the AFDC are generally designed for one-parent households, and one-parent households are typically headed by women.

The aggregate statistics hide immense variation in welfare participation behavior among national-origin groups. Immigrant households originating in Europe or in some Asian countries have low welfare participation rates, while immigrant households originating in Latin America tend to have very high participation rates. For instance, the welfare participation rate ranges from a low of 3 percent (households originating in India) to a high of 26 percent (households originating in the Dominican Republic). Within the population of female-headed immigrant households, the dispersion is even more striking, from a low of 7 percent to a high of 41 percent.

Therefore, among female-headed households in some national-origin groups, welfare is not a rare occurrence. It is, instead, a disturbingly common feature of the immigrant experience. For three national-origin groups (persons born in Cuba, the Dominican Republic, and Mexico), the welfare participation rates among female-headed households is about 30 percent or higher.

Surely part of the variation in welfare participation rates among national-origin groups is due to cultural differences. Some nationalities view welfare in a somewhat old-fashioned way and would refuse to apply for public assistance unless (and perhaps even if) they were in dire economic conditions. Part of the variation, however, is due to skill differentials among the various groups. The relation between the skill composition of a national-origin group and its participation in the welfare system is discussed below.

In addition to differences in welfare participation rates among national-origin groups, significant dispersion is also introduced by the assimilation process and by skill differences among immigrant waves. By tracking immigrant households belonging to specific cohorts between the 1970 and 1980 Censuses, it is possible to determine the extent to which the welfare participation rate of households in a single cohort changes (relative to that of natives) as assimilation occurs.

As table 9.2 shows, at the time of entry into the United States, female-headed households that migrated in the late 1970s are slightly less likely to be on welfare than natives. The longer these immigrant households have been in the United States, however, the higher their welfare participation rate. At the time of entry, female-headed immi-

TABLE 9.2

Difference in Welfare Participation Rate Between Immigrants and Natives

	Female-Headed Households		Male-Headed Households	
Group	At Time of Entry	Thirty Years After Entry	At Time of Entry	Thirty Years After Entry
1950–1959 cohort	−10.6	2.3	−1.5	.3
1960–1964 cohort	−4.6	8.3	.7	2.5
1965–1969 cohort	−1.7	11.2	1.4	3.2
1970–1974 cohort	−.6	12.3	.9	2.7
1975–1979 cohort	−2.6	10.3	2.3	4.1

SOURCE: Adapted from George J. Borjas and Stephen J. Trejo, "Immigrant Participation in the Welfare System," mimeograph, Univerisity of California, Santa Barbara, September 1988, table 3. The statistics are based on maximum likelihood logit regressions in which the dependent variable is the welfare participation propensity of the household. The data are drawn from the 1970 and 1980 Public Use Samples of the U.S. Census and use the samples of immigrant and native households in which the head is at least eighteen years of age. The regressors include age, an indicator of whether the observation was drawn from the 1970 or the 1980 Census, the cohort of immigration, and the number of years since immigration.

grant households have a welfare participation rate that is 3 percentage points below that of natives. After thirty years, the welfare participation rate of these households will exceed that of natives by 10 percentage points. It is ironic that an assimilation process that improves immigrant earnings and employment opportunities also seems to increase their propensities to enter the welfare system.

The strong impact of assimilation on welfare participation is partly due to the lifting of restrictions that prevent newly arrived foreigners from participating in some welfare programs. In principle, immigrants are deportable if they become public charges within a five-year period after entry, unless the immigrant can show that "the causes for dependency arose after entry."[14] Even though this provision of immigration law is seldom enforced, newly arrived immigrants may believe that welfare participation jeopardizes their legal status in the country, hence they avoid applying for welfare even if they qualify.

The concern over immigrant abuse of the welfare system led Congress to enact statutes that explicitly limit immigrant participation in welfare programs in the first few years after entry. The first of these restrictions, included in the 1980 amendments to the Social Security Act, requires that immigrants who apply for welfare in the first three years after entry "have their sponsor's income and resources imputed to them in the application," thus reducing the chances that the immigrants will qualify for public assistance.[15] More recently, IRCA prohibits illegal aliens granted amnesty from receiving most types of public assistance in the five-year period following their legalization.[16]

As immigrants age in the United States, they also accumulate information about relevant characteristics of the welfare sector. Over time, immigrants learn about the types of welfare programs available, the income opportunities associated with these programs, the qualification requirements, and the bureaucratic quagmire through which persons apply for these benefits. Therefore, it is not surprising to find that as immigrants qualify and learn about the income-transfer programs available, they make increasing use of these entitlements. As a result, most immigrant waves, including those who arrived prior to the 1965 amendments, have higher welfare participation rates than natives within three decades after arrival.

The empirical evidence also reveals that welfare participation rates differ among immigrant waves: the new immigrants are more likely to be welfare recipients than the old. At the time of entry into the United States, households that migrated in the late 1970s were about 2 percentage points more likely to be on welfare than households that migrated in the early 1960s, and 4 to 8 percentage points more likely than households that migrated in the 1950s.

In view of the evidence presented in previous chapters, it is not at all surprising that the new immigrants have high welfare participation rates. After all, recent immigrant waves have weaker labor market attachment, fewer skills, lower lifetime earnings, and higher poverty rates than earlier waves. The changes that have occurred in the immigration market in the past two or three decades inevitably led to the immigrant population's increasing use of the American welfare system.

There is obviously a strong link between the increase in welfare participation rates among successive immigrant waves and the changing national-origin mix of the immigrant flow. Recent immigrant waves are more likely to originate in Asian and Latin American countries and much less likely to originate in European countries. Immigrant groups originating in Europe tend to have lower welfare participation propensities than groups originating in some Asian countries or in Latin America. In fact, the empirical evidence suggests that the changing national-origin mix of the immigrant flow is largely responsible for the increase in welfare participation among successive immigrant waves.[17]

Are Immigrants More Welfare-Prone Than Natives?

To some extent, differences in welfare participation rates between immigrants and natives reflect differences in demographic characteristics and household composition between the groups. For example, households with large numbers of small children and elderly or disabled persons or households whose members have relatively little schooling are more likely to be welfare recipients than other households, and these demographic characteristics vary substantially between immigrants and natives.

It may also be the case, however, that for any particular set of demographic characteristics some groups are more prone than others to go on welfare. In other words, some groups may simply have a higher underlying propensity to enter the welfare system than other demographically comparable groups. Do recent immigrant households have higher welfare participation rates than demographically comparable native households?

The data do not provide a clear-cut answer to this question.[18] In particular, female-headed immigrant households are less likely to be on welfare than their demographically comparable native counterparts, while the opposite is true for male-headed households. The evidence, therefore, does not support the conjecture that immigrant households are generally more welfare-prone than native households.

I should add, however, that although the question of whether immigrants are more welfare-prone than demographically comparable natives is interesting, it has little relevance to policy.[19] Policy makers are (or should be) more concerned with the calculation of the welfare costs attributable to specific changes in immigration policies. The pertinent issue is whether immigrants are more likely to receive welfare than natives (and by how much), not whether they are more likely to receive welfare than demographically comparable natives. From the taxpayer's point of view, whether immigrants get more welfare because they happen to have less education or to be less skilled, or because they are particularly attracted to the welfare system, is somewhat beside the point. Either way, the immigrant household enters the welfare system, the costs of maintaining the welfare state rise, and taxes increase to pay for the expanded government programs.

National Origin and Welfare

There are significant differences in the welfare participation rates of the various national-origin groups, even after controlling for differences in demographic characteristics among the groups. What characteristics of the source country are most influential in determining the group's welfare participation rate?

Perhaps the most important characteristic is the source country's level of economic development. There is a strong negative correlation between the immigrant group's welfare participation rate and the per capita GNP in the country of origin. In other words, immigrants originating in the less developed countries have higher welfare participation rates than immigrants originating in highly industrialized economies, even after accounting for the differences in the demographic characteristics of the groups. In fact, a doubling of the source country's per capita GNP decreases the group's welfare participation rate by between 2 and 4 percentage points.[20] Because income levels vary widely among countries, these differences play a crucial role in generating dispersion in welfare participation among national-origin groups. For example, the per capita GNP in the United Kingdom is more than six times greater than that in the Dominican Republic. It is not surprising that immigrant households originating in the Dominican Republic are about five times more likely to be on welfare than those originating in the United Kingdom.

The strong negative correlation between a source country's income level and welfare participation propensities arises because persons who originate in countries with highly developed, industrialized economies perform quite well in the U.S. labor market. As we saw in previous chapters, these are the national-origin groups who tend to have high earnings and low poverty rates. These immigrants have skills that are easily transferable to the American economy, and it is unlikely that many of them even qualify for welfare payments. By the same token, persons originating in less developed countries generally fare poorly in the American labor market. These national-origin groups, therefore, are much more likely to qualify for and receive welfare.[21]

The American offer in the immigration market is also much more generous, in terms of the availability of welfare programs, for immigrants admitted into the country as refugees or asylees. These immigrants qualify for a relatively large number of entitlement programs immediately upon arrival into the United States. For instance, newly arrived refugees qualify for AFDC or SSI on the same basis as U.S. citizens, and even those who do not qualify for these programs are eligible for special assistance designed especially for them, such as the Refugee Cash Assistance and the Medical Assistance programs.[22]

The availability of particularly generous income-transfer programs to refugees and asylees implies that persons originating in countries that recently underwent political upheaval (such as Vietnam in the 1970s, or Cuba in the 1960s) are much more likely to be in the welfare rolls. In fact, the welfare participation rate of immigrants originating in a country that recently underwent a political upheaval is 2 to 3 percentage points higher than that of immigrants originating in other countries.[23]

Welfare Costs and Declining Immigrant Skills

Because the new immigrants are more likely to be on welfare than the old, the changing conditions in the immigration market have obviously increased the costs of maintaining the welfare state. Nonetheless, it is likely that the dollar costs associated with increasing immigrant participation in the welfare system are small. Welfare incomes, whether those of immigrants or those of natives, tend to be very low. In 1979, the typical native household on welfare received about $2,500, while the corresponding immigrant household received about $2,800. The $300 differential in welfare incomes between the two groups is mainly attributable to the immigrants' different residential location and relatively unfavorable socioeconomic characteristics.[24] Because supporting a welfare family is relatively inexpensive, and because immigrants are a small fraction of the U.S. population, the new immigration is unlikely to have a major impact on welfare expenditures.

It is easy to get a rough estimate of the cost increase associated with the declining skills among successive immigrant cohorts. Households that immigrated in the 1970s are about 2 percentage points more likely to be on welfare than households that immigrated in the early 1960s. During the 1970s, 311,000 female-headed and 1.3 million male-headed households immigrated to the United States (as enumerated by the 1980 Census). The relatively low skill level of these households, therefore, accounts for the entry of an additional 6,000 female-headed and 26,000 male-headed immigrant households into the welfare rolls. The decline in the skills of successive immigrant cohorts accounts for a $147-million rise in welfare costs per year (in 1988 dollars). In other words, the fact that persons who immigrated in the 1970s are less skilled than those who came in the early 1960s is responsible for only a $147-million increase in the costs of welfare.

It turns out that this cost increase is small by almost any measuring rod. In 1979, despite all of the attention devoted to the problem of welfare in America, total expenditures on the main welfare programs (AFDC, SSI, and General Assistance) were only $33 billion (in 1988 dollars).[25] Approximately $2.3 billion of this total, or about 7 percent, was distributed to immigrant households. The $147-million increase attributable to declining immigrant skills, therefore, represents a 6.4 percent increase in the immigrant welfare bill, but only a .4 percent increase in total welfare expenditures. It is worth stressing, however, that these welfare expenditures are a very small component of the costs associated with maintaining a welfare state. Expenditures on other programs, such as Social Security and health maintenance, are much higher than the costs of the welfare programs analyzed in this chapter. For instance, in 1979, public expenditures on health and medical care were $142 billion (in 1988 dollars), and the total cost of all the programs in the welfare state was $702 billion.[26] Unfortunately, little is known about immigrant participation in most of these programs. Nevertheless, as noted in the previous chapter, because government spending benefits the poor, the declining skills of immigrant flows almost certainly led to an increase in the costs of maintaining the welfare state. In view of the size of these programs, the increase in expenditures associated with unskilled immigration may have been substantial.

There is, of course, a more general question underlying this type of accounting exercise. Are social expenditures on immigrants offset by the taxes they put into the system? This problem is difficult to address because the data and conceptual framework needed to conduct such

160

a cost/benefit calculation are not available. Nevertheless, a recent study by economist Julian Simon attempts to tackle this monumental task.[27] He basically finds that immigrants, on aggregate, put as much into the tax system as they take out of it. In other words, immigrants pay their way in America's welfare state. Unfortunately, Simon's conclusion depends on a number of unverifiable conceptual and empirical assumptions, and it is almost certainly the case that his finding is sensitive to variations in these assumptions.

Because of data limitations, for example, Simon assumes that the income transfers received by the most recent immigrant waves will be the same as those received by earlier waves. There are, in other words, no differences in welfare participation behavior among immigrant cohorts. The data presented here, however, indicate otherwise. Because the Simon study assumes that the recent cohorts are exactly like the earlier cohorts, it underestimates the extent to which welfare costs will be increasing in the future.

In addition, this type of cost/benefit calculation must account for the fact that immigrants help reduce the tax burden of natives. In particular, a portion of immigrant taxes is used to pay for such public goods as national defense, scientific research, and national parks. Expenditures on these government programs are basically independent of the size of the U.S. population and would be incurred even if immigration did not take place. Because immigrants share in the costs of these programs, natives gain from the increase in the tax base associated with immigration. Of course, the cost/benefit calculation must classify which types of government programs are public goods and which are not. Inevitably, any such categorization is open to question, and any conclusion can be easily reversed by an appropriate reclassification of government programs.

Moreover, even if Simon's conclusions are correct and the immigrant flow indeed "pays its way," there remains the question whether current immigration policy is most beneficial for the United States, at least in terms of the balance between additional tax revenues and increased expenditures in government programs. Put differently, should the United States pursue an immigration policy in which the immigrant flow more than pays its way? As shown in the previous chapter, tax revenues would have been higher if the U.S. had attracted a more skilled immigrant flow in the late 1970s. Moreover, government spending would have been smaller because unskilled workers receive a disproportionate share of the government's resources. Therefore, changing the parameters of America's offer in the immigration market so as to attract a more skilled immigrant flow could lead to substantial financial benefits for the country.

CHAPTER 10

Immigrant Entrepreneurship
and Immigrant Enclaves

E̲NTREPRENEURSHIP is an important aspect of the immigrant experience. Observers of the contemporary American scene are often struck by the fact that a relatively large number of immigrants run their own businesses. Immigrant entrepreneurs manage large numbers of ethnic restaurants and shops, sell goods and services to members of their own national group and to others, and provide employment opportunities for many workers.

Some immigrants probably begin their climb up the ladder of economic success by opening up small shops and catering to the consumption needs of their compatriots. It is obvious that immigrants have a comparative advantage in fulfilling the needs of this consumer group because they share the same language, culture, and preferences, and immigrants are particularly well suited to meet these consumer demands. Moreover, the existence of immigrant enclaves in many American cities generates a high level of demand for these ethnic and cultural goods in a compact geographic area. This concentration makes it easy for immigrant entrepreneurs to serve the enclave economy. If these entrepreneurs are successful, focusing solely on the relatively poor performance of their counterparts in the salaried labor market provides an incomplete and perhaps misleading picture of the economic contribution of immigration to the United States.

This chapter describes the role that immigrant entrepreneurship plays in the American economy. Consistent with the stereotypical image, self-employment rates for many national-origin groups are quite large: the self-employment sector evidently provides many economic opportunities to foreign-born persons. There is no evidence, however, that immigrant entrepreneurs are particularly successful. The presumption that many immigrant entrepreneurs begin with small shops, and through their ability and hard work accumulate substantial wealth, is a myth.

The Self-Employment Sector

On average, immigrants are slightly more likely to be self-employed than natives (see table 10.1).[1] The immigrant self-employment rate is 12 percent, while that of natives is 11 percent. Within the immigrant population, however, self-employment rates vary widely among national-origin groups. In some groups, such as Mexican and Jamaican immigrants, self-employment is a relatively rare occurrence, while in others, such as Greek and Korean immigrants, one-quarter or more of the labor force participants are self-employed. For some national-origin groups, therefore, self-employment is a remarkably common feature of the immigrant experience.

The incomes of self-employed workers appear to be higher than the incomes of their salaried counterparts. Self-employed immigrant men, for instance, earn about 48 percent more than salaried immigrants, while self-employed native men earn about 28 percent more than their salaried counterparts. These data, however, should not be interpreted as evidence that immigrants are particularly successful in the self-employment sector. Self-employment incomes reflect not only the returns to the entrepreneur's human capital, but also the returns to a perhaps sizable investment in equipment and inventory required to open and run a business. The incomes of salaried workers, by contrast, only reflect the returns to the worker's human capital. Hence the incomes of salaried and self-employed workers are not truly comparable. There is no information on the size of the financial investment that immigrant and native entrepreneurs make in their businesses. Thus, it is impossible to adjust the self-employment income data and subtract the returns to the entrepreneur's financial investment to make it comparable to the earnings data available in the salaried sector.

Moreover, the income advantage of self-employed over salaried workers disappears after controlling for the large differences in demographic characteristics between the two groups. Subsequent discussion

164

Immigrant Entrepreneurship and Immigrant Enclaves

TABLE 10.1

The Self-Employment Sector in 1980

Group	Fraction of Workers Who Are Self-Employed	Average Annual Income of Self-Employed Workers (in 1,000s)	Average Annual Income of Salaried Workers (in 1,000s)
Native Men	11.4	23.2	18.0
All Immigrant Men	12.2	23.9	16.2
Immigrant Men Born in Europe			
Germany	16.1	27.3	21.9
Greece	29.5	19.6	15.3
Italy	18.2	19.8	16.7
Poland	15.6	25.6	18.2
United Kingdom	10.2	23.9	23.4
Immigrant Men Born in Asia			
China	16.2	19.7	15.3
India	11.1	37.1	20.8
Japan	10.0	20.8	21.6
Korea	24.6	23.0	16.0
Philippines	6.3	43.5	14.8
Immigrant Men Born in the Americas			
Canada	15.5	27.2	21.2
Cuba	15.7	21.6	15.0
Dominican Republic	5.9	19.5	9.6
Jamaica	5.9	17.5	13.0
Mexico	5.1	16.5	11.4

SOURCE: Author's tabulations from the 1980 Public Use Sample of the U.S. Census. These statistics refer to the population of working men aged twenty-five to sixty-four. Self-employment status is given by the class of work characterizing the person's main job. The income figures give the total receipts from all jobs in either sector.

will show that the comparison of demographically similar persons in the two sectors indicates that self-employed workers, whether immigrants or natives, actually have somewhat lower incomes than salaried workers. There also exists substantial variation in self-employment incomes among national-origin groups. For some nationalities, such as men born in the Philippines or India, self-employment incomes are quite high, while for others, such as Jamaican or Mexican immigrants, self-employment incomes are much lower. To some extent, income differentials

165

among national-origin groups in the self-employment sector mirror the income differentials observed in the salaried sector. In particular, there is a positive correlation between the average earnings of salaried workers and the incomes of entrepreneurs originating in the same source country: the same national-origin groups that are successful in the salaried labor market tend to be successful in the self-employment sector.

What do self-employed workers do? Four industries account for about two-thirds of entrepreneurs in both the immigrant and the native populations: construction, retail trade, business services, and professional services.[2] But immigrant entrepreneurs are much more likely to be working in the retail-trade industry than their native counterparts. More than 27 percent of self-employed immigrants are in this single industry, compared with only 17 percent of self-employed natives. Because the retail-trade industry contains such types of firms as variety stores, grocery stores, and eating and drinking places, the data confirm the observation that a large number of immigrants enter the self-employment sector by opening small shops and catering to specialized consumer groups.

Who are the self-employed? Labor force participants, whether immigrants or natives, have the option of obtaining work in the wage and salary sector or of becoming self-employed. Obviously, people choose whichever option provides better opportunities, taking into account the human capital and financial assets available to the worker.

One crucial difference between the two sectors plays a major role in determining who becomes self-employed: opening up a business, unlike getting a job, often requires a considerable financial investment. Individuals with little collateral or without an established credit history have trouble borrowing funds from banks. These persons find it difficult to finance the investment required in opening a firm, such as leasing (or buying) space for the business, obtaining the necessary equipment and machinery, and purchasing the inventory needed to run a successful shop. The worker's wealth and financial resources, therefore, are a major obstacle restricting entry into the self-employment sector.

Regardless of whether workers are immigrants or natives, recent studies point to three demographic characteristics as the main determinants of which persons become self-employed: education, age, and marital status.[3]

There is a strong positive correlation between educational attainment and self-employment propensities. College graduates, for instance, have self-employment rates that are at least 1 percentage point higher than those of high school graduates.[4] There are many reasons why such a correlation exists. Higher education levels are associated with higher wealth, and thus highly educated individuals face fewer financial constraints in starting a business. Higher education levels may also increase a worker's ability to anticipate consumer needs and to provide a service that other persons desire (and are willing to pay for), or they may increase the organizational and managerial skills of potential entrepreneurs. In addition, for certain types of occupations that have large self-employment rates, such as accounting, the law, and medicine, high education levels are a prerequisite.

Self-employment rates also increase with age. If other factors are held constant, the self-employment rates of men at age forty are about 3 percentage points higher than the self-employment rates of men ten years younger.[5] This correlation arises because as people age, they accumulate wealth and remove many of the financial constraints that restrict their ability to open a business. Furthermore, they also learn about consumer preferences and about the availability and profitability of self-employment options.

Finally, men who are married with a spouse present in the household have a self-employment rate that is about 2 percentage points higher than that of single men or of men who are separated.[6] This differential probably arises because married entrepreneurs can usually count on the spouse as an inexpensive source of labor and financial resources. In addition, because all family members are concerned about the household's economic welfare, an entrepreneur who employs relatives can devote less time to monitoring the employees' activities than entrepreneurs who hire unrelated workers. This increases the gains to self-employment and leads to higher self-employment rates.

Generally, immigrant self-employment rates exceed those of natives even after controlling for these (and other) demographic characteristics. Just as variations in demographic characteristics do not fully account for the wage and employment differentials observed in the salaried sector, they also do not explain the differences in self-employment propensities between immigrants and natives, or within the immigrant population. The reasons for the higher self-employment rates of immigrants, and for the variations in self-employment rates among national-origin groups, lie elsewhere.

The Impact of Assimilation on Self-Employment

As table 10.2 shows, assimilation has a strong impact on the self-employment rates of immigrants.[7] Immigrants are more likely to be self-employed the longer they have resided in the United States. Moreover, the increase in the self-employment propensity of immigrants over the working life greatly exceeds the increase experienced by demographically comparable natives. The typical immigrant who arrived between 1965 and 1969, for instance, entered the labor market with a self-employment rate that is 5 percentage points below that of comparable native men. After thirty years in the United States, the immigrant's self-employment rate is predicted to be 3 percentage points above that of natives.

Newly arrived immigrants usually lack the financial resources and business connections required to open a business. Over time, their chances of qualifying for loans and having the financial resources to

TABLE 10.2

The Impact of Assimilation on Self-Employment

| Group | Difference Between the Self-Employment Rates of Immigrant and Comparable Native Men at: | |
	Time of Entry	Thirty Years After Entry
1950–1959 cohort	−5.4	3.0
1960–1964 cohort	−5.0	3.4
1965–1969 cohort	−5.3	3.1
1970–1974 cohort	−4.2	4.2
1975–1979 cohort	−3.9	4.5

SOURCE: Author's tabulations from the 1970 and 1980 Public Use Samples of the U.S. Census. The estimated differentials are based on regressions using the linear-probability model wherein the dependent variable is the self-employment propensity of the worker. The data are restricted to workers aged twenty-five to sixty-four. The regressors include education, age, marital status, health status, an indicator of metropolitan residence, an indicator of whether the observation was drawn from the 1970 or the 1980 Census, the cohort of immigration, and the number of years since immigration.

start a successful firm increase, and immigrants find it easier to enter the self-employment sector. It is also unlikely that newly arrived immigrants know much about the types of income opportunities available in self-employed jobs in the United States. Over time, as immigrants learn about these opportunities, many discover that entrepreneurship can be a profitable endeavor.

Even though assimilation has a strong impact on the self-employment propensity of immigrants, it cannot explain why immigrants eventually have higher self-employment rates than natives. After all, natives also learn about income opportunities available in the various sectors of the economy as they age; they accumulate wealth, develop business connections, and establish credit histories; and they behave in ways that motivate them to choose the best option available.

In addition, the data indicate that the new immigrants are more likely to enter the self-employment sector than the earlier ones. Men who entered the United States in the late 1970s have a self-employment rate that is 1.4 percentage points higher than that of men who immigrated in the late 1960s.

The increasing self-employment propensities of immigrants among successive waves suggest a shift in relative labor market opportunities between the salaried and the self-employment sectors. I argue subsequently that entrepreneurial opportunities for the immigrant population have increased in the past two or three decades. This expansion in entrepreneurial opportunities is related to the increasing size of the foreign-born population in the United States and to the growing economic importance of immigrant enclaves.

The Enclave Economy

Immigrants have a comparative advantage over natives in operating certain types of businesses. A native born, raised, and living in Milwaukee, for instance, will find it quite difficult to open up, staff, and run a small family restaurant serving Korean food. An immigrant from Korea obviously knows much more about Korean cuisine and is better skilled at operating this type of business. This skill gap between immigrants and natives implies that certain types of businesses will be run largely by immigrants from particular national backgrounds.

In general, immigrants have a comparative advantage at providing goods and services to specific segments of the population, particularly other persons of the same national origin. This skill advantage arises because immigrant entrepreneurs know the language, business customs, and consumption preferences of their compatriots much better than natives do. Therefore, immigrant entrepreneurs have an economic incentive to operate businesses that cater largely to other immigrants of the same national origin. In addition, immigrants are unlikely to be as familiar with American culture and consumption preferences as U.S.-born workers. In short, there are gains to specialization.

The fact that immigrants have an advantage over natives in carrying out certain types of business activities, however, does not necessarily imply that immigrants will indeed go ahead and open up these types of firms. In order to make the self-employment option economically viable, there must also exist a strong demand for these cultural or ethnic goods and services. Immigrant enclaves, populated by people who share a language, cultural habits, and consumption preferences, generate a market for goods and services that native entrepreneurs find difficult to tap.

The enclave makes it profitable for immigrants to enter the self-employment sector and specialize in catering to the consumption needs of their compatriots. The economic gains to this activity may be sizable because a large number of relatively similar persons live together in a small geographic region, and immigrant entrepreneurs can serve the market at a very low cost.

One of the most heavily studied enclaves in the United States is that of the Cubans in Miami.[8] A series of important studies by sociologist Alejandro Portes and his associates describes the size, growth, and economic impact of this enclave.[9] Among Hispanic groups, Cuban immigrants tend to have the highest self-employment rates. The Portes studies reveal that in the early 1980s, there were 25,000 Cuban-owned firms in the Miami area alone, with more than 90 percent of these firms employing fewer than ten employees. The pervasive economic and social influence of the enclave on Miami's Cuban community is clearly described by Portes:

The economic importance of this set of enterprises is minuscule on a national scale, but it has had significant consequences for the ethnic group. As consumers, it allows immigrants who speak little English to conduct economic transactions and meet their demand for culturally defined goods. A survey of recently arrived Mariel refugees in Miami found, for example, that 86% lived in Cuban neighborhoods, 75% patronized mostly stores owned by conationals, and 82% read exclusively Spanish-language newspapers.[10]

These studies document that immigrants have consumer needs that cannot be easily satisfied by native entrepreneurs. The size of Miami's Cuban enclave indicates that there are significant economic gains associated with opening up businesses that specifically cater to these needs. The birth and continuing growth of the Cuban enclave, along with enclaves of many other national-origin groups (Koreans, Japanese, Filipinos, Vietnamese, and Mexicans), have radically altered the character of many American cities. Because of the large size of these immigrant flows, the socioeconomic importance of ethnic enclaves has increased in the past two or three decades. As a result, economic opportunities for self-employed immigrants have expanded substantially.

How important are the enclaves in attracting ever-increasing numbers of immigrants to the self-employment sector? There is evidence that the growth of Hispanic enclaves is an important factor contributing to the high self-employment rates of some of the Spanish-speaking immigrant groups.[11]

To the extent that immigrant enclaves increase the gains to becoming self-employed for specific types of persons, the self-employment rates of Hispanic immigrants should be larger when they reside in cities with relatively large numbers of Hispanic residents. In fact, an increase of 10 percentage points in the fraction of the city's population that is Hispanic increases the self-employment rate of Cuban immigrants by about 2 percentage points, and that of other Hispanic immigrants by about 1 percentage point.[12]

Moreover, the positive correlation between the size of the Hispanic community and the Hispanic self-employment rate does not arise because immigrants live in expanding areas that offer more economic opportunities to all potential entrepreneurs, not just Hispanic entrepreneurs. In fact, there is no correlation between the self-employment rates of non-Hispanics and the size of the city's Hispanic population. In other words, the presence of Hispanics in the marketplace increases the self-employment rates of Hispanics, but does not affect the self-employment rates of others. The enclave economy expands entrepreneurial opportunities only for its own members.

The impact of the enclave on self-employment propensities generates major differences between the self-employment rates of Hispanic immigrants and those of natives. The typical Hispanic immigrant lives in an SMSA that is about 20 percent Hispanic. The typical non-Hispanic native lives in an SMSA that is only about 6 percent Hispanic.[13] The geographic concentration of Hispanic immigrants in a few localities implies that they are 2 to 3 percentage points more likely to be self-employed than non-Hispanic natives. Therefore, the effect of the enclave on economic opportunities probably accounts for the relatively higher self-employment rates found among immigrants and for the increase in entrepreneurial activity among successive immigrant waves.

Salaried Employment in the Enclave

Enclaves affect not only the economic opportunities available to immigrants in the self-employment sector, but also the wage and salary opportunities of immigrant workers. After all, immigrant entrepreneurs are likely to hire a large number of their compatriots.

The economic importance of the employment of immigrants by other immigrants is established in a series of surveys conducted by Portes. Even six years after immigration, about 40 percent of Cuban immigrants are employed by Cubans, and 15 percent of Mexican immigrants are employed by Mexicans.[14] Because of data limitations, this aspect of the immigrant experience has not been explored carefully, but it is sure to have an important effect on the economic well-being of the immigrant population.

It is not at all clear, however, whether this hiring of immigrants by their compatriots is a "good" thing for the typical immigrant living and working in the enclave. On the one hand, by working for immigrant entrepreneurs, immigrants avoid the labor market discrimination that may be operating against them outside the enclave. Immigrant entrepreneurs and native employers probably also have a very different perception of the skills and productivities of immigrant workers. Immigrant entrepreneurs may view their conational employees as being more valuable and more productive. Because people of the same national origin share the same culture, language, and work habits, immigrant employers could use the cultural idiosyncrasies of the national-origin group to the advantage of the work environment, whereas these cultural differences may create friction and reduce productivity in a nonenclave working environment. In this view, immigrants working in the enclave would be paid relatively higher wage rates (because they are more productive and face less discrimination) than immigrants who take a chance and find a job outside the "womb."

Immigrants who work outside the enclave, on the other hand, have a greater set of job opportunities to choose from. Typically, these immigrants are more proficient with the English language and can trade with a much larger number of employers in the mainstream American economy. Because they have more job opportunities and can pick a job from among more diverse offers, these peregrinators may be more successful than immigrants who remain in the enclave. Although there is only limited evidence on this important point, and that evidence is based on small surveys of only two national-origin groups (Cubans and Mexicans), the data suggest that immigrants who work in the enclave earn less than immigrants who work outside it. Studies by Portes and Robert Bach indicate that Mexican immigrants working for Mexican (or other ethnic) employers earn about $142 less per week than demographically comparable Mexican immigrants who work for non-Mexican employers. Among Cuban immigrants, the earnings differential is much smaller, but it still favors Cubans who work for American employers.[15]

Because these results are based on small samples of only two national-origin groups, it is unknown whether they can be generalized to the typical immigrant in the population. Nevertheless, the findings are important: they indicate the types of economic costs associated with enclave economies. The relatively low wages received by immigrants working in the enclave retard the group's economic progress in the United States. There are gains to be made by learning the culture, language, and skills that can be traded in the much larger labor market looming outside the ethnic enclave. Immigrant assimilation into American society pays. It expands the extent of the labor market facing the typical immigrant and gives immigrants a much broader menu of economic choices.

Are Immigrant Entrepreneurs Successful?

There is clearly a growing movement in the immigrant population away from salaried work and toward self-employment. How successful are immigrant entrepreneurs? Are their incomes so high that a reassessment of the relatively negative portrait of immigrant performance in the salaried sector is required?

The answer is no. Even though immigrant entrepreneurs earn about 48 percent more than immigrants in the salaried sector, the demographic characteristics of the two populations are quite different. In particular, immigrant entrepreneurs are more highly educated, are older, and are more likely to be married with a spouse present in the household than salaried immigrants. All of these demographic characteristics are associated with higher incomes in the self-employment sector. Once the differences in demographic characteristics are controlled for, the earnings advantage of immigrant entrepreneurs entirely disappears. In fact, immigrant entrepreneurs earn about 4 percent less than demographically comparable immigrants in the wage and salary sector.[16] Moreover, because the incomes of entrepreneurs include a return to their financial investment in the business, the 4-percent income gap actually underestimates the relatively poor performance of immigrants in the self-employment sector.

Several factors account for the surprising result that immigrant entrepreneurs, on average, have lower incomes than comparable salaried immigrants.[17] The first is that self-employment provides substantial psychological benefits to entrepreneurs. These benefits include independence in the work environment and the ability to perform tasks that the entrepreneur finds enjoyable. Entrepreneurs are willing to purchase these job advantages through a reduced income. Despite the fact that higher income opportunities are available elsewhere, the emotional benefits accruing to entrepreneurs running their own businesses compensate for the relatively low incomes and prevent them from switching over to the salaried sector.[18]

Second, for specific demographic characteristics, the self-employment sector may be attracting relatively unskilled immigrants. Because of their comparative advantage in the production of ethnic and cultural goods, most immigrant entrepreneurs decide to cater solely to the consumption needs of their compatriots and necessarily restrict their services to a relatively small enclave market. Highly skilled workers are less likely to find this type of segregation profitable, for by serving a small market, they are prevented from operating at their full potential.[19] Highly skilled immigrants, therefore, have weaker incentives to stay in the enclave and enter the self-employment sector.

Recent evidence, in fact, suggests that the sorting of less skilled minority workers into self-employment is quite prevalent in the U.S. economy, particularly among Hispanics and Asians.[20] Self-employed workers in these minority groups are not favorably selected: they are not the persons with the highest productivity and skills in their populations. This type of skill sorting between the salaried and self-employment sectors leads to immigrant entrepreneurs having relatively lower earnings than comparable immigrants working in the salaried sector.

In addition, a large fraction of immigrant entrepreneurs open firms in the retail-trade industry. Their concentration in this industry reflects the comparative advantage that immigrants have at providing these types of services. Unfortunately, this industry is characterized by some of the lowest wage levels in the interindustry wage structure of the United States.[21] Work in the retail-trade industry is simply not very profitable.

Finally, and perhaps most importantly, the incomes of individuals in the self-employment sector may be artificially low due to the systematic misreporting of self-employment incomes.[22] Misreporting occurs either because it is difficult for respondents to state their self-employment incomes precisely in the census surveys or because the respondents may be attempting to hide the actual income figures from auditors at the Internal Revenue Service. In fact, it is likely that the most successful entrepreneurs have the most incentive to underreport their incomes.[23] Unfortunately, the extent of this misreporting among immigrant entrepreneurs is unknown.

Conclusions about the performance of immigrant entrepreneurs in the U.S. economy are also clouded by the lack of information regarding the impact of assimilation on self-employment incomes. Both immigrants and natives are likely to move in and out of the self-employment sector as economic opportunities change. The composition of the pool of immigrants and natives who are self-employed, therefore, will change substantially over time. Only those persons who are best adapted to the entrepreneurial environment survive the experience, and those whose firms die out are replaced by others who have recently discovered income opportunities in the self-employment sector.[24] Estimating the impact of assimilation on self-employment incomes thus requires an analysis of longitudinal data. This data base would track specific immigrant firms over time and would record the "natural selection" process, the births and deaths of firms, and the movements in and out of the self-employment sector. Unfortunately, no currently available data set, with sufficiently large samples, allows a statistically reliable study.

In sum, immigrant entrepreneurs do not seem to be particularly successful in the American economy. Even though this conclusion is obviously affected by what is probably substantial underreporting of self-employment incomes, there simply is no empirical evidence suggesting that the economic success of immigrant entrepreneurs offsets the relatively poor performance of immigrants in the salaried labor market.

CHAPTER 11

The Ties That Bind:
The Immigrant Family

IMMIGRATION is a family affair. The 1965 amendments to the Immigration and Nationality Act ensure that the family plays a major role in the immigration market. First of all, 80 percent of all numerically restricted visas are reserved for close relatives of U.S. residents and citizens.[1] In addition, any person residing abroad who is an immediate relative (a spouse, minor child, or parent) of an adult U.S. citizen can enter the country without having to qualify for one of the numerically restricted visas. To a great extent, the American offer in the immigration market is one in which visas are literally given away to persons who happen to be related in certain ways to American residents or citizens, and visas are prohibitively expensive for practically everyone else.

Even if immigration policy did not specifically encourage "chain immigration"—the staggered migration of family units—economic factors are at work that would nevertheless generate this type of migration flow. After all, immigration is likely to be cheaper for persons with relatives already residing in the United States. The family ties that reach across international boundaries form a network transmitting valuable, reliable, and inexpensive information about economic and social conditions in the United States to relatives residing abroad, which greatly reduces the uncertainty associated with the immigration decision.[2] In effect, family ties lower the costs of immigration, and persons who are part of the network are more likely to migrate than persons who are not. Therefore, chain immigration is likely to be a prevalent characteristic of immigrant flows.

The family-reunification provisions of the 1965 amendments reinforce these economic incentives and, as a result, may have a potentially explosive impact on the size of the immigrant flow. As noted above, American citizens can sponsor the entry of relatives currently residing abroad. These relatives, upon naturalization, can in turn sponsor the entry of additional relatives, and so on. Current immigration policy, therefore, creates a potential for an ever-increasing immigrant flow. Each layer of the inverted pyramid sponsors more and more relatives, with each new link in the chain being more distantly related to the original immigrants. A population time-bomb may be slowly ticking away.

An immigration policy that allocates visas on the basis of specific types of family ties is also likely to change the skill composition of the immigrant flow. Obviously, because only a fixed number of visas are awarded annually, the allocation of most visas to relatives of U.S. residents or citizens must mean that many highly skilled applicants are denied visas simply because there are no entry slots available.

Furthermore, the fact that the immigration decision is made collectively by the family changes the composition of the immigrant flow. In particular, single or unattached persons decide to immigrate by comparing their own economic opportunities among potential countries of residence. Families make the immigration decision by comparing the *family's* economic welfare among the various countries. The family must also determine the placement of its members in the immigration chain (who goes first?). Finally, all members of the family unit must decide whether to go along with the family's immigration decision or to break away from the family altogether and do what is personally best for them. In the end, persons immigrating as part of a family unit, whether they came at the same time or in sequence, will differ from persons who moved on their own.

This chapter analyzes the impact of the kinship provisions in the 1965 amendments on the size and skill composition of the immigrant flow entering the United States. The empirical evidence is surprising. First, there is no evidence that the size of the immigrant flow is growing explosively as a result of our current immigration policy. Second, the data indicate that persons who migrate as part of a family unit are more skilled and have higher earnings than persons who migrate on their own.

The Immigration Multiplier

There are two general types of kinship provisions in current U.S. immigration policy. The first permits the entry of the offspring, spouse, and parents of adult U.S. citizens or legal residents, either through the use of numerically restricted visas or through visas that are exempt from these restrictions. The second, the so-called fifth-preference provision, allocates 24 percent of the numerically restricted visas (64,800 visas in 1987) to the siblings, and to the families of the siblings, of adult U.S. citizens.

Obviously, repeated use of these kinship provisions introduces the potential for explosive growth in the size of the immigrant flow. The main source of this concern is the fifth-preference provision. This preference can sprout many new "branches" (that is, new households) in the immigration tree. The new family units can then begin their own immigration chains.

It is easy to see how the number of persons who qualify to enter the United States under the family-reunification provisions can multiply very quickly. The Reverend Theodore Hesburgh, chairman of the U.S. Select Commission on Immigration and Refugee Policy, clearly states the argument:

The inclusion of a preference for brothers and sisters of U.S. citizens creates a runaway demand for visas. . . . Once any person enters the country under any preference and becomes naturalized, the demand for the admission of brothers and sisters increases geometrically. . . . To illustrate the potential impact, assume one foreign-born married couple, both naturalized, each with two siblings who are also married and each new nuclear family having three children. The foreign-born married couple may petition for the admission of their siblings. Each has a spouse and three children who come with their parents. Each spouse is a potential source for more immigration, and so it goes. It is possible that no less than 84 persons would become eligible for visas in a relatively short period of time.[3]

The family-reunification provisions, therefore, create the potential for a Malthusian geometric growth in the size of the immigrant flow. Many additional persons eventually qualify for entry into the United States because of one single admission. Thus the "immigration multiplier," the number of future admittances attributable to the admission of one immigrant today, may be quite large. If Reverend Hesburgh is right, the multiplier is at least eighty-four. It is theoretically possible that at some point in the not-too-distant future, a large fraction of the world's population would qualify for entry into the United States under one of the provisions of the 1965 amendments.[4]

Nevertheless, the fact that the number of *potential* entrants increases explosively does not necessarily imply that the number of *actual* immigrants will increase correspondingly. There is no reason to presume that every person who qualifies for entry into the United States indeed wants to reside here. So the true immigration multiplier cannot be calculated by mechanically grinding through the formulas specified in the 1965 amendments. Legislatures enact laws; individuals respond to them. In other words, the law gives some persons the opportunity to migrate to the United States. Potential migrants must decide on their own whether to take advantage of this opportunity. It is this behavioral response, alongside the fact that only U.S. citizens can give birth to new branches in the immigration tree, that determines the actual size of the immigration multiplier. Therefore, the calculation of the multiplier requires a systematic analysis of immigrant-flow data that accounts for the naturalization behavior of immigrants and for the extent to which the kinship provisions in the 1965 amendments are actually used.

Estimates of the Immigration Multiplier

The observed immigration multiplier is likely to be far below its theoretical potential for three reasons. First, the 1965 amendments place numerical limits on the number of visas that are allocated to certain types of relatives, even though many additional persons may qualify. In 1987, there were 270,000 numerically restricted visas available, and only 64,800 visas for fifth-preference applicants. The number of persons who qualify for these visas greatly exceeds the number of entry slots available, and there are long queues of applicants waiting for the visas. In January 1984, for instance, 1.6 million persons were in the queue for the numerically restricted visas, and 1 million persons in this queue were waiting for one of the scarce fifth-preference visas.[5] Even if no further visa applicants showed up at U.S. embassies around the world, it would take more than fifteen years to admit all applicants for fifth-preference visas.

The existence of long queues obviously delays the potential immigration of many qualified applicants. This delay increases immigration costs because persons in the queue must basically put their personal lives on hold for a relatively long time, while deferring important economic and investment decisions until after the move. In addition, long queues reduce the economic benefits of immigration. The older the immigrant, the shorter the time period over which the economic gains to immigration can be collected. Because they reduce the attractiveness of the American offer in the immigration market, the queues are likely to discourage the immigration of many persons who are otherwise qualified to enter the United States.

A second factor attenuating the size of the immigration multiplier is that the crucial fifth-preference provision requires that the sponsor be an American citizen. A remarkably large number of immigrants choose not to become citizens. For example, only half of the foreign-born persons enumerated in the 1980 Census are naturalized.[6] Further, a recent longitudinal survey tracked the naturalization behavior of immigrants who entered the country in 1971, and found that only 37 percent had naturalized by 1981, even though the residence requirement for naturalization is only five years.[7] Moreover, most of the immigrants who became citizens had done so in the first six or seven years after immigration. It is, therefore, unlikely that the naturalization rate of the 1971 cohort would increase much above 37 percent. Because many immigrants never naturalize, the number of foreign-born persons in the U.S. population who qualify to use the fifth preference is relatively small.

Finally, the size of the immigration multiplier is further attenuated because not all persons who qualify for entry wish to immigrate, even in the absence of queues. Most Americans find it hard to understand how anyone, when given the choice, would rather reside elsewhere. Yet, it is clearly the case that many persons choose not to migrate to the United States. Differences in economic, political, social, and cultural conditions among countries imply that not every person in the world is better off living in the United States. As an example, just prior to the enactment of the 1965 amendments, the United Kingdom was

181

allocated 65,000 visas. Yet only 32,000 British residents chose to take advantage of these visas and migrate to the United States.[8] Even though the American offer in the immigration market literally gave visas away to British residents, there were relatively few takers. Simply because some people qualify for certain entitlements under the law does not imply that they will use those entitlements.

These three important points imply that the size of the immigration multiplier is probably much smaller than the eighty-four entrants conjectured by Reverend Hesburgh. In fact, it is easy to show through a back-of-the-envelope calculation that the numerical magnitude of the immigration multiplier is unlikely to be greater than one.

In 1970, there were 9.7 million foreign-born persons residing in the United States.[9] These foreign-born persons presumably have relatives still residing in the various source countries. If each of these persons had sponsored the entry of only one immigrant during the next decade, the size of the immigrant flow between 1970 and 1980 would also have been 9.7 million persons. In fact, the size of the immigrant flow was only about 4.5 million during the decade. Therefore, even if every new immigrant who came in the 1970s was sponsored by a relative, only one immigrant came for every two foreign-born persons already here. These calculations, crude as they are, imply a short-run multiplier of slightly less than .5 (assuming that the 9.7 million immigrants present in the United States in 1970 did not sponsor the entry of any additional relatives during the 1980s and beyond).

The story does not end here, though. The 4.5 million persons who were sponsored into the United States during the 1970s, and who form the second link in the immigration chain, will themselves wish to sponsor the entry of their relatives, who will in turn wish to sponsor the migration of additional relatives, and so on. It is conceivable that this chaining of immigrant generations will lead to incredibly large numbers of entrants despite the fact that the first-round, or short-run, multiplier is relatively small.

This argument, it turns out, is not correct. Because the magnitude of the short-run multiplier is less than one, the chaining of different generations of foreign-born persons, even until doomsday, will not lead to an explosion in the size of the immigrant flow. If the magnitude of the short-run multiplier remains at .5, the 4.5 million persons who entered the United States in the 1970s will sponsor 2.25 million relatives after their arrival (4.5 million times .5). The 2.25 million immigrants who form the third link in the chain will, in turn, sponsor 1.13 million relatives (4.5 million times .5 times .5), and so on.

It is evident that the size of the immigrant flow decreases rapidly among the various links in the chain. Thus, the total number of immigrants admitted as a result of the sponsoring behavior of the 9.7 million original immigrants converges to a relatively small number. In fact, it converges to 9.7 million, so that the long-run multiplier is approximately one.[10] After everything is said and done, therefore, each immigrant present in the United States in 1970 was responsible for the entry of one additional immigrant.

Because these rough calculations make one crucial assumption—that the immigrants present in the United States in 1970 stopped sponsoring the entry of their relatives after 1980—this conclusion may be incorrect. Yet this assumption may not be as unrealistic as it seems. More than 80 percent of the immigrants enumerated in the 1970 Census arrived prior to 1965, hence they had at least fifteen years over which to sponsor the entry of their relatives. Furthermore, INS data suggest that most of the reunification of immigrant families takes place within ten years after the immigrant's arrival.[11]

Although this example is useful because it provides a simple understanding of the technical issues involved in estimating the immigration multiplier, the accuracy of the calculations can be greatly improved by incorporating key elements of American immigration policy. After all, the current visa-allocation system requires a specific pattern of age/naturalization/kinship relationships. The calculation of the immigration multiplier should take into account such factors as the naturalization rates of immigrants and the ages of the sponsors and applicants.

The important work of sociologist Guillermina Jasso and economist Mark Rosenzweig provides a methodological framework for estimating the immigration multiplier that takes many of these factors into account.[12] Using a longitudinal data set created by the INS, Jasso and Rosenzweig track the naturalization behavior of the immigrants who entered the United States in 1971 for a ten-year period. Because these data indicate the types of visas and family ties used by cohort members to enter the United States, they also allow the determination of which immigrant flows tend to have high sponsorship rates. Using these data, along with the demographic characteristics of the immigrants in the

1971 cohort, Jasso and Rosenzweig predict the number of relatives who entered the United States before 1981 for each member of the 1971 cohort. It turns out that the estimated short-run multiplier is less than one: it is on the order of .2 to .4 for immigrants who entered the United States under one of the family-reunification provisions and between .6 and .7 for immigrants who entered under one of the skill preferences.[13] Because most immigrants enter the country using a kinship provision, the results imply that for every two immigrants in the 1971 cohort, at most one additional immigrant enters the United States.

The Jasso and Rosenzweig study, therefore, confirms what the rough calculations suggest. It is not the case that the 1965 amendments will eventually lead to explosive growth in the size of the immigrant flow. Many other factors influence the immigration incentives of individuals, and these factors greatly attenuate the size of the immigration multiplier.

Families, Networks, and International Migration: Evidence from Mexico

The finding that the immigration multiplier is small does not imply that family ties are unimportant in encouraging further migration. In fact, persons are much more likely to migrate to the United States if they have relatives residing here. In other words, even though the typical foreign-born person residing in the United States sponsors few additional relatives, those persons who do come generally have family ties with immigrants already here.

The family is a network through which all types of economic, social, and cultural exchanges and interactions take place.[14] In the context of international migration, once a member of that network reaches the United States, reliable information about economic and social conditions here is transmitted back to the country of origin and is easily available to all other members of the network. Successful migration by one household member, therefore, increases the migration incentives of other members even in the absence of any policies that explicitly encourage the migration of additional members of the family unit.

The Ties That Bind: The Immigrant Family

Of course, the network need not be limited to nuclear or even extended families. It can also encompass friends and entire small communities. In some Mexican rural villages, for instance, a very large fraction of the households have a family member who is either residing in the United States or resided here at some point in the past.[15] This communal experience creates a much wider network, where information about economic and social conditions in the United States is a public good. This information is easily available to all members of the community and greatly increases the immigration propensities for members of that network.

A recent study by Douglas Massey and Felipe Garcia España documents that these family and social networks are important determinants of the immigration flow originating in Mexico.[16] Using a survey of rural Mexican households, they determined the relation between the migration propensities of individuals and the prior history of immigration to the United States by members of the household and by members of the community. As table 11.1 shows, an individual is much more likely to immigrate to the United States if either a family member or other members of the community already reside here.

The numerical impact of family and community networks on immigration propensities is large. People belonging to a household with no prior history of immigration and residing in a locality that also has no prior history of immigration have only a 2-percent probability of migrating to the United States over the study period. This probability

TABLE 11.1

Family and Social Networks and the Emigration Propensity of Mexicans

	Probability That a Mexican Migrates to the United States Between 1979 and 1981, if the Percent of the Community's Members Who Migrated to the United States Between 1976 and 1979 is:		
	0	5	10
Individual does not have a relative in the United States	.015	.032	.069
Individual has a relative in the United States	.072	.142	.277

SOURCE: Douglas S. Massey and Felipe Garcia España, "The Social Process of International Migration," *Science* 237 (August 14, 1987): table 2.

increases to 7 percent if the household already has a member residing in the United States, and to 28 percent if one-tenth of the households in the community have a history of immigration to the United States.

The Incidence of Chain Immigration

Additional evidence that family ties play a major role in immigration is available in the decennial U.S. censuses. As shown in table 11.2, most immigrants enumerated in the 1970 and 1980 Censuses either had a relative who resided in the United States prior to their migration, or migrated with a relative, or had a relative who immigrated subsequently.[17] The immigration of family units, whether in chains or contemporaneously, is the rule rather than the exception.

The census data indicate that the frequency of chain immigration has been increasing rapidly over time. For instance, 14 percent of the persons who immigrated to the United States between 1960 and 1964 had a relative residing here prior to their arrival, but almost twice as many of the persons who came in the late 1970s already had relatives here. Similarly, 14 percent of the immigrants in the 1960–1964 cohort sponsored the entry of a relative in the subsequent five years, as compared to 23 percent of the immigrants in the 1970–1974 cohort. The

TABLE 11.2
The Incidence of Chain Immigration

| Group | Percentage of Immigrants Residing with Relatives Who Migrated: | | |
	Prior to Immigrant	With Immigrant	In Five-Year Period After Immigrant
1960–1964 cohort	14.0	61.2	13.5
1965–1969 cohort	17.8	69.1	—
1970–1974 cohort	22.2	58.7	22.7
1975–1979 cohort	26.5	65.9	—

SOURCE: George J. Borjas and Stephen G. Bronars, "Immigration and the Family," mimeograph, University of California, Santa Barbara, January 1989, table 2. The data for the 1960–1964 and 1965–1969 cohorts are obtained from the 1970 Public Use Sample of the U.S. Census, while the data for the 1970–1974 and 1975–1979 cohorts are obtained from the 1980 Public Use Sample. Relatives who migrated "prior" to the immigrant arrived in an earlier cohort, while those who migrated "with" the immigrant arrived in the same cohort.

The Ties That Bind: The Immigrant Family

family-reunification provisions in the 1965 amendments, therefore, almost doubled the incidence of chain immigration. A large fraction of the current immigrant flow involves the reunification of family units that are separated by international boundaries.

It is remarkable that the chain-immigration process includes not only the staggered migration of siblings and other more distant relatives, but also the staggered migration of spouses and children. For instance, about 16 percent of the immigrants who came in the early 1970s, and who were married at the time of migration, had their spouse or children residing in the United States prior to their arrival, and 15 percent had their spouse or children join them in the subsequent five-year period.[18]

The importance of family ties in the immigration decision differs dramatically among national-origin groups. As table 11.3 shows, 28 percent of the Mexicans who arrived in the early 1970s had a relative residing in the United States prior to their migration, as compared to only 11 percent of the Canadians. In addition, 31 percent of the Mexicans sponsored the migration of a relative in the subsequent five-year period, while the sponsorship rate for Canadian immigrants was only 6 percent. The immigration multiplier appears to be significantly higher for immigrants originating in the less developed countries (such as Mexico, Korea, and the Philippines).[19]

This finding suggests that the multiplier, found to be small in the

TABLE 11.3

Differences in Chain-Immigration Propensities Among National-Origin Groups

	Percent of Immigrants in the 1970–1974 Cohort Residing with Relatives Who Migrated:		
Country of Origin	Prior to Immigrant	With Immigrant	In Five-Year Period After Immigrant
Canada	11.0	47.1	5.8
Italy	20.2	70.1	7.9
Korea	8.6	62.9	23.6
Mexico	28.3	64.3	31.4
Philippines	27.6	64.9	33.1
United Kingdom	10.9	51.3	5.4

SOURCE: George J. Borjas and Stephen G. Bronars, "Immigration and the Family," mimeograph, University of California, Santa Barbara, January 1989, table 3. The data are obtained from the 1980 Public Use Sample of the U.S. Census. Relatives who migrated "prior" to the immigrant arrived in an earlier cohort, while those who migrated "with" the immigrant arrived in the same cohort.

1970s data discussed above, may increase significantly in the future. After all, the national-origin groups represented by the new immigration have a much higher propensity for chain immigration than the old immigrants. Unfortunately, it is too early to estimate precisely what the immigration multiplier will be, for it will depend on the naturalization behavior of the new immigrants, on the frequency with which they use the sponsorship provisions of the law, and on economic and political conditions in the source countries.

In sum, family and community networks are important determinants of the immigration incentives of individuals. In view of the central role played by these social networks in the migration decision, it is necessary to analyze explicitly the ties that bind families across international boundaries in order to obtain a complete understanding of the immigrant experience in the United States.

Tied Movers

Thus far, I have stressed a conceptual approach to immigration that focuses on the economic incentives underlying an individual's decision to migrate. The individual compares alternative options and chooses the one that is best for him. In fact, it is *families* who enter the immigration market, compare the various offers, and choose the option that maximizes the household's economic well-being.[20] Put simply, the family as a whole and individual members within the household take actions that maximize total family income and avoid actions that lower family income levels.[21]

It is unlikely that the "private" immigration incentives of each member of the household—the incentives that would exist if there were no other family members involved in the decision—exactly coincide with the family's incentives to immigrate. Some individuals would probably prefer to take a specific course of action if they were on their own, but because of family ties they choose a different option. This unavoidable conflict between what is best for an individual and what is best for the family implies that family ties generate a different immigrant pool than would have been observed if immigration were purely an individual matter. Some persons who would not have migrated on their own will migrate as part of the family. By contrast, other persons who would have preferred to immigrate will stay behind in order to remain with their relatives. Therefore, the composition of the immigrant flow may be significantly affected by the fact that families, not individuals, make the immigration decision.

It is easy to see how family ties alter the immigration incentives of the various members of the household by considering the simple example of a family that contains two persons, a husband and a wife. In the country of origin, the husband earns $10 and the wife earns $5. If they were to move to the United States, the husband would earn $17 and the wife would earn $3. If they decided to remain in the source country, therefore, family income would be $15, while if they decided to immigrate, family income would be $20. In this hypothetical world, no costs are incurred when the family moves to the United States. What should this couple do?

If there were no family ties between the two persons, the man would obviously decide to immigrate and the woman would choose to stay in the country of origin. The existence of family ties implies that, as long as the family wants to act as a unit, one of the two parties must take an action detrimental to his or her private interests, regardless of the outcome of the immigration decision.

If the couple does not consider the possibility of divorce, the family will inevitably decide to immigrate, even though the wife loses $2 as a result of the move.[22] This loss, however, is more than offset by the husband's gain of $7. The husband can compensate his wife for her loss and thus "buy" her approval to immigrate to the United States. Because the family unit as a whole is better off after the move, both members of the household willingly agree to the immigration decision.

In this example, the wife is a "tied mover."[23] She is basically following her husband in his search for better economic opportunities, and even though her income is lower in the United States, in the end she too gains from the immigration of the family unit. It is clear that tied movers incur a private loss as a result of immigration, but that the loss is more than outweighed by the economic gains of other family members. Because income is redistributed within the household, all family members approve of and benefit from immigration. Generally, members of a family often take actions that are not privately beneficial, but that are best for the economic well-being of the family unit.

This example indicates that each worker in the pool of persons who migrate on their own, without family ties restricting the outcome of the migration decision, moves because he himself found it best to do so. There are no tied movers among single immigrants. None of these immigrants loses as a result of immigration.

In contrast, the pool of persons who migrate as part of a family unit includes a number of tied movers. This pool contains some persons who, had they not been part of a family unit, would rather have remained in the country of origin and incur private losses as a result of immigration. On average, therefore, the typical family immigrant has less to gain from the move than the typical single immigrant.

The presence of tied movers in the immigrant flow has a major impact on the skill composition of the foreign-born population. As shown earlier, the flow of single immigrants originating in countries with relatively egalitarian income distributions is composed of highly productive workers. But the flow of family immigrants contains some tied movers, persons who migrate not because they found it worthwhile to move on their own but because their spouse (or a relative) found that they could do much better in the United States. So the pool of family immigrants includes some persons who are not as well suited for the U.S. labor market. On average, therefore, the typical family immigrant originating in these countries is less skilled and has lower earnings than the typical single immigrant, because some of the family immigrants are tied movers. In effect, family ties attenuate the favorable selection that characterizes the immigrant flow originating in countries with egalitarian income distributions. Policies that favor the immigration of family units, therefore, lower the skill content of these immigrant flows.

Alternatively, single immigrants originating in countries with high levels of income inequality are relatively unskilled. Again, family ties distort the incentives that guide the immigration decision; they imply that some persons migrate simply because their spouse (or relative) gains significantly from the migration. But who are the tied movers? Clearly not the unskilled workers, because they gain substantially from immigration. Instead, the tied movers are relatively skilled workers. These workers do relatively well in countries characterized by a sizable amount of income inequality (and high payoffs for their skills), and they have few incentives to migrate to the United States.

Therefore, the flow of family immigrants originating in countries with high levels of income inequality will be more skilled and have higher earnings, on average, than the flow of single immigrants. The family ties that influence the immigration decision attenuate the unfavorable selection characterizing the immigrant flow. Policies that favor the immigration of families, therefore, may actually increase the average skills of immigrants.

The empirical analysis of the skills and earnings of immigrants indicates that men who migrate in family units tend to be more skilled and have higher wage rates than men who do not. Immigrant men who migrated to the United States entirely on their own earn about 4 percent less than immigrants who migrated contemporaneously with relatives.[24] Therefore, family immigrants are more skilled than single immigrants.

In addition, the data indicate that men who were married at the time of migration are more skilled and have higher earnings than men who were single at the time of migration.[25] In fact, men who were married at the time of entry earn about 5 to 10 percent more than men who did not have these family ties.[26] Presumably, the immigration of married men is more strongly influenced by family ties than that of single men. Thus, the empirical evidence again suggests that family ties increase the average skill level of the immigrant flow.

In sum, there is no evidence to support the conjecture that the family context of the immigration decision lowers the productivities or skills of immigrants. After all, persons who migrate as part of a family unit tend to have higher earnings than persons who do not.

Even so, it is not the case that our current immigration policy leads to a more skilled flow than would a policy requiring high levels of education or particular occupational skills as a condition for entry. Instead, the results indicate that because of the national-origin mix of the immigrant flow, the family context of the immigration decision attenuates the unfavorable selection characterizing immigrant skills. As shown in chapter 7, the redistribution of visas away from Western European countries to Asian and Latin American countries led to an adverse change in the nature of the skill sorting generated by the immigration market. Because most immigrants now originate in countries with high levels of income inequality (and high payoffs to skills), the immigrant flow tends to be composed of relatively unskilled persons. Had the flow consisted solely of persons who immigrated for purely private gains, the decline in immigrant skills documented in earlier chapters would have been much steeper.

Who Comes First?

To a great extent, chain immigration occurs because once an immigrant establishes a foothold in the United States, the remaining members of the household can easily obtain visas as the various sponsorship restrictions in the 1965 amendments are satisfied. Which family members have the greatest incentive to be the first link in the immigration chain? How does the skill level of the immigrant flow differ among various links in the chain? What are the implications of chain immigration for the long-run trends in the skill composition of the immigrant flow?

Much of the concern over chain immigration is generated by the fear that later links in the immigration chain tend to be relatively unskilled. These persons migrate only because they have relatives in the United States who can protect them from poor labor market outcomes, who can tide them over long spells of unemployment, and who can help them in periods of financial need. Hence later links in the chain may have relatively high probabilities of becoming public charges. In this view, the long-run prospects for the skill composition of immigrant flows are disturbing. Because the 1965 amendments greatly encourage chain immigration, future immigrants are likely to be even less skilled than current immigrants.

In fact, the trend in the skills of successive links in the chain depends on the economic incentives that determine the family's immigration decision. Suppose, for instance, that the family can choose whichever family member they want to be the first link in the chain. This is obviously a restrictive assumption because U.S. immigration policy allows the entry only of the person who qualifies under the explicit restrictions in the law, and this visa is not transferable to other family members. Nevertheless, it is a useful thought experiment that easily illustrates the impact of chain immigration on the skill composition of the immigrant flow.

If families can choose whomever they want to be the first link in the chain, and if the objective of the family is to maximize its economic welfare, it is evident that the family will "nominate" the person who has the most to gain from immigration to move to the United States first. Through this choice, the household ensures that it maximizes family income: that is, the total income of all family members in both countries.[27]

But who has the most to gain from immigration? If the household originates in a country with a relatively egalitarian income distribution, the person with the most to gain is the most skilled person in the family. This worker is the one who benefits most by moving to a country that offers higher rewards to skills. Immigrant flows originating in these countries, therefore, should have the characteristic that the first link in the immigration chain will be more skilled and more successful in the U.S. labor market than subsequent links in the chain.

By contrast, if the household resides in a country that has substantial income inequality, the family member with the most to gain from immigration is the person with the fewest skills. This individual has the most to gain because the United States provides better insurance against poor labor market outcomes for unskilled workers. Therefore, the first link in immigration chains originating in these countries will be less successful than subsequent links.

Therefore, the first link in the chain, the person who has the most to gain from immigration, need not be the most skilled person in the family. As long as a family's immigration decision is motivated by the search for better economic opportunities, the first link is the most skilled family member if the flow originates in countries with egalitarian income distributions, and it is the least skilled if the flow originates in countries with substantial income inequality. This insight contradicts many of the presumptions usually voiced in the debate over the economic impact of the family-reunification provisions in immigration policy. The traditional argument assumes that the family wants to send the most skilled person to the United States so that this person can then sponsor and subsidize the immigration of the remaining family members. But this is not the way that families wishing to maximize their economic well-being behave. Family income is increased when the household first "ships out" the family member who has the most to gain from immigration, and this person may well be the least skilled worker in the household.

Of course, the assumption that families can choose whomever they want to be the first link in the chain is clearly unrealistic because U.S. entry visas cannot be exchanged among family members. The first link must be the family member who can qualify for a visa under the law, and not necessarily the person who has the most to gain from immigration (which is what the family would prefer). Obviously, families whose preference for the first link in the chain coincides with the arbitrary choice imposed by government policies will still choose to immigrate. The government constraint is not binding and simply confirms a choice the family would have made anyway. But if the family's preference for the first link differs from the government's dictate, the family has fewer incentives to migrate to the United States. Some of these families may even find that immigration is no longer profitable. After all, government regulations require them to ship out a family member whose departure may lead to lower family incomes than if the family simply stayed in the country of origin. Thus, the pool of households undertaking the chain immigration process is likely to be dominated by families whose preference for the first link coincides with that imposed by the immigration statutes. On average, these chains are characterized by the first link being the person with the highest gains from immigration.

The data in the 1970 and 1980 Censuses allow the identification of three links in the immigration chain: relatives who arrived prior to the immigrant, the immigrant himself, and relatives who arrived after the immigrant. The comparison of the educational attainment and earnings of immigrant men in each of these links indicates that early links in the immigration chain actually have less education and lower wages than subsequent links in the chain. At the time of entry into the United States, immigrants who are the first link in the chain have about half a year less schooling and earn about 4 percent less than immigrants who are the last link in the chain.[28]

These differentials in skills and earnings among links in the chain are also evident in comparisons of husbands who immigrated prior to their wives with those who immigrated after their wives. At the time of entry, husbands who immigrated prior to their wives have about one

194

year less schooling and earn 10 percent less than husbands who immigrated after their wives.[29] The empirical evidence, therefore, is unequivocal. The first link in the chain is less skilled than subsequent links.[30]

This finding may partly reflect an informational advantage associated with coming to the United States after some relatives have already established a beachhead. For instance, early links can convey information about the U.S. labor market to later links, a form of intergenerational transfer of wealth, and thus improve the chances of successful labor market outcomes for later links in the chain. This explanation of the empirical evidence, however, is not satisfactory. If the information being transmitted across links is valuable, what prevents the first arrivals from using this information to increase their own earnings? Moreover, the data indicate that first-link immigrants are less educated than subsequent links. It is difficult to see how the transmission of information about the United States would lead to an increase in education levels across links in the chain. There is little doubt, therefore, that early links are inherently less skilled than later links.

The result that households residing in countries with large levels of income inequality first send the least successful and unskilled family members to the United States is confirmed by J. Edward Taylor's study of the migration decisions of rural Mexican households.[31] His analysis indicates that, prior to any immigration taking place, the household members who remained in Mexico had higher earnings than the household members who eventually migrated to the United States.

The empirical evidence, therefore, presents an unexpected picture of the ways that the family-reunification provisions in U.S. immigration policy affect the skill composition of the immigrant flow. The first link in the immigration chain is not, on average, the person who is most successful in the labor market, but is in fact the person who is the least successful. Over time, the unfavorable selection characterizing the early links in the immigration chain is attenuated. In a sense, the family-reunification provisions in immigration policy insure a "regression toward the mean" in immigrant skills among the various links in the chain. Even though the early links in the chain were relatively unskilled because the immigrant flows originate in countries with high levels of income inequality, subsequent links in the chain are more favorably selected.

This result has obvious implications for the long-run trend in the skill level of the immigrant flow. As long as the national-origin mix of the immigrant population is dominated by persons who originate in countries with relatively high payoffs to skills, family ties play the important role of attenuating the extent of unfavorable selection that characterizes these immigrants. As the chain-immigration process unfolds, each new link is more skilled than the previous one.

Therefore, the two main components of the 1965 amendments, the redistribution of visas among source countries and the allocation of the scarce visas to persons with family members residing in the United States, had conflicting impacts on immigrant skills. The redistribution of entry visas to countries with relatively high payoffs to skills clearly lowered the skill level of the immigrant flow. At the same time, however, the allocation of the scarce visas to persons with families in the United States, and to persons who migrate as part of family units, attenuated this unfavorable selection.

Although the analysis in this chapter (along with most of this book) focuses on the skills, labor market performance, and economic impact of first-generation migrants, the immigrant family also plays the important role of transmitting skills and information about the old and new cultures to future generations. There has been little study, within an economic framework, of the practical importance of this transmission and of its impact on the American economy. It will be interesting to see whether the differences in economic performance so evident among the various immigrant waves and national-origin groups are transmitted to their children and grandchildren, persisting across generations.

PART III

THE INTERNATIONAL COMPETITION FOR IMMIGRANTS

CHAPTER 12

American Competitiveness in the Immigration Market

Up to this point, the book has analyzed the composition of the immigrant flow allocated to the United States by the immigration market and the economic impact of this allocation on the American economy. It is likely that the socioeconomic characteristics of immigrants in the United States differ substantially from those of the foreign-born populations in other countries. Immigrants in the United States could have migrated to other host countries but chose not to because the American offer in the immigration market presumably dominated the alternative offers. Similarly, many foreign-born persons in other host countries probably considered immigrating to the United States but did not. The sorting of immigrants among host countries, therefore, is not random, and there are likely to be significant differences in the characteristics of persons who choose to migrate to different countries.

Are we competitive in the immigration market? Are the immigrants attracted to the United States more skilled and productive than immigrants who decide to go elsewhere? How is U.S. competitiveness in this marketplace affected by changes in immigration policy?

By comparing the skills and labor market performance of immigrants in the United States with those of immigrants in two competing host countries, Australia and Canada, this chapter reviews the available evidence on these key issues. The empirical evidence is striking and unambiguous. As a result of fundamental changes in immigration policies in all three host countries, the United States began to attract a relatively less skilled immigrant flow than did the other countries. To the extent that countries benefit from the entry of skilled workers, the evidence indicates a significant decline in U.S. competitiveness in the immigration market.

199

Immigrant Flows to Competing Host Countries

There are many migration flows across national boundaries going on in the world today. The United Nations reports that nearly 5 million persons migrated to a different country between 1975 and 1980.[1] These persons are of diverse national origins. Practically every country in the world contributes to the pool of persons who believe that better opportunities exist elsewhere and who are willing to incur the costs required to experience those opportunities firsthand. Nevertheless, these peregrinators tend to seek only a handful of destinations. In fact, about two-thirds of all international migrants moved to one of three countries: Australia, Canada, and the United States.[2]

Each of these host countries has a long history of immigration. At the turn of the century, immigrants comprised 14 percent of the U.S. population, 22 percent of the Canadian population, and 18 percent of the Australian population. By the early 1980s, the share of foreign-born persons had declined to 6 percent in the United States and to 16 percent in Canada, while it had increased to 21 percent in Australia.[3]

As table 12.1 indicates, large numbers of immigrants have entered each of these countries in recent years. Between 1959 and 1981, nearly 15 million persons migrated to one of the three host countries. Of these migrants 61 percent chose the United States as their destination, 22 percent Canada, and 18 percent Australia.

TABLE 12.1

Immigration to the United States, Canada, and Australia, 1959–1981

Origin	Number of Immigrants (in 1,000s)	Percent Choosing: United States	Canada	Australia
Africa	335.5	44.6	31.5	23.9
Americas	4,799.3	82.7	14.8	2.5
Asia	3,289.0	72.7	18.0	9.3
Europe (excluding United Kingdom)	3,892.6	50.3	27.9	21.8
United Kingdom	2,074.0	19.6	29.9	50.5
Oceania	300.5	21.6	24.8	53.6
Total	14,690.9	60.8	21.7	17.5

SOURCE: George J. Borjas, *International Differences in the Labor Market Performance of Immigrants* (Kalamazoo, Mich.: W. E. Upjohn Institute for Employment Research, 1988), table 1.2.

There are substantial differences in the national-origin composition of the immigrant flows to the three host countries. Even though the United States was chosen by more than 60 percent of all migrants, only 20 percent of those originating in the United Kingdom and 50 percent of those originating in other European countries came here. By contrast, the United States was very likely to attract immigrants originating in Asia or in the Americas. About 70 to 80 percent of the immigrants originating in these regions chose the United States.

Australia, meanwhile, received a disproportionately high share of the immigrants from the United Kingdom and other European countries. Half of the 2 million British emigrants moved to Australia, but only 9 percent of the persons originating in Asia and 3 percent of those originating in the Americas did the same.

It seems sensible to presume that people tend to migrate to neighboring countries, simply because these types of moves are not very costly. Moreover, individuals probably have more reliable information about economic opportunities and social conditions in nearby countries. Thus, the fact that potential migrants originating in the Americas pick the United States over Australia seems quite reasonable.

Other aspects of the immigration flows into the three host countries, however, are not consistent with this conjecture. For instance, Canada attracts few immigrants from Latin America. It would seem that transportation costs from Latin America to Canada or to the United States are not significantly different, and the two host countries offer relatively similar cultures and economies. Moreover, even though Australia is much closer to the Asian continent, the United States attracts many more Asian immigrants than does Australia.

Clearly, the size and direction of population flows also depend on the policies enacted by the various host countries to restrict or encourage the immigration of particular types of persons. Host countries make offers to potential migrants, including both economic incentives and entry permits. Individuals participating in the immigration market compare the offers and choose the one that is most favorable.

Immigration Policies in Canada and Australia

Canada

Until 1961, Canadian immigration policy only permitted the entry of persons originating in a few selected countries—such as the United Kingdom, Ireland, the United States, and Australia—or of persons who were dependents of Canadian residents.[4] Major policy changes in 1962 and 1967 removed the national-origin restrictions and shifted the emphasis in the visa-allocation system toward skill requirements. Under the new regulations, applicants for entry into Canada were classified into three categories: sponsored immigrants (which included close relatives of Canadian residents), nominated relatives (which included more distant relatives of Canadian residents), and independent immigrants.

Visa applicants in the last two of these categories were screened by means of a point system. Potential migrants were graded on a scale of zero to one hundred. Points were awarded according to the applicant's education (a point per year of schooling, up to twenty), occupational demand (up to fifteen points if the applicant's occupation was in strong demand in Canada), age (up to ten points for applicants under the age of thirty-five, minus one point for each year older), arranged employment (ten points if the applicant had a job offer from a Canadian employer), a "personal assessment" by the immigration officer based on the applicant's motivation and initiative (up to fifteen points), and other factors. Generally, an applicant needed to obtain at least fifty points in order to pass the test and be awarded an entry visa.[5]

In 1976, Canada amended its Immigration Act and made it easier for the families of Canadian residents to migrate there by revising the point system in order to award extra points to nominated relatives. To some extent, Canada enacted a weak version of the 1965 amendments eleven years after the United States' law was passed.

These policy changes led to a major redistribution of Canadian entry visas among source countries. For instance, 70 percent of immigrants entering Canada in the 1960s originated in the United Kingdom or in other European countries. During the 1970s, the fraction of the immigrant flow originating in Europe was cut by half, to 37 percent. At the same time, the fraction of immigrants originating in Asia almost quad-rupled, from 8 percent in the 1960s to 29 percent in the 1970s.[6]

Canada and the United States, therefore, experienced a somewhat similar change in the national-origin mix of their immigrant flows. Generally, European countries became a less important source of immi-gration, while Asian countries became a more important source. Of the immigrant pool reaching the United States in the 1960s, 34 percent originated in European countries, but in the 1970s this fraction was cut by about half, to 18 percent. Similarly, the fraction of immigrants originating in Asian countries almost tripled, from 13 to 35 percent, over the same period.

Australia

Prior to World War II, immigration policy in Australia almost ex-clusively emphasized the recruitment of migrants from Great Brit-ain.[7] Because of its geographic isolation, Australia took its role in the immigration market one step farther than did the United States or Canada. To make its offer more lucrative and outbid its competitors, the Australian government assisted many immigrants by incurring part of the migration and resettlement costs. The financial-assistance program was substantial. Of the 2.5 million settlers who migrated to Australia between 1788 and 1939, nearly half did so with government assistance.[8]

The prohibitions on immigration from countries other than those in northwestern Europe became known as the "White Australia Policy." For the most part, these restrictions were not statutory but operated through the power of administrators to accept or reject potential appli-cants without justifying their decisions. In addition, financial assistance to cover transportation and resettlement costs was rarely granted to Asians or other "undesirable" immigrant groups.

World War II raised doubts about the ability of the small Australian population to defend the vast continent. In response, the Australian government instituted a policy designed to increase population by about 2 percent per year, with half of the increase to be accomplished through immigration. Initially, the government strictly adhered to the principles of the White Australia Policy: the objective was for the immigrant flow to be more than 90 percent British. These national-origin restrictions were taken quite seriously: the Australian government even refused to let its soldiers bring back their Japanese wives after the war.[9]

But it was impossible to populate postwar Australia solely with British immigrants. Even though financial aid and entry visas were easily available to British citizens, there were few takers. As a result, Australia signed formal arrangements with a number of European countries (such as Germany, the Netherlands, Italy, and Greece) to recruit potential migrants. These national-origin groups, however, were generally given a lower level of financial assistance than British citizens. It was only in the early 1970s that parity was reached in the subsidies of transportation costs and other settlement benefits among national-origin groups.

Political changes in Australia led to the formal abolition of the White Australia Policy in 1972 and to the enactment of an immigration policy that did not discriminate on the basis of national origin or race. Visas are now allocated among the many applicants through a point system, similar to that used by Canada, which generally emphasizes educational background and occupational skills.[10]

These policy changes obviously had an impact on the national-origin composition of the immigrant flow. Although the United Kingdom accounted for nearly half of the immigrants in the 1960s, it "only" accounted for one-third of the immigrants during the 1970s. There was also a comparable decline in the fraction of immigrants originating in other European countries, from 41 percent to 22 percent. Simultaneously, the fraction of immigrants originating in Asia quadrupled, from 5 to 21 percent.[11]

Therefore, the change in the national-origin mix of the immigrant flow entering Australia somewhat resembles the experiences of Canada and the United States. Even after the major shifts in immigration policy, however, the Australian immigrant flow is much more European in origin than the flows reaching the other two host countries. During the 1970s, 57 percent of Australian immigrants originated in Europe, as compared to only 37 percent in Canada and 18 percent in the United States. In effect, the national-origin mix of the immigrant flow entering Australia was more stable over time than that of the other host countries.

Immigrant Performance in the Host Countries

Apart from the fact that Australia, Canada, and the United States are the three most important host countries participating in the immigration market, they also have publicly available census data that allow a comparative analysis of immigrant labor market performance.[12] Data similar in quality and coverage to the 1970 and 1980 U.S. Censuses are available for Canada (in 1971 and 1981) and for Australia (in 1981). As table 12.2 shows, there are significant differences in the annual earnings of immigrant men (relative to those of natives) among host countries.[13] As we have seen, the relative earnings of immigrants in the United States declined substantially between 1970 and 1980. In 1970, immigrants who had arrived in the five-year period prior to the census earned about 17 percent less than natives, but in 1980 the most recent immigrants earned about 29 percent less than natives.

Surprisingly, the trend in the labor market performance of immigrants in Canada bears some resemblance to that experienced by the United States. Even though the average earnings of immigrants in Canada did not change much between 1971 and 1981 (relative to the earnings of Canadian natives), the most recent immigrants enumerated in the 1971 Census earned only about 7 percent less than natives, while

TABLE 12.2

Labor Market Performance of Immigrants

Host Country	Percentage Difference in Annual Earnings Between Immigrant and Native Men	Percentage Difference in Annual Earnings Between Recent Immigrant and Native Men
United States in 1970	−1.5	−17.3
United States in 1980	−8.7	−29.4
Canada in 1971	2.6	−6.6
Canada in 1981	1.9	−17.3
Australia in 1981	−3.6	.3

Source: Adapted from George J. Borjas, *International Differences in the Labor Market Performance of Immigrants* (Kalamazoo, Mich.: W. E. Upjohn Institute for Employment Research, 1988), table 5.1. These statistics are obtained from the Public Use Samples of the censuses available in each of the host countries and give the earnings differentials among men aged twenty-five to sixty-four. The group of recent immigrants refers to individuals who migrated to the host country during the five-year period prior to the census. The percentage earnings differentials are calculated from the antilogs of the mean differences in log annual earnings.

the most recent immigrants in the 1981 Census earned about 17 percent less. It appears that Canada, like the United States, has experienced a decline in the relative skills of immigrants over successive cohorts. Even so, immigrants in Canada do have a much smaller earnings disadvantage than immigrants in the United States. There is less of a skill gap between immigrants and natives in Canada than in the United States.

The labor market performance of immigrants in Australia differs from that observed in the other two host countries. In 1981, the typical immigrant in Australia earned about 4 percent less than natives. But persons who had just migrated to Australia earned about the same as natives. The most recent immigrant wave in Australia, therefore, had higher earnings than earlier waves. If anything, Australia experienced an increase in the skill level of its immigrant flow.

There is also substantial variation in the labor market performance of national-origin groups among the host countries (see table 12.3). In Canada and the United States, recent European immigrants earn slightly less than the typical native, while in Australia they earn about 9 percent more than natives. In addition, recent Asian immigrants earn about 30 percent less than natives in both Canada and the United States, but in Australia they earn only 18 percent less than the typical native. Immigrant groups that tend to do well in the United States and Canada, therefore, tend to do even better in Australia. Immigrant

TABLE 12.3

National-Origin Differentials in the Labor Market Performance of Immigrants in 1980–1981

| | Percentage Difference in Annual Earnings Between Recent Immigrant Men and Native Men in: | | |
Origin	United States	Canada	Australia
Africa	−26.9	−18.5	5.1
Asia	−30.0	−31.5	−18.2
Europe	−1.9	−3.3	9.0
Latin America	−49.1	−34.1	4.9

SOURCE: Adopted from George J. Borjas, *International Differences in the Labor Market Performance of Immigrants* (Kalamazoo, Mich.: W. E. Upjohn Institute for Employment Research 1988), table 5.1. The statistics are obtained from the Public Use Samples of the censuses available in each of the host countries and give the earnings differentials among men aged twenty-five to sixty-four. The group of recent immigrants refers to individuals who migrated to the host country during the five-year period prior to the census. The percentage earnings differentials are calculated from the antilogs of the mean differences in log annual earnings.

groups that tend to perform badly in North America tend not to do as badly in Australia.[14]

These data suggest that, even from specific national-origin groups, some host countries attract immigrants who are relatively successful in the labor market. The nonrandom sorting of immigrants among host countries thus implies that global generalizations about the productivity or skills of particular national-origin groups are misleading. In other words, there is no such thing as "the" impact of immigrant status or a particular national origin on earnings, because the skill levels of these groups may differ markedly among host countries.

Immigration Policy and Immigrant Skills

Obviously, the different immigration policies pursued by the three host countries since 1960 must have had a differential impact on the skills and earnings of the immigrant flow allocated to each of the countries by the immigration market.

Figure 12.1 illustrates the by now familiar finding that the new immigrants in the United States are less skilled than the old.[15] The typical man who came here between 1960 and 1964 has about 7 percent lower lifetime earnings than natives, while men who migrated in the late 1970s have a (predicted) lifetime earnings disadvantage of approximately 30 percent. Surprisingly, figure 12.1 also shows that, as in the United States, recent immigrant waves choosing Canada have lower lifetime earnings than earlier waves. In fact, persons who migrated to Canada in the early 1960s have about 2 percent lower lifetime earnings than natives, while those who migrated in the late 1970s have about 13 percent lower earnings. By contrast, the trend in the lifetime earnings of immigrants choosing Australia is quite different: the typical person who migrated to Australia in the late 1970s has higher lifetime earnings than immigrants in earlier waves. Immigrants who entered Australia in the early 1960s have a lifetime earnings disadvantage of about 8 percent, while persons who immigrated in the 1970s have roughly the same lifetime earnings as Australian natives.

There are, therefore, a number of important differences and similari-

FIGURE 12.1

The Trend in the Lifetime Earnings Differential Between Immigrant Waves and Natives

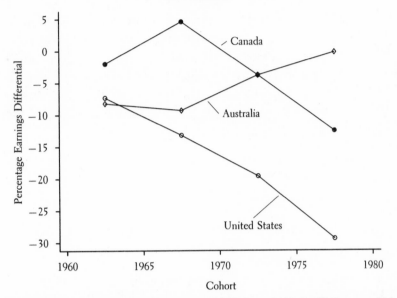

SOURCE: Adapted from George J. Borjas, "Immigration and Self-Selection," in Richard B. Freeman and John M. Abowd, eds., *Immigration, Trade, and the Labor Market* (Chicago: University of Chicago Press, 1990), table 15. The predicted lifetime earnings differentials are based on log annual earnings regressions estimated in the samples of immigrant and native men aged twenty-five to sixty-four, and they use a 5-percent rate of discount. The regressors include age, an indicator of whether the observation was drawn from the 1970 or the 1980 Census, the cohort of immigration, and years since migration. For details on the construction of the lifetime earnings differentials using the only available Australian census, see Borjas, "Immigration and Self-Selection."

ties among host countries in the skills of the various immigrant waves. The two host countries (Australia and Canada) that screen immigrants on the basis of demographic characteristics "recruit" persons who tend to be relatively more successful in the labor market. Nevertheless, the trend in the lifetime earnings of successive immigrant waves choosing Canada resembles the trend observed in the United States despite the major differences in immigration policies between the two countries.

As noted above, both Australia and Canada now use a point system to screen visa applicants on the basis of such observable characteristics as education and occupation, and only those persons who pass the test are permitted to enter the country. This visa-allocation mechanism should ensure that immigrants admitted to these countries are relatively well educated and have a favorable demographic background.

It is certainly the case that immigrants in Australia and Canada are better educated than immigrants in the United States. The typical recent immigrant in both Australia and Canada has about thirteen years of schooling, compared to twelve years for his American counterpart. Moreover, in both Australia and Canada, unlike the United States, the typical recent immigrant has more schooling than natives. Natives have only about eleven or twelve years of education in Australia and Canada, as compared to thirteen years in the United States.[16] These differences in educational attainment, therefore, partly explain why immigrants in the United States have lower earnings (relative to natives) than immigrants in the other host countries.

It is evident, however, that the entry obstacles imposed by the point system in Canada, unlike those in Australia, were unable to prevent a sizable decline in immigrant skills among successive immigrant waves. The lifetime earnings of immigrants in Canada fell by 11 percent between 1960 and 1980. Despite its point system, Canada's historical experience in the immigration market has much in common with the American one. Even so, the point system greatly dampened the extent of the decline in immigrant skills in Canada. The data suggest that this decline would have been much steeper in its absence. As figure 12.2 shows, the lifetime earnings differential between the various immigrant waves and *demographically comparable* natives is not all that different in Canada and the United States. Persons who migrated to Canada in the late 1970s, like those who migrated to the United States, have much lower earnings than comparable natives. For instance, the typical person who migrated to the United States in the late 1970s earns about 23 percent less over his lifetime than a comparable American native. The typical person who migrated to Canada in the same period earns about 20 percent less than a comparable Canadian native. If it were not for their relatively more favorable demographic characteristics, the new immigrants in Canada would have performed about as badly in that labor market as the new immigrants in the United States performed in the American labor market.

The contrast between figures 12.1 and 12.2, therefore, clearly demonstrates both the benefits and the limitations of an immigration policy based on a point system. The Australian and Canadian point systems attracted a typical immigrant who is better educated, who has more favorable demographic characteristics, and who has higher (relative)

FIGURE 12.2

The Trend in the Lifetime Earnings Differential Between Immigrant Waves and Demographically Comparable Natives

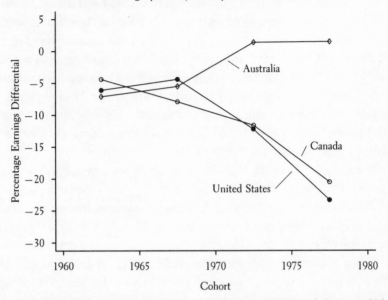

SOURCE: Adapted from George J. Borjas, "Immigration and Self-Selection," in Richard B. Freeman and John M. Abowd, eds., *Immigration, Trade, and the Labor Market* (Chicago: University of Chicago Press, 1990), table 15. The predicted lifetime earnings differentials are based on log annual earnings regressions estimated in the samples of immigrant and native men aged twenty-five to sixty-four, and they use a 5-percent rate of discount. The regressors include education, age, marital status, health status (when available), an indicator of metropolitan residence, an indicator of whether the observation was drawn from the 1970 or the 1980 Census, the cohort of immigration, and years since migration.

earnings than immigrants to the United States. The filtering of Australian and Canadian visa applicants, therefore, greatly increased the skill qualifications of the immigrant flow.

Nevertheless, the point system could not prevent a sizable decline in the skills of immigrants entering Canada. Even though the recent immigrants in Canada tend to be well educated, they simply do not perform as well in the labor market as do comparably educated natives. Holding demographic characteristics constant, the labor market performance of recent immigrants is equally poor in the United States and in Canada. Two factors account for this surprising finding. First, the changes in immigration policies that occurred in all three countries, but particularly in Canada and the United States, led to a major shift in the national-origin mix of immigrant flows. The new immigrants are more likely to originate in countries with less developed economies, and with labor market institutions and industrial structures that differ from those found in the host countries. Because skills acquired in less developed economies are not easily transferable to industrialized economies, immigrants originating in many Asian and Latin American countries tend to have relatively lower earnings than demographically comparable natives in all of the host countries.[17]

Because Canada and the United States experienced somewhat similar changes in the national-origin composition of the immigrant flow, it is not surprising that, in both countries, the lifetime earnings of earlier immigrant waves greatly exceed those of the more recent waves. In contrast, Australia is the one host country that experienced a more modest shift in the national-origin mix of its immigrant flow, and it is also the one in which recent immigrant waves do not have lower earnings than earlier waves.

The point system, with its emphasis on such characteristics as education, age, and occupation, ignores the fact that skills obtained in different countries of origin are valued differently by the host country's labor market. For example, it is likely that the economic value of a certificate indicating a particular type of occupational skill differs among national-origin groups. Even though this certificate may be sufficient to pass the test and qualify for entry under the point system, the actual skill level implied by the certificate depends on the immigrant's country of origin. We have seen throughout this book that skills acquired in some source countries are valued much more by the U.S. labor market than skills acquired in other countries. Because the point system does not take into account the transferability of skills between the country of origin and the host country in awarding entry visas, it is unable to prevent a change in skills due to the shifting national-origin mix of the immigrant flow.

In addition, there is an inherent shortcoming in the screens used by a point system, which severely limits its effectiveness: the point system restricts entry according to the applicant's *observable* demographic characteristics, such as education, age, and occupation. This type of visa-allocation system, however, imposes no restrictions whatsoever on the unobserved traits of applicants, such as drive, ability, and motivation. For instance, Canadian immigration policy clearly encourages the migration of highly educated workers. This does not necessarily imply that the sample of highly educated persons who choose to go to Canada are the most productive highly educated workers in the populations of the source countries.

It is evident that there is a great deal of dispersion in skills even among highly educated workers. Some physicists, for instance, are quite productive and make fundamental discoveries, but other physicists are not, even if they concentrated in the same field and graduated in the same year from the same university. A point system that awards entry visas to highly educated persons can do little to ensure that only the most productive highly educated workers are attracted to that host country.

This conclusion has far-reaching policy implications. The Canadian experience suggests that a key factor in determining the labor market success of immigrants cannot be regulated through a point system based on observable demographic characteristics. Though better than nothing, screens based on these demographic factors, and independent of national origin, are imperfect predictors of skills and productivity. In fact, at least two-thirds of all dispersion in wage rates among individuals cannot be attributed to variations in observable demographic characteristics.

Therefore, even if a point system is used to regulate the entry of immigrants, the skill composition of the immigrant flow also depends on whether the host country has a wage structure that rewards skills. If so, the host country attracts the most productive workers from the pool of persons who, given a particular immigration policy, have the acceptable demographic characteristics. If not, the host country attracts the least skilled workers from the acceptable pool. Point system or not, a host country can only attract those persons who find it worthwhile to reside there.

The analysis of international differences in the labor market performance of immigrants thus provides important evidence about the competitiveness of America's offer in the immigration market. In the early 1960s, there was relatively little variation in the labor market performance of immigrants (relative to natives) among host countries. This type of sorting, however, changed drastically after 1965. During the late 1970s, Australia attracted immigrants with the highest lifetime earnings, and the United States attracted immigrants with the lowest lifetime earnings.[18] It is no coincidence that the deterioration (from the U.S. point of view) in the nature of the skill sorting allocating immigrants among host countries occurred about the time that U.S. immigration policy underwent radical changes. If a more skilled immigrant flow is beneficial to the host country, the 1965 amendments are responsible for a sizable decline in American competitiveness in the immigration market.

The Emigration of Americans to Canada

There is another dimension to the immigration market that has not been addressed. The United States competes in this marketplace not only in terms of attracting persons from many source countries, but also in terms of retaining the physical and human capital of its native population. After all, other countries offer Americans alternative sets of social, cultural, and economic opportunities. Some of these offers may be substantially better than the U.S. offer, and perhaps a sizable number of Americans migrate elsewhere. Which types of Americans move out of the United States? Is this country also losing in the competition for its indigenous labor?

These questions are difficult to address because so little is known about the quantity and skill composition of the people who leave the United States. There are practically no exit restrictions on Americans. As long as the country of destination consents, an American citizen is free to move to whatever country he wishes, whenever he wants, without reporting that fact to anyone in the United States. Therefore, no data are generally available describing the size and skill composition of the emigrant flow.

But a large number of Americans have migrated to Canada, and their skills and labor market characteristics are recorded in the Canadian census. In 1981 there were 3.9 million foreign-born persons in Canada, of whom 316,000, or 8 percent, were born in the United States.

As figure 12.3 shows, the lifetime earnings of American immigrants in Canada do not suggest that, for the most part, they are a successful group. The Americans who migrated between 1965 and 1975, for instance, have lifetime earnings that are similar to those of Canadian natives, while the ones who migrated in the late 1970s have about 22

FIGURE 12.3

Trends in Lifetime Earnings of Waves of Transnational Migrants Between
Canada and the United States

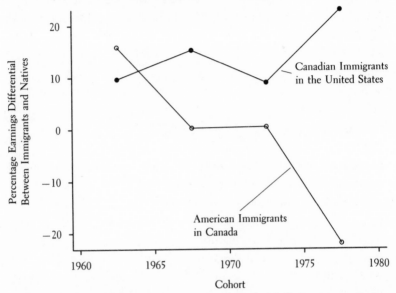

SOURCE: Author's tabulations from the 1970 and 1980 Public Use Samples of the U.S. Census, and the 1971 and 1981 samples of the Canadian Census. The predicted lifetime earnings differentials are based on log annual earnings regressions estimated in the samples of immigrant and native men aged twenty-five to sixty-four, and they use a 5-percent rate of discount. The regressors include age, an indicator of whether the observation was drawn from the 1970 or the 1980 Census, the cohort of immigration, and years since migration.

percent lower earnings than natives.[19] The lackluster economic performance of Americans in Canada is somewhat surprising because they tend to be well educated. American émigrés have about three more years of schooling than Canadian natives. Yet, despite their high level of education, American immigrants earn no more and sometimes earn less than Canadian natives. This fact implies that the labor market performance of Americans in Canada is quite poor.[20]

Therefore, the evidence indicates that workers who moved from the United States to Canada in the late 1970s are not successful in the Canadian labor market. It seems reasonable to conjecture that these individuals are also likely to be relatively unsuccessful in the United States, so that the pool of persons migrating from the United States to Canada is not favorably selected.

It is unlikely that Americans in Canada have relatively low earnings because their skills are not transferable to the Canadian economy. After

214

all, there is little difference in the aggregate economic indicators that characterize the two countries. In 1980, per capita GNP in the United States was only 9 percent larger than in Canada, and the two economies had relatively similar industrial structures.[21] Thus, there is little reason to suspect that Americans migrating to Canada have the same economic disadvantage in the Canadian labor market as immigrants from Asia or Latin America.

But the United States has a less egalitarian income distribution than Canada.[22] Unskilled Americans are relatively better off in Canada, and more skilled American workers are better off in the United States. As long as individuals migrate in search of better economic opportunities, the immigrant flow from the United States to Canada is likely to be composed of relatively unskilled workers seeking the protection and insurance that the Canadian economy provides.

It is worth reiterating that Canadian immigration policy places a high premium on the admission of highly educated individuals through its use of the point system. The data suggest that the Canadian offer in the immigration market does indeed attract highly educated American workers. These highly educated Americans, however, are not as productive as their Canadian counterparts. As noted above, there is little that immigration policies that award entry visas on the basis of observable demographic characteristics can do to prevent that outcome, because there is much unobserved dispersion in the skills of highly educated workers.

An additional insight into just what it is that immigration policies can and cannot do is given by the labor market performance of Canadian immigrants in the United States. Just as large numbers of Americans immigrate to Canada, large numbers of Canadians come to the United States. In 1980, 843,000, or 6 percent, of the 14.1 million foreign-born persons residing in the United States were born in Canada.

As shown in figure 12.3, Canadian men who migrated to the United States in the late 1970s are predicted to have lifetime earnings that are 23 percent higher than those of American natives. The contrast with the labor market outcomes experienced by Americans in Canada is striking. The sorting generated by the immigration market is one in which the United States exports relatively unskilled labor, while the Canadians export highly skilled workers.

This finding is remarkable. Because of the skill filters explicitly built into Canadian immigration policy and the absence of such filters in American policy, it would not be unreasonable to expect a different outcome in the immigration market. Canada's point system would presumably ensure that only the most skilled workers enter Canada, and Americans in Canada would be expected to be relatively successful in that labor market. The almost complete absence of skill requirements in the awarding of U.S. entry visas would be expected to dilute the skill level of immigrants entering the United States, hence Canadians in America would be relatively unsuccessful.

The facts are exactly the opposite. In the end, regardless of what immigration policy says, only those persons who gain from immigration do so. Governments legislate, but it is people who immigrate.

International trade in the goods market leads to an allocation of the available goods among competing countries. Japanese cars, for instance, "migrate" to whichever country is willing to pay the highest price for them. Likewise, the immigration market allocates potential migrants among the various countries. In this marketplace, both source and host countries compete for the physical and human capital of workers, and persons move to (or stay in) countries that offer the best economic opportunities.

During the 1980s, the United States suddenly awoke to the notion that we compete against other countries in the international market for goods and services. The Japanese invasion of cars, electronic equipment, and high-technology items led to an unprecedented trade deficit, motivated discussions about the extent of U.S. competitiveness in the global market, and initiated a heated political debate over our trade policy, over why we lost the competitive edge to the Japanese, and over what we can do to get the edge back.

The empirical evidence presented in this chapter suggests that the United States should also awaken to the notion that we are competing against other countries in the immigration market. The comparative analysis of immigrant skills and earnings in three host countries indicates that the overall performance of the United States in the immigration market was not much better than its performance in the goods market. We attracted much less skilled immigrants in the late 1970s than did Australia and Canada, our main competitors for the human capital and wealth of potential migrants.

216

Prior to the 1965 amendments, the typical immigrant choosing the United States as his destination was about as successful in the labor market as the typical immigrant choosing Australia and slightly less successful than his counterpart in Canada. By the late 1970s, however, the immigrant flow into the United States was composed of individuals who, on average, performed poorly in the American labor market, while the immigrant flow into Australia was composed of highly skilled persons who were relatively successful in the Australian economy.

CHAPTER 13

Implications for Policy

Wнат should be the nature of America's offer in the immigration market? Should we continue a policy that stresses the reunification of families, or should we shift to a skill-based admissions policy? Should we openly sell entry visas, or should we allocate them to persons who satisfy a number of arbitrary requirements? Should we encourage the immigration of the skilled, or should we continue the admission of relatively unskilled workers?

American immigration policy attempts to balance a number of economic, political, and humanitarian tradeoffs. The policy dilemma implicit in these tradeoffs is clearly delineated by Elliott and Franklin Abrams: "If we emphasize the economic role of immigration and admit more and more skilled workers, we sacrifice the goal of reuniting families; if we stress (as is now the case) the admission of relatives, we lose control of the effect of immigration on our labor markets. If we admit highly skilled immigrants, we may be hurting their home countries and our own less privileged citizens; if we fail to admit the highly skilled immigrants, we deprive our country of their badly needed talents."[1]

An immigration policy, reached through a political compromise that chooses from these conflicting alternatives, consists of two provisions: How many persons should we admit? And who should get the scarce visas? Existing research does not directly address the first of these questions. In fact, the available empirical evidence has little to say about what the optimal size of the immigrant flow should be. Obviously, because of the existence of a welfare state, the proposition that the United States should admit anyone who wishes to come is not taken seriously by participants in the debate over immigration policy. Therefore, there will be some limitation on the size of the immigrant flow. The research findings presented in this book, and summarized in chapter 1, have implications for the second question: in view of the limited number of entry visas, what characteristics should the United States look for when picking the winners from the applicant pool?

Implications for Policy

Two basic conclusions emerge from the empirical evidence. First, immigrants have little impact on the earnings and employment opportunities of natives. Thus, the concern that has fueled much of the movement toward a more restrictionist immigration policy is, in terms of recent immigration, unjustified. Second, the skill level of successive immigrant waves admitted to the United States has declined precipitously in the past two or three decades. On average, immigrants in recent waves have relatively less schooling, weaker labor market attachment, higher unemployment rates, lower wage rates, higher poverty rates, and higher rates of welfare participation than immigrants in the waves that arrived in the 1950s and 1960s. The new immigrants simply do not perform as well in the U.S. labor market as do natives, or as did the earlier immigrants.

In effect, the United States has become an importer of relatively unskilled labor. Economic and political changes here and in the many other countries participating in the immigration market significantly altered the nature and attractiveness of the American offer to potential migrants. Our offer is not what it used to be, and we do not get the types of immigrants that we used to get. As a result, the United States has lost its competitive edge in the international marketplace for the human capital of potential migrants.

These conclusions summarize the evidence uncovered by state-of-the-art econometric studies and are not based on ad hoc theorizing about the role that immigrants play or should play in the American economy. Further, these conclusions are robust. They withstand a series of experiments designed to determine their sensitivity to a number of technical assumptions and to variations in the type of data analyzed. There seems to be little doubt, therefore, about what the facts are.

Unfortunately, much of the debate over immigration policy in the past decade, unaware of these facts, has focused on the problem of undocumented workers. This heated discussion, fed by charges that perhaps 10 million illegal aliens were overrunning the country and taking jobs away from natives, culminated in the enactment of the Immigration Reform and Control Act of 1986. We do not yet know whether this legislation will actually stop the flow of illegal aliens, but early signs are not encouraging.[2]

When apprehended, illegal aliens are simply deported. This punishment is unlikely to deter a persistent migrant. He has little to lose by attempting to reenter the United States one more time and, if caught again, try yet once more. For many illegal aliens, therefore, apprehension is just a minor inconvenience. Any additional punishments, such as incarceration, are likely to be extremely costly to the American taxpayer. Further, even though the legislation imposes sanctions on employers who knowingly hire illegal aliens, the enforcement provisions of the law are relatively weak.[3] Preliminary reports from the Mexican border suggest that the size of the illegal flow was not greatly affected by the legislation. In both 1987 and 1988, about 1 million persons were apprehended trying to enter the United States illegally.[4] It is likely, therefore, that the policy debate over illegal immigration will resurface in the next few years.

If nothing else, the enactment of IRCA inspired a much-needed reevaluation of the legal immigration process. Because changing conditions in the immigration market led to major shifts in the size, national-origin mix, and skill composition of legal immigrant flows, a consensus is beginning to form that our immigration policy is in need of reform. Several proposals designed to overhaul the visa-allocation system in existence since the 1965 amendments are now under discussion.[5] They include a reduction in the number of visas allocated to relatives of U.S. residents; establishing a firm ceiling on the size of the immigrant flow; the enactment of a point system, similar to the Canadian one, that favors the entry of workers with particular skill characteristics, such as education, occupation, and English proficiency; and the selling of visas.

I do not know what our immigration policy should be. As noted above, the immigration statutes reflect a political consensus, a consensus that attempts to accommodate the conflicting interests of various demographic and ethnic groups, the humanitarian aspects of family reunification and asylum for oppressed persons, the economic impact of immigration both on the United States and on the countries of origin, and the foreign-policy ramifications of immigrant flows that drain source countries of particular types of workers.

The analysis presented in this book focuses solely on the economic impact of immigrants on the United States. Perhaps the main lesson of the study is that because the American offer attracts many relatively unskilled workers, current immigration policy imposes costs on American society. Although some would argue that these economic issues are precisely the ones that should determine the future of American immigration policy, the research findings certainly do not suggest that economic factors must take precedence over political and humanitarian considerations.[6] This is a value judgment that has little to do with the empirical evidence. The important question facing policy makers is whether these economic costs are sufficiently high to warrant a reevaluation and redirection of U.S. immigration policy.

Is the Immigration of Unskilled Workers All That Bad?

Different types of immigrant flows have different impacts on the American economy. Which type of immigrant flow, skilled or unskilled, is most beneficial to the United States?

Because a skilled person is more productive, he contributes more to the gross national product. As long as nothing else in the economy changes, national income is inevitably higher if the immigrant flow is mainly composed of highly skilled workers. For example, the empirical evidence indicates that if immigrants who came to the United States in the late 1970s had been as skilled as those who came in the early 1960s, national income would have been at least $6 billion higher in each year of the cohort's working life.

But other things do change. The admission of an immigrant affects national income not only because he produces additional output, but also because the immigrant flow alters the productivity of natives. If the two groups have similar skills and are interchangeable in the production process, native productivity and wages decline as a result of immigration. Alternatively, immigrants and natives may be complements in production, in which case the entry of immigrants into the U.S. labor market increases native productivity and wages. To determine the total impact of immigration on national income, therefore, it is necessary to ascertain how different types of immigrants and natives interact in the labor market. The empirical evidence indicates that immigrants only have a minor impact on the earnings and employment opportunities of natives. Hence, national income is not greatly affected by the labor market interactions between immigrants and natives.

There are, however, other channels through which immigrants alter the real incomes of Americans. For example, it is likely that consumers benefit greatly from the entry of unskilled immigrants. The United States has a comparative advantage at producing relatively skilled labor, and it is costly to attract skilled natives to certain types of occupations, such as the harvesting of seasonal crops. Unskilled immigrants can fill these jobs at a relatively low wage. In effect, the specialization of unskilled immigrants in particular industries reduces the prices of these goods and increases the real incomes of American consumers.

The practical importance of this increase in real income has not been empirically documented. It is also unclear whether American consumers benefit more from the entry of unskilled immigrants than from the entry of skilled workers. After all, highly skilled immigrants may have a comparative advantage in the production of different goods, and real incomes will increase because of the reduction in the costs of producing those goods. No one knows which type of immigration is more beneficial to American consumers. Put bluntly, do we gain more from having cheaper agricultural produce or from having cheaper (or more advanced) electronic and technical equipment?[7]

The admission of unskilled immigrants (as opposed to skilled immigrants), therefore, reduces potential national income simply because they are less productive, and it has an indeterminate impact on the real incomes of natives. We have seen that if the immigrant wave admitted in the late 1970s had been as skilled as the wave admitted in the early 1960s, national income would have been at least $6 billion higher annually. This loss in potential national income has important fiscal implications, because, for instance, tax revenues are reduced by $1.5 billion per year. Therefore, to provide an economic justification of our current offer in the immigration market, one must conjecture that the entry of relatively unskilled workers increases the real income of native consumers by substantially more than would the entry of skilled immigrants.

In addition to unskilled immigration's impact on national income, the immigration of unskilled workers can create or exacerbate a number of potentially serious socioeconomic and political problems. For example, the empirical evidence indicates that a large number of persons in the unskilled immigrant groups end up below the poverty line. In fact, poverty rates in some of these groups are sometimes as large as poverty rates among black natives. Moreover, because the assimilation process is relatively slow, many of these immigrants will find it impossible to reach economic parity with natives during their lifetimes. As a result, unskilled immigrant groups have higher welfare participation rates than natives. The immigration of unskilled workers, therefore, aggravates the economic and social problems associated with poverty and welfare.[8]

The weight of the empirical evidence thus suggests that the new immigrants impose costs on the American economy. Further, it is unclear whether the economic benefits resulting from the new immigration exceed the benefits that would accrue from a more skilled immigrant flow. It appears that a prudent course of action would be to redirect U.S. immigration policy so as to attract a different mix of immigrants, a mix that would be relatively more skilled. In other words, the empirical evidence summarized in this book justifies the inference that a central objective of any reform in immigration policy should be to stop, if not reverse, the decline in immigrant skills that has occurred during the past two or three decades.

How Can We Attract More Skilled Immigrants?

The simplest way of increasing the skill level of the immigrant flow would be for the United States to follow the lead of Australia and Canada and institute a point system that grades visa applicants on the basis of observable skills. Points could be awarded according to the applicant's education, age, occupation, English fluency, and other demographic characteristics, and entry visas would be given to those persons who receive a high enough score.

The enactment of a point system would also link immigration policy and America's economic needs. For instance, if labor needs in particular sectors or occupations arise, extra points could be easily awarded to persons who are urgently needed. This flexibility would ensure that the economic impact of immigration would be more predictable and more closely targeted to the country's labor requirements.

As I showed above, however, the skill filters implicit in this type of point system are very imperfect. There is significant dispersion in the productivities of individuals even among persons who have exactly the same demographic characteristics. For instance, the point system may only permit the entry of highly educated persons, but it does not ensure that the most productive highly educated persons are the ones who choose to come to the United States. Similarly, the point system may encourage the immigration of individuals with particular types of occupational certificates, but it ignores the variation in the actual skill content of these certificates between immigrants and natives, as well as among national-origin groups.

The Canadian experience with the point system is instructive. Entry restrictions on persons with unfavorable demographic characteristics generated a more skilled immigrant flow than that admitted by the United States. At the same time, however, Canada's point system was unable to prevent (though it did dampen) a decline in skills among successive immigrant waves, a decline similar to that experienced by the United States. Because of major changes in the national-origin mix of the immigrant flow, and because the point system cannot screen visa applicants along every dimension of the skills embodied in individuals, Canada could not stop the deterioration in the skill composition of its immigrant flow.

Thus, the screens used to filter out unskilled applicants in a point system, though better than none, do not address a more fundamental problem. Persons who want to immigrate are the ones who have the most to gain by doing so. It is not necessarily the case that only the most productive and the most skilled have the most to gain by coming to the United States. The only sure way to attract highly skilled workers is to make an offer in the immigration market that is particularly attractive to those workers and that is unattractive to unskilled workers.

This insight has far-reaching policy significance. American immigration policy cannot force persons in the source countries to migrate to the United States. If economic conditions in the source countries and in America are such that skilled workers have little to gain by coming here, they will simply decide to remain in the source countries (or

224

migrate elsewhere). Other countries are also making offers in the immigration market, and for many potential migrants these alternative offers are more attractive than the American one. Therefore, the effectiveness of any immigration policy in filtering the applicant pool is diminished by the fact that the host country is not the only player in the immigration market.

The United States, however, can have a major impact on economic conditions abroad through its import/export policies and through such programs as debt-repayment subsidies and foreign aid. These programs affect economic development and economic growth in many source countries, and they may also affect how different skills are rewarded in those countries. Clearly, these economic policies alter the attractiveness of America's offer in the immigration market and help determine not only who comes to the United States but also what impact those immigrants have when they get here.

Moreover, the U.S. government influences economic conditions in this country through its domestic policies. Changes in income-tax rates, in subsidies to certain industries, and in the economic insurance provided by the welfare state change the rewards to skills in the American economy. Different domestic policies generate different offers in the immigration market and attract different types of immigrants. For example, economic policies that increase wage differentials between skilled and unskilled workers, such as a reduction in the progressivity of income-tax rates, make America's offer more lucrative for skilled workers residing abroad and increase the skill level of the immigrant flow.

Therefore, there is an intimate connection between the economic policies pursued by the U.S. government and the economic impact of immigration. In a very important sense, economic policies are part of our overall immigration policy, and the desirability of major changes in economic policy should be partly assessed in terms of their impact on America's offer in the immigration market. Put differently, American immigration policy should be regarded as more than just the listing of arbitrary rules allocating visas among applicants.

As an alternative to (or in conjunction with) the point system, it has been suggested that the United States sell visas to potential migrants.[9] Presumably, because of the entry fees imposed on the immigrants, this policy would tend to improve the skill composition of the immigrant flow. To an economist, the idea that visas should be bought and sold in the open market is quite appealing. After all, the price system leads to a well-functioning economy and to an efficient allocation of resources in the markets for goods and services, and will also lead to an efficient allocation of resources in the immigration market.

Many noneconomists find this idea unnatural, if not repulsive. As I have already noted, however, we already participate in the visa market. For better or worse, the U.S. government "sells" visas, but it uses a peculiar pricing scheme. In particular, the United States gives visas away to persons fortunate enough to have certain types of family ties with U.S. residents, and it makes the visas prohibitively expensive for those who happen to lack those ties. One useful reform of our immigration policy would be to make the pricing scheme more consonant with the market system. The price of visas would then reflect the supply of entry slots and the demand for those slots.

An open market in American visas would certainly make our immigration policy more responsive to changes in economic and political conditions here and abroad. The inflexibility of current policy, and the missed opportunities implied by this inflexibility, are costly. For example, a large number of Hong Kong residents, apprehensive of the changes that are bound to occur when Hong Kong becomes part of the People's Republic of China in 1997, recently entered the immigration market. Australia and Canada quickly began to sell visas to those residents who have substantial financial resources and who are willing to invest part of these resources in the host countries.[10] The inflexible immigration policy of the United States, combined with the very long queues for the scarce skill-based visas, implies that these motivated and prosperous persons have little chance of being admitted here.

One serious criticism of this proposed deregulation of the market for visas is that persons in many countries of origin have little chance of ever accumulating enough resources to buy visas. It is doubtful that many of our ancestors could have purchased the entry permits and immigrated to the United States. Similarly, it is unlikely that even skilled persons originating in less developed countries can compete in this marketplace. After all, per capita incomes in many of these countries are so low that most applicants would literally have to work a lifetime to be able to afford a visa selling for what most Americans would consider a modest price.

Implications for Policy

Although these concerns are justifiable, they are easily addressed. For example, if the United States wished to encourage the entry of persons from less developed countries, it could set the price of the visa in terms of the source country's per capita income, and migration to the United States would then be financially feasible for many persons residing in these countries.

Unfortunately, it is not clear that the selling of visas to potential applicants would necessarily generate a highly skilled immigrant flow. Clearly, the buyers will be the persons who not only can afford to purchase the visas at the going price but also have the largest incentives to migrate to the United States. One could argue that because unskilled persons typically lack the financial resources required to enter the visa market, the entry fee would automatically filter the pool of potential migrants, and the skill level of the immigrant flow would increase as a result. But it is often the case that unskilled workers in the source countries are the persons who have the most to gain by coming to the United States. These workers, therefore, have a major incentive to finance the purchase of the visa through any available means, such as borrowing from financial institutions and their families, or by making implicit contracts with their future U.S. employer. Conversely, if skilled workers have little to gain from immigration, they will remain in the country of origin regardless of the system used to allocate visas. The sale of visas, therefore, does not solve the problem that our offer of economic opportunity often seems most attractive to unskilled workers in the countries of origin.

Although the empirical evidence suggests that the objective of any reform in immigration policy should be to increase the skill level of the immigrant flow, these policy changes need not completely ignore humanitarian considerations. To a great extent, emigration and immigration statutes reflect what a society believes about liberty, human rights, and family values. These concerns can be easily incorporated into the policy reforms. For example, extra points could be awarded to visa applicants who have close relatives residing in the United States, or visas could be sold at a discount to buyers who have these family ties. Similarly, these policies can be easily adjusted to account for sudden political changes in the source countries and to permit the entry of persons seeking refuge from political or religious oppression.

Of course, a visa-allocation system based on the person's ability to pay discriminates against applicants who lack these financial resources. Similarly, a point system discriminates against applicants who lack the favored demographic characteristics. But any visa-allocation system is bound to lead to inequities, and the inequities created by an open market for visas or by the point system are certainly no more egregious than those associated with current or previous immigration policies. Throughout the first half of the century, the national-origins quota system simply prohibited the entry of Asians. The 1965 amendments prevent the entry of most persons who do not have relatives in the United States. Moreover, they also discriminate against persons who originate in populous countries, for no more than 20,000 (numerically restricted) visas are allocated to any country, regardless of the source country's population.

Immigration policy is inherently discriminatory. The statutes describe a set of rules designed to select from the many applicants. These rules may stress national origin, or skills, or financial resources, or family ties, or any combination of characteristics that Americans deem economically and politically desirable and consistent with the country's values and beliefs. Because there are only a limited number of visas, the policy has to restrict or prohibit the entry of many classes of persons. Inevitably, difficult choices must be made.

APPENDIX

Differences Among National-Origin Groups

THIS appendix presents summary statistics describing the skills and economic performance of immigrants belonging to a large number of national-origin groups. These data are presented here in order to provide additional evidence of the significant differences that exist among national-origin groups and to satisfy the curiosity readers may have regarding the performance of specific groups.

Most of the tables that follow report statistics for immigrants originating in forty-two different countries. The potential lifetime earnings differences between immigrants and natives (presented in tables A.4 and A.5) are calculated by tracking the groups between the 1970 and 1980 censuses and are reported for only forty-one countries. Because of the small number of Vietnamese immigrants residing in the United States in 1970, the sample sizes available in the 1970 Census are too small to allow a statistically reliable analysis.

TABLE A.1

Legal Immigrant Flow to the United States

	Number of Immigrants (in 1,000s) by Year of Immigration			
Country of Birth	1951–1960	1961–1970	1971–1980	1981–1986
Europe				
Austria	29.7	13.7	4.7	2.4
Czechoslovakia	28.8	21.4	10.2	6.2
Denmark	13.7	11.8	4.5	3.1
France	38.0	34.4	17.8	12.6
Germany	345.5	200.0	66.0	41.6
Greece	48.4	90.2	93.7	18.8
Hungary	64.5	17.3	11.6	4.7
Ireland	64.4	42.4	14.1	7.4
Italy	188.0	206.7	130.1	20.9
Netherlands	47.2	27.8	10.7	6.9
Norway	24.7	16.4	4.0	2.3
Poland	128.0	73.3	43.6	44.8
Portugal	20.4	79.3	104.5	25.2
Romania	17.4	14.9	17.5	22.0
Spain	10.7	30.5	30.0	9.2
Sweden	18.9	16.7	6.3	5.8
Switzerland	17.2	16.3	6.6	3.9
United Kingdom	208.9	230.5	123.5	85.4
USSR	46.5	15.7	43.2	42.1
Yugoslavia	58.7	46.2	42.1	10.1
Asia and Africa				
China	32.7	96.7	202.5	219.3
Egypt	3.7	17.2	25.5	17.2
India	3.1	31.2	176.8	145.9
Iran	2.5	10.4	46.2	79.0
Israel	8.6	12.9	26.6	20.1
Japan	44.7	38.5	47.9	24.0
Korea	7.0	35.8	272.0	201.8
Philippines	17.2	101.5	360.2	273.8
Vietnam	2.0	4.6	179.7	264.8
Americas				
Argentina	14.3	42.1	25.1	12.4
Brazil	8.9	20.5	13.7	11.0
Canada	274.9	286.7	114.8	66.6
Colombia	17.6	70.3	77.6	63.0
Cuba	78.3	256.8	276.8	92.0
Dominican Republic	9.8	94.1	148.0	130.8
Ecuador	9.5	37.0	50.2	26.7
Guatemala	4.1	15.4	25.6	25.1
Haiti	4.0	37.5	58.7	56.6
Jamaica	8.7	71.0	142.0	120.1
Mexico	319.3	443.3	637.2	401.7
Panama	9.7	18.4	22.7	17.6
Trinidad and Tobago	1.6	24.6	61.8	19.9

SOURCE: U.S. Bureau of the Census, *Statistical Abstract of the United States* (Washington, D.C.: Government Printing Office, various issues).

Appendix

TABLE A.2
Average Years of Education of Immigrant Men

Country of Birth	Education of Group as of 1980	Education of 1965–1969 Wave as of 1970	Education of 1975–1979 Wave as of 1980
Europe			
Austria	14.3	13.4	14.8
Czechoslovakia	13.5	14.1	15.4
Denmark	13.5	16.1	15.5
France	13.9	14.5	15.6
Germany	13.7	13.3	15.2
Greece	10.9	8.8	11.1
Hungary	13.4	12.3	13.6
Ireland	12.3	12.9	13.8
Italy	9.9	6.8	10.6
Netherlands	14.1	14.1	15.9
Norway	13.4	14.0	15.2
Poland	11.5	10.7	12.7
Portugal	7.2	5.2	6.6
Romania	13.1	11.6	13.7
Spain	12.2	10.3	13.2
Sweden	14.1	15.5	15.4
Switzerland	14.7	14.5	15.4
United Kingdom	14.1	13.7	15.1
USSR	12.8	10.5	14.3
Yugoslavia	11.0	10.7	11.0
Asia and Africa			
China	13.0	12.8	11.3
Egypt	16.3	15.5	15.9
India	17.3	16.7	16.1
Iran	15.8	15.3	15.2
Israel	14.7	13.5	14.2
Japan	15.3	15.4	15.7
Korea	15.0	15.8	14.0
Philippines	14.2	14.8	14.2
Vietnam	12.8	—	12.8
Americas			
Argentina	13.1	12.0	13.6
Brazil	13.6	12.6	15.4
Canada	12.9	12.9	14.6
Colombia	12.1	10.6	11.9
Cuba	11.6	9.5	11.3
Dominican Republic	9.2	8.4	8.9
Ecuador	11.5	10.4	10.9
Guatemala	10.1	10.4	10.9
Haiti	12.2	12.0	10.2
Jamaica	11.5	10.7	11.3
Mexico	7.2	6.1	6.5
Panama	13.1	12.4	13.1
Trinidad and Tobago	12.3	11.0	11.7

SOURCE: Author's tabulations from the 1970 and 1980 Public Use Samples of the U.S. Census. The statistics refer to working immigrant men aged twenty-five to sixty-four.

TABLE A.3

Percentage Difference in Hourly Wage Between Immigrant Men and
White Native Men

| | 1970 Census | | 1980 Census | | |
Country of Birth	All Immigrants	1965–1969 Cohort	All Immigrants	1965–1969 Cohort	1975–1979 Cohort
Europe					
Austria	21.8	24.4	23.5	43.3	−11.8
Czechoslovakia	13.1	4.8	16.0	12.1	2.8
Denmark	12.8	19.8	27.0	42.9	52.8
France	11.7	−7.4	11.3	12.3	25.1
Germany	17.4	11.6	17.1	26.5	30.3
Greece	−15.8	−31.0	−17.1	−22.6	−28.8
Hungary	13.9	−6.1	11.2	10.8	−16.5
Ireland	−3.6	−2.6	7.1	7.6	−13.2
Italy	−1.5	−15.7	−1.2	−7.6	−14.9
Netherlands	6.6	15.2	18.7	24.3	32.6
Norway	18.0	30.1	30.9	51.9	27.7
Poland	4.0	−9.1	1.7	2.1	−30.9
Portugal	−17.4	−21.4	−19.0	−17.7	−27.7
Romania	12.2	−17.4	5.7	9.7	−25.3
Spain	−14.5	−29.4	−4.1	−1.8	−19.3
Sweden	16.0	29.3	27.0	57.9	17.6
Switzerland	27.4	1.0	39.2	23.6	60.6
United Kingdom	18.2	20.9	23.5	37.5	21.2
USSR	8.5	−9.9	−5.2	−5.6	−24.8
Yugoslavia	3.6	−12.9	5.6	−1.9	−15.7
Asia and Africa					
China	−14.3	−29.2	−19.8	−12.4	−41.6
Egypt	−0.7	−19.2	7.6	38.0	−25.1
India	18.1	4.2	13.0	49.9	−18.8
Iran	−1.2	−29.9	−5.3	14.7	−20.0
Israel	7.3	−17.7	−2.7	−3.8	−22.0
Japan	5.5	5.3	14.6	16.1	22.4
Korea	−7.5	−19.6	−8.4	27.2	−26.0
Philippines	−17.5	−21.3	−6.8	7.2	−27.0
Vietnam	—	—	−44.7	—	−45.8
Americas					
Argentina	3.2	−15.2	−1.0	0.9	−13.3
Brazil	2.1	−9.5	5.0	15.1	4.9
Canada	11.3	11.4	13.4	15.5	19.0
Colombia	−13.5	−20.8	−20.6	−18.3	−36.0
Cuba	−24.6	−36.0	−16.7	−23.6	−41.7
Dominican Republic	−30.1	−40.3	−37.9	−35.1	−49.3
Ecuador	−20.9	−36.3	−21.9	−24.9	−40.7
Guatemala	−17.6	−41.6	−29.0	−19.6	−45.0
Haiti	−26.2	−26.4	−31.1	−20.5	−48.0
Jamaica	−15.2	−21.8	−19.2	−11.7	−30.3
Mexico	−33.6	−45.2	−32.8	−29.0	−47.3
Panama	−1.9	−17.3	−7.3	−11.9	−30.7
Trinidad and Tobago	−14.5	−25.2	−13.8	−6.6	−34.0

SOURCE: Adapted from George J. Borjas, "Immigration and Self-Selection," in Richard B. Freeman and John M. Abowd, eds., *Immigration, Trade, and the Labor Market* (Chicago: University of Chicago Press, 1990), table 1. The statistics refer to working men aged twenty-five to sixty-four. The percentage wage differentials are calculated from the antilogs of the mean differences in log wages.

Appendix

Percentage Difference in Potential Lifetime Earnings Between Immigrant
and White Native Men

Country of Birth	1950–1959 Cohort	1960–1964 Cohort	1965–1969 Cohort	1970–1974 Cohort	1975–1979 Cohort
Europe					
Austria	5.5	12.3	36.4	22.0	1.4
Czechoslovakia	12.6	13.8	8.4	0.5	5.8
Denmark	3.2	4.2	35.4	9.8	82.3
France	1.2	−8.1	1.7	15.8	30.4
Germany	5.4	3.7	9.8	11.1	18.2
Greece	−3.6	−5.2	−20.8	−25.9	−18.0
Hungary	9.7	4.2	4.5	−7.7	−10.7
Ireland	3.0	7.0	13.7	3.1	1.5
Italy	0.1	−1.3	−5.1	−9.0	−6.2
Netherlands	3.0	10.6	23.6	0.4	51.7
Norway	22.4	31.7	39.4	52.7	35.0
Poland	5.8	1.9	7.6	4.9	−18.9
Portugal	−11.9	−14.3	−17.8	−22.3	−24.6
Romania	7.5	8.4	12.1	26.4	−10.9
Spain	−12.5	−0.8	2.2	6.2	12.5
Sweden	9.1	15.3	37.3	22.3	20.0
Switzerland	17.2	21.0	26.9	18.7	33.2
United Kingdom	9.5	12.7	20.9	18.6	20.6
USSR	4.4	−1.2	−2.9	−0.6	−18.8
Yugoslavia	9.8	11.7	1.2	0.4	−1.1
Asia and Africa					
China	1.6	−3.7	−10.6	−23.3	−30.9
Egypt	12.2	9.6	16.9	6.0	1.0
India	32.1	38.3	29.9	14.3	−6.8
Iran	22.8	14.3	16.2	11.4	10.6
Israel	19.1	−7.4	−16.1	−17.2	−23.6
Japan	5.1	9.7	5.8	7.1	20.4
Korea	−1.7	12.1	8.6	0.5	−8.1
Philippines	−10.3	−1.1	2.5	2.4	−13.2
Americas					
Argentina	7.6	−1.2	−16.5	−26.8	−20.1
Brazil	6.3	8.4	7.4	−7.8	17.1
Canada	7.1	6.8	11.3	6.1	20.5
Colombia	19.6	−5.1	−17.3	−27.0	−35.9
Cuba	−15.3	−2.3	−17.1	−15.6	−29.2
Dominican Republic	−14.3	−26.2	−32.7	−36.6	−49.3
Ecuador	1.9	−3.3	−24.3	−21.6	−33.1
Guatemala	−9.7	−22.4	−30.3	−33.2	−38.9
Haiti	−5.1	0.7	−12.3	−26.2	−44.6
Jamaica	−4.6	−19.1	−13.1	−21.2	−32.6
Mexico	−20.9	−24.4	−26.5	−29.7	−38.0
Panama	−4.2	−8.7	−12.9	−6.3	−27.8
Trinidad and Tobago	19.0	7.2	−4.3	−11.0	−28.2

SOURCE: Adapted from George J. Borjas, "Immigration and Self-Selection," in Richard B. Freeman and John M. Abowd, eds., *Immigration, Trade, and the Labor Market* (Chicago: University of Chicago Press, 1990), table 6. The potential lifetime earnings differentials are calculated from regressions estimated in the sample of working men aged twenty-five to sixty-four using the hourly wage rate as the dependent variable. For details, see the discussion in chapter 7.

TABLE A.5

Percentage Difference in Potential Lifetime Earnings Between Immigrant
Men and Demographically Comparable White Native Men

Country of Birth	1950–1959 Cohort	1960–1964 Cohort	1965–1969 Cohort	1970–1974 Cohort	1975–1979 Cohort
Europe					
Austria	0.0	7.3	21.5	14.4	−8.1
Czechoslovakia	1.8	6.3	−0.4	−5.3	−1.4
Denmark	−4.2	−0.1	16.4	6.4	55.8
France	−6.1	−11.1	−4.1	8.6	20.7
Germany	1.5	1.2	3.9	6.6	7.6
Greece	−3.7	−3.9	−12.6	−16.6	−10.1
Hungary	3.9	−3.8	−1.3	−10.7	−14.3
Ireland	−2.5	7.0	19.2	8.5	13.5
Italy	7.2	8.8	7.2	4.3	5.1
Netherlands	−4.3	2.7	9.8	−8.8	32.5
Norway	15.5	22.3	19.2	28.0	20.7
Poland	5.4	3.9	8.2	7.5	−17.5
Portugal	9.1	10.0	8.2	3.5	3.0
Romania	5.5	−2.5	−0.5	9.5	−18.4
Spain	−11.2	−0.2	5.3	13.7	11.0
Sweden	0.0	7.5	24.7	17.6	12.1
Switzerland	6.1	10.2	15.1	11.3	27.1
United Kingdom	1.0	4.6	9.9	9.5	11.1
USSR	2.1	−4.5	−3.3	−3.0	−23.2
Yugoslavia	11.5	14.9	6.4	7.7	6.2
Asia and Africa					
China	−11.6	−16.8	−20.3	−28.6	−30.7
Egypt	−8.6	−9.3	−5.7	−11.2	−14.8
India	3.8	4.0	−4.8	−15.1	−28.6
Iran	−2.0	−4.6	2.2	−0.8	7.8
Israel	0.6	−17.9	−24.2	−20.9	−28.1
Japan	−7.7	−3.9	−4.8	−1.4	7.7
Korea	−19.9	−7.1	−9.2	−11.0	−16.8
Philippines	−16.9	−10.2	−6.7	−7.5	−17.2
Americas					
Argentina	−4.8	−7.9	−17.4	−23.8	−22.4
Brazil	−0.1	8.1	6.4	−9.0	7.0
Canada	3.7	7.0	12.2	5.1	15.5
Colombia	9.6	−6.0	−14.5	−21.1	−31.4
Cuba	−16.1	−6.6	−12.8	−8.1	−23.7
Dominican Republic	−3.1	−3.3	−3.9	−6.1	−14.5
Ecuador	−7.8	−6.4	−20.9	−16.0	−25.7
Guatemala	−9.1	−18.8	−22.5	−23.6	−27.1
Haiti	−10.0	−1.9	−11.5	−21.7	−37.6
Jamaica	−7.5	−19.6	−10.2	−14.0	−25.6
Mexico	−3.1	−3.3	−3.9	−6.1	−14.5
Panama	−10.7	−9.3	−11.9	−2.2	−23.8
Trinidad and Tobago	10.3	0.0	−4.3	−7.4	−21.6

SOURCE: Adapted from George J. Borjas, "Immigration and Self-Selection," in Richard B. Freeman and John M. Abowd, eds., *Immigration, Trade, and the Labor Market* (Chicago: University of Chicago Press, 1990), table 3. The potential lifetime earnings differentials are calculated from regressions estimated in the sample of working men aged twenty-five to sixty-four using the hourly wage rate as the dependent variable. For details, see the discussion in chapter 7.

Appendix

Employment Characteristics of Immigrant Men in 1980

Country of Birth	Labor Force Participation Rate	Unemployment Rate	Annual Hours Worked
Europe			
Austria	90.4	3.6	2,008
Czechoslovakia	90.4	2.9	1,920
Denmark	87.8	3.0	1,920
France	92.5	3.7	1,939
Germany	93.4	3.0	2,006
Greece	91.6	4.4	1,850
Hungary	92.4	4.0	1,951
Ireland	90.9	3.7	1,895
Italy	89.9	5.8	1,846
Netherlands	92.5	2.4	2,024
Norway	86.8	4.9	1,933
Poland	89.0	4.5	1,910
Portugal	93.4	7.1	1,846
Romania	90.7	5.3	1,865
Spain	92.5	4.4	1,867
Sweden	87.8	3.0	2,004
Switzerland	93.5	2.1	2,045
United Kingdom	92.0	2.9	1,990
USSR	84.8	6.4	1,657
Yugoslavia	93.4	5.4	1,910
Asia and Africa			
China	90.2	2.5	1,848
Egypt	91.6	4.0	1,808
India	95.5	3.2	1,876
Iran	64.9	7.3	1,357
Israel	90.7	4.1	1,843
Japan	90.4	2.1	1,880
Korea	90.1	3.3	1,715
Philippines	92.4	3.3	1,762
Vietnam	77.7	7.1	1,817
Americas			
Argentina	93.7	4.2	1,878
Brazil	86.9	3.7	1,867
Canada	87.7	3.8	1,941
Colombia	92.8	4.0	1,781
Cuba	92.0	4.0	1,878
Dominican Republic	88.6	9.0	1,679
Ecuador	92.6	6.4	1,763
Guatemala	95.6	5.3	1,812
Haiti	90.7	9.8	1,711
Jamaica	91.2	6.9	1,693
Mexico	92.1	7.7	1,739
Panama	92.0	6.7	1,758
Trinidad and Tobago	90.9	6.2	1,681

SOURCE: Author's tabulations from the 1980 Public Use Sample of the U.S. Census. The statistics refer to men aged twenty-five to sixty-four.

TABLE A.7

Poverty and Welfare in the Immigrant Population in 1980

Country of Birth	Poverty Rate	Welfare Participation Rate		
		All Households	Female-Headed Households	Male-Headed Households
Europe				
Austria	7.8	7.1	10.2	4.9
Czechoslovakia	8.3	5.2	7.0	4.2
Denmark	7.3	3.8	6.5	2.7
France	10.0	6.5	9.0	4.8
Germany	8.2	4.6	7.5	3.0
Greece	10.4	6.4	12.9	4.9
Hungary	8.7	6.1	9.3	4.5
Ireland	7.8	6.5	9.9	4.2
Italy	8.2	7.1	12.1	5.2
Netherlands	7.1	4.7	7.8	3.8
Norway	8.5	6.8	8.6	5.9
Poland	8.1	6.3	9.1	4.9
Portugal	8.2	7.9	21.1	5.6
Romania	10.2	6.7	11.5	5.0
Spain	11.2	15.7	19.8	14.7
Sweden	7.9	5.8	8.5	4.4
Switzerland	8.2	4.4	7.1	3.2
United Kingdom	7.2	5.3	9.2	3.1
USSR	14.8	9.6	12.8	7.7
Yugoslavia	7.8	6.6	11.2	5.2
Asia and Africa				
China	12.5	8.4	15.0	7.2
Egypt	9.8	5.0	15.3	3.6
India	6.0	2.8	6.5	2.5
Iran	31.1	2.0	6.8	1.3
Israel	17.5	5.0	9.6	4.2
Japan	13.0	5.7	9.0	4.0
Korea	13.5	6.3	8.7	5.7
Philippines	5.8	10.3	12.2	9.8
Vietnam	37.0	29.4	39.2	27.1
Americas				
Argentina	11.2	7.1	13.2	5.6
Brazil	11.3	5.5	9.9	3.8
Canada	7.7	6.2	11.1	3.7
Colombia	13.6	9.5	15.8	7.3
Cuba	12.2	17.3	31.7	13.1
Dominican Republic	33.7	25.9	41.0	12.9
Ecuador	16.9	11.9	30.2	6.9
Guatemala	18.3	9.6	17.7	6.5
Haiti	21.7	10.0	17.5	6.1
Jamaica	14.4	7.4	12.1	3.9
Mexico	26.0	12.7	29.3	9.0
Panama	16.7	11.8	20.3	5.9
Trinidad and Tobago	15.7	10.1	15.1	6.5

SOURCE: Author's tabulations from the 1980 Public Use Sample of the U.S. Census; and George J. Borjas and Stephen J. Trejo, "Immigrant Participation in the Welfare System," mimeograph, University of California, Santa Barbara, September 1988. The poverty rate gives the fraction of individuals below the poverty line. The welfare participation rate gives the fraction of households (where the head is at least eighteen years old) in which at least one household member receives public assistance.

Appendix

TABLE A.8
Self-Employment Among Immigrant Men

Country of Birth	Percent Self-Employed	Self-Employed Annual Income (in 1,000s of dollars)	Salaried Annual Income (in 1,000s of dollars)
Europe			
Austria	20.0	30.9	23.6
Czechoslovakia	21.3	25.9	21.3
Denmark	21.9	26.6	23.4
France	14.4	23.6	21.4
Germany	16.1	27.3	21.9
Greece	29.5	19.6	15.3
Hungary	19.5	24.9	20.6
Ireland	12.2	23.3	19.1
Italy	18.2	19.8	16.7
Netherlands	16.0	21.5	22.3
Norway	18.5	26.9	24.1
Poland	15.6	25.6	18.2
Portugal	5.6	18.9	13.2
Romania	17.9	25.1	19.5
Spain	12.8	25.7	17.2
Sweden	17.7	24.1	23.4
Switzerland	16.2	24.2	27.3
United Kingdom	10.2	23.9	23.4
USSR	11.5	22.5	15.7
Yugoslavia	11.5	24.4	18.5
Asia and Africa			
China	16.2	19.7	15.3
Egypt	16.1	33.5	19.9
India	11.1	37.1	20.8
Iran	22.2	32.9	14.8
Israel	28.3	25.4	18.1
Japan	10.0	20.8	21.6
Korea	24.6	23.0	16.0
Philippines	6.3	43.5	14.8
Vietnam	3.3	13.0	11.0
Americas			
Argentina	18.1	24.5	18.6
Brazil	12.7	25.7	18.8
Canada	15.5	27.2	21.2
Colombia	8.7	23.2	13.6
Cuba	15.7	21.6	15.0
Dominican Republic	5.9	19.5	9.6
Ecuador	6.6	17.2	13.0
Guatemala	3.6	15.0	11.1
Haiti	4.9	18.9	10.9
Jamaica	5.9	17.5	13.0
Mexico	5.1	16.5	11.4
Panama	6.8	15.9	15.1
Trinidad and Tobago	4.8	21.1	13.4

SOURCE: Author's tabulations from the 1980 Public Use Sample of the U.S. Census. The statistics refer to working men aged twenty-five to sixty-four.

NOTES

Chapter 1

1. U.S. Immigration and Naturalization Service, *Statistical Yearbook of the Immigration and Naturalization Service, 1987* (Washington, D. C.: Government Printing Office, 1988), p. 1. This statistic includes only legal immigrants and excludes both persons who were involuntarily brought into the country and persons who entered the country illegally.

2. A classic history of immigration to the United States and the reception faced by immigrants in this country is given by Maldwyn Allen Jones, *American Immigration* (Chicago: University of Chicago Press, 1960). An interesting historical survey of the media's attitudes about immigration is given in Rita J. Simon, *Public Opinion and the Immigrant: Print Media Coverage, 1880–1980* (Lexington, Mass.: D. C. Heath, 1985).

3. This quote is from a 1752 letter cited by Marion T. Bennett, *American Immigration Policies* (Washington, D.C.: Public Affairs Press, 1963), p. 5.

4. There was one brief attempt by the federal government, the Aliens Act of 1798, to regulate certain aspects of immigration. This law, however, was not enforced and expired after its two-year term. But there were restrictions adopted by state and local authorities, such as a head tax, designed to discourage poor immigrants from entering the localities. See Jones, *American Immigration*, p. 250; and E. P. Hutchinson, *Legislative History of American Immigration Policy, 1798–1965* (Philadelphia: University of Pennsylvania Press, 1981).

5. The text of the People's Party platform is included among the historical documents reprinted in Daniel J. Boorstin, *An American Primer* (Chicago: University of Chicago Press, 1966), p. 519.

6. Richard D. Lamm and Gary Imhoff, *The Immigration Time Bomb* (New York: E. P. Dutton, 1985), pp. 76–77.

7. The scarcity of data on immigration led to the recent convening of a National Academy of Sciences panel specifically designed to study the issue and to recommend ways of alleviating the problem in the future. The panel's final report is given in Daniel B. Levine, Kenneth Hill, and Robert Warren, editors, *Immigration Statistics: A Story of Neglect* (Washington, D.C.: National Academy Press, 1985).

8. Levine, Hill, and Warren, editors, *Immigration Statistics*, p. 2.

9. This approach to the study of immigration was introduced by George J. Borjas, "Self-Selection and the Earnings of Immigrants," *American Economic Review* 77 (September 1987): 531–53; and idem, "Immigration and Self-Selection," in Richard B. Freeman and John M. Abowd, eds., *Immigration, Trade, and the Labor Market* (Chicago: University of Chicago Press, 1990).

10. The market approach to the behavior of political parties has been influential in political science and originates with the work of Gary S. Becker, "Competition and Democracy," *Journal of Law and Economics* 1 (1958): 105–109; and Anthony Downs, *An Economic Theory of Democracy* (New York: Harper & Row, 1957). The operation of the marriage market is discussed in Gary S. Becker, "A Theory of Marriage," in Theodore W. Schultz, editor, *Economics of the Family: Marriage, Children, and Human Capital* (Chicago: University of Chicago Press, 1975), pp. 299–344. Additional examples of the usefulness of this approach to the study of what many consider noneconomic problems are given in Gary S. Becker, *The Economic Approach to Human Behavior* (Chicago: University of Chicago Press, 1976). Technical discussions of sorting models are given by Sherwin Rosen, "Hedonic Prices and Implicit Markets," *Journal of Political Economy* 82 (January–February 1974): 34–55; and Alvin E. Roth, "The Evolution of the Labor Market for Medical Interns and Residents: A Case Study in Game Theory," *Journal of Political Economy* 92 (December 1984): 991–1016.

Notes

11. Australia's Business Migration Program was the focus of a recent article in *Newsweek,* "Capitalism's Last Frontier," May 16, 1988, pp. 53–55.

12. The United States also has provisions for issuing "investor" visas. But these visas are available only if the slots allocated for family reunification and for attracting certain types of workers are not used. No such openings have been available for more than a decade.

13. These implications of the economic theory of migration were first derived by John R. Hicks, *The Theory of Wages,* 2d ed. (New York: St. Martin's Press, 1968, orig. 1932); and Larry A. Sjaastad, "The Costs and Returns of Human Migration," *Journal of Political Economy* 70 (October 1962 Supplement): 80–93.

14. Immigration and Naturalization Service, *Statistical Yearbook . . . 1987,* p. 63.

15. Borjas, "Self-Selection and the Earnings of Immigrants," p. 514.

16. See Giora Hanoch, "An Economic Analysis of Earnings and Schooling," *Journal of Human Resources* 2 (Summer 1967): 310–29; Robert J. Willis, "Wage Determinants: A Survey and Reinterpretation of Human Capital Earnings Functions," in Orley C. Ashenfelter and Richard Layard, editors, *Handbook of Labor Economics,* vol. 1 (Amsterdam: North-Holland, 1986), pp. 525–602; and George Psacharopoulos, *Returns to Education: An International Comparison* (San Francisco: Jossey-Bass, 1973).

17. Although much of the literature identifies the rate of return to schooling as the percentage increase in earnings attained by persons with one more year of schooling, there are difficult conceptual and statistical issues involved in correctly estimating the rate of return. See Sherwin Rosen, "Human Capital: A Survey of Empirical Research," *Research in Labor Economics* 1 (1977): 3–39; and Zvi Griliches, "Estimating the Returns to Schooling," *Econometrica* 45 (February 1977): 1–22.

18. Psacharopoulos's *Returns to Education* presents an encyclopedic treatment of international differences in the impact of education on earnings. The statistics cited in the text are drawn from George Psacharopoulos, "Returns to Education: An Updated International Comparison," *Comparative Education* 17.3 (1981): 327–28.

19. A voluminous literature analyzes the related question of why migration flows seem to be dominated, on average, by highly educated individuals. The usual explanation is that high education levels reduce mobility costs, presumably because of increased information about the opportunities available in the destination. See, for example, Aba Schwartz, "Migration and Lifespan Earnings in the U.S." (Ph.D. diss., University of Chicago, 1968).

20. A classic econometric analysis of income distributions is given by Jacob Mincer, *Schooling, Experience, and Earnings* (New York: Columbia University Press, 1974). See also Christopher Jencks et al., *Inequality* (New York: Basic Books, 1972).

21. In fact, if the distribution of skills were constant among countries, international variation in income inequality would be entirely determined by differences in the prices attached to the various skills.

22. George J. Borjas and Stephen G. Bronars, "Immigration and the Family," mimeograph, University of California, Santa Barbara, January 1989.

23. The analysis of how individuals are sorted among different alternatives according to their skills is due to Andrew D. Roy, "Some Thoughts on the Distribution of Earnings," *Oxford Economic Papers* 3 (June 1951): 80–93. This approach was first applied to the immigration decision by Borjas, "Self-Selection and the Earnings of Immigrants." Other applications include Robert J. Willis and Sherwin Rosen, "Education and Self-Selection," *Journal of Political Economy* 87 (October 1979 Supplement): S7–S36; and James J. Heckman and Guilherme Sedlacek, "Heterogeneity, Aggregation, and Market Wage Functions: An Empirical Model of Self-Selection in the Labor Market," *Journal of Political Economy* 93 (December 1985): 1077–125. These models typically assume that earnings are log-normally distributed in the population. It has been shown recently, however, that the central insights of the theory hold for a much more general family of statistical distributions. See James J. Heckman and Bo E. Honoré, "The Empirical Content of the Roy Model" (mimeograph, University of Chicago, August 1987). It is also easier to work out the technical details of the models in the case where there are only two countries competing in the immigration market. As noted in Roy's original work, this assumption is not necessary. Under a simplifying set of conditions, the models can be easily generalized to any number of countries, without fundamental changes in the insights provided by the approach.

24. The discussion in the text assumes that the most skilled individuals in any source country remain the most skilled individuals in the host country, while the least skilled remain unskilled wherever they go. The possibility of a negative correlation, which permits the possibility that what

Notes

passes for a "skill" in one country is not considered a skill in another, is discussed in Borjas, "Self-Selection and the Earnings of Immigrants," p. 534. Data on international differences in income inequality are available in World Bank, *World Development Report* (New York: Oxford University Press, 1988), pp. 272–73.

25. An interesting study of the Swedish tax system is given by Charles Stuart, "Swedish Tax Rates, Labor Supply, and Tax Revenues," *Journal of Political Economy* 89 (October 1981): 1020–38.

Chapter 2

1. E. P. Hutchinson, *Legislative History of American Immigration Policy, 1798–1965* (Philadelphia: University of Pennsylvania Press, 1981), p. 577.

2. Quoted in Hutchinson, *Legislative History*, p. 623.

3. Ibid., p. 624.

4. The most thorough discussion of the history of American immigration policy is contained in Hutchinson, *Legislative History*. Other studies include Marion T. Bennett, *American Immigration Policies: A History* (Washington, D.C.: Public Affairs Press, 1963); John Higham, *Strangers in the Land: Patterns of American Nativism, 1860–1925* (New York: Atheneum, 1963); and Leonard Dinnerstein and David M. Reimers, *Ethnic Americans: A History of Immigration*, 3d ed. (New York: Harper & Row, 1988). Briefer summaries include David M. Reimers, "Recent Immigration Policy: An Analysis," in Barry R. Chiswick, editor, *The Gateway: U.S. Immigration Issues and Policies* (Washington, D.C.: American Enterprise Institute, 1982), pp. 13–53; and Daniel B. Levine, Kenneth Hill, and Robert Warren, editors, *Immigration Statistics: A Story of Neglect* (Washington, D.C.: National Academy Press, 1985), chap. 2. Several interesting discussions of immigration policy are contained in Nathan Glazer, editor, *Clamor at the Gates: The New American Immigration* (San Francisco: Institute for Contemporary Studies, 1985).

5. The history of these Supreme Court decisions is given in Roy L. Garis, *Immigration Restriction* (New York: Macmillan, 1928), and is briefly reviewed in Hutchinson, *Legislative History*, p. 403.

6. Quoted in Barbara Benton, *Ellis Island* (New York: Facts on File Publications, 1987), p. 34.

7. Quoted in Higham, *Strangers in the Land*, p. 143. See also the discussion regarding the "scientific" studies of changes in the ability level of immigrants in Stephen Jay Gould, *The Mismeasure of Man* (New York: Norton, 1981), pp. 224–32.

8. The quotation comes from a 1920 article written by Kenneth Roberts for the *Saturday Evening Post*, quoted in Rita J. Simon, *Public Opinion and the Immigrant: Print Media Coverage, 1880–1980* (Lexington, Mass.: D. C. Heath, 1985), p. 83.

9. A fascinating account of how the national-origins formula came about is given by Higham, *Strangers in the Land*, chap. 11.

10. A minimum of 100 visas was given to each nationality, regardless of its proportional representation in the U.S. population.

11. These are the quotas for the 1930 fiscal year. See Hutchinson, *Legislative History*, p. 485.

12. Quoted in Higham, *Strangers in the Land*, p. 300; and Gould, *Mismeasure of Man*, p. 232.

13. A preference system was already in place as a result of the statutes enacted in the 1920s. See Hutchinson, *Legislative History*, p. 580.

14. Elliott Abrams and Franklin S. Abrams, "Immigration Policy—Who Gets in and Why?" *Public Interest* 38 (Winter 1975): 7.

15. Quoted in Simon, *Public Opinion*, p. 39.

16. The 1965 amendments preserved the distinction in immigration policies between the Eastern and Western Hemispheres. The 20,000 numerical limitation for immigration from any single country and the preference system did not apply to Western Hemisphere countries until after 1976.

17. U.S. Immigration and Naturalization Service, *Statistical Yearbook of the Immigration and Naturalization Service, 1987* (Washington, D.C.: Government Printing Office, 1988), pp. 8–11.

18. Quoted in Abrams and Abrams, "Immigration Policy," p. 12.

19. U.S. Immigration and Naturalization Service, *Statistical Yearbook . . . 1987*, pp. 8–11.

An interesting discussion of this fact is given by Barry R. Chiswick, "Legal Aliens: Toward a Positive Immigration Policy," *Regulation* 12 (1988): 17–22.

20. Quoted in Reimers, "Recent Immigration Policy," p. 35.

21. Quoted in Abrams and Abrams, "Immigration Policy," p. 8.

22. See Reimers, "Recent Immigration Policy," pp. 38–41, for a discussion of how Asian immigration grew after the 1965 amendments.

23. The connection between foreign policy and refugee policy is clearly delineated by Christopher Mitchell, "International Migration, International Relations and Foreign Policy," *International Migration Review*, forthcoming.

24. U.S. Department of Health and Human Services, Office of Refugee Resettlement, *Refugee Resettlement Program, Annual Report FY 1982* (Washington, D.C.: Government Printing Office, 1983), pp. 1–2. Presidential action is required in order to classify a person who is still living in his country of normal residence as a refugee. For a history of refugee policy up to 1965, see Hutchinson, *Legislative History*, chap. 17.

25. U.S. Immigration and Naturalization Service, *Statistical Yearbook . . . 1987*, p. 50.

26. Ibid., p. 63.

27. "Soviet Jews to Be Pressed to Go to Israel, Cabinet Decides," *Los Angeles Times*, June 20, 1988, p. 7.

28. Ibid., p. 1.

29. The U.S. government, however, no longer automatically grants refugee status to Soviet Jews. The applicants must now prove that they are being persecuted, under the definition provided by the Refugee Act of 1980. See Robert S. Greenberger, "Now That Soviet Jews Are Freer to Emigrate, U.S. Is Less Hospitable," *Wall Street Journal*, June 23, 1989, p. 1.

30. See U.S. Department of Health and Human Services, Office of Refugee Resettlement, *Refugee Resettlement Program . . . 1982*, for a description of the social programs available to refugees.

31. U.S. Department of Health and Human Services, Office of Refugee Resettlement, *Refugee Resettlement Program, Annual Report* (Washington, D.C.: Government Printing Office, annual).

32. Minor exceptions are the statutes restricting the travel of American citizens to such countries as Cuba and North Vietnam.

33. Robert Warren and Jennifer Marks Peck, "Foreign-Born Emigration from the United States: 1960 to 1970," *Demography* 17 (February 1980): 71–84; Guillermina Jasso and Mark R. Rosenzweig, "Estimating the Emigration Rates of Legal Immigrants Using Administrative and Survey Data: The 1971 Cohort of Immigrants to the United States," *Demography* 19 (August 1982): 279–90; Robert Warren and Ellen Percy Kraly, "The Elusive Exodus: Emigration From the United States," *Population Trends and Public Policy* (March 1985, no. 7); and Kit Chum Lam, "An Analysis of the Outmigration of Foreign Born Members in a Population" (Ph.D. diss., Harvard University, 1987).

34. George J. Borjas, "Immigrants in the U.S. Labor Market: 1940–1980" (mimeograph, University of California, Santa Barbara, September 1988, table 2).

35. U.S. Immigration and Naturalization Service, *Annual Report of the Immigration and Naturalization Service, 1965* (Washington, D.C.: Government Printing Office, 1965), p. 34.

36. Throughout most of the postwar period, the INS did not differentiate between China and Taiwan in its reporting of immigration statistics. Because of the restrictive emigration policies pursued by the People's Republic of China before the 1980s, it is likely that most "Chinese" immigrants originated in Taiwan. Table 2.3, therefore, uses Taiwan's population as the base for calculating the emigration rate.

37. See George J. Borjas, "Self-Selection and the Earnings of Immigrants," *American Economic Review* 77 (September 1987): 531–53; and Guillermina Jasso and Mark R. Rosenzweig, "Immigration, Emigration and Sample Selection: Comment on Borjas" (mimeograph, University of Minnesota, 1987).

Chapter 3

1. Almost all of the original empirical research reported in this book uses the Public Use Samples of the decennial U.S. censuses available since 1940. All of these data sources contain very

large numbers of observations on the immigrant population and allow for statistically reliable estimates of the differences between immigrants and natives, as well as within the immigrant population. For instance, the 1980 Census file contains a 5-percent random sample of the immigrant population. This sampling proportion generates extremely large sample sizes. There are, for instance, 134,252 salaried immigrant men (aged between twenty-five and sixty-four) in the 1980 data set. The 1970 Census extract contains a 2-percent random sample of the immigrant population, while the pre-1970 Public Use Samples contain a 1 percent random sample of the immigrant and native populations. Because of the very large sample sizes, the study of the 1970 and 1980 censuses uses subsamples of the native population: a .001 percent random sample in the 1970 Census, and a .0004 percent random sample in the 1980 Census. For details on the construction of these data sets, see George J. Borjas, "Self-Selection and the Earnings of Immigrants," *American Economic Review* 77 (September 1987): 531–53. The 1980 Census is also the most recently available data set that allows the comparison of the immigrant and native populations and that has sufficiently large numbers of observations to allow statistically reliable comparisons among the various immigrant groups. More recent data sets, such as the annual Current Population Survey (CPS) or the Survey of Income and Program Participation, have much smaller samples of immigrants and often do not permit a disaggregation of the immigrant population by country of origin or year of immigration. For a statistical profile of the immigrant population using the matched March–April 1983 CPS, see Ellen Sehgal, "Foreign-Born in the U.S. Labor Market: The Results of a Special Survey," *Monthly Labor Review* 108 (July 1985): 18–24.

2. I should add that because relatively few immigrants are under the age of sixteen, the costs associated with their participation in the public-school system may be low, and these "savings" may offset the additional costs incurred by the older population.

3. A classic study of the "brain drain," the immigration of highly educated persons to the United States, is given by Walter Adams, *The Brain Drain* (New York: Macmillan, 1968).

4. See Ann P. Bartel, "Location Decisions of the New Immigrants to the United States," National Bureau of Economic Research Working Paper no. 2049 (October 1986).

5. For analyses of immigrant enclaves, see Alejandro Portes, "The Social Origins of the Cuban Enclave Economy of Miami," *Sociological Perspectives* 30 (October 1987): 340–72; and Walter McManus, "Labor Market Effects of Ethnic Enclaves: Hispanic Men in the United States" (mimeograph, University of Florida, April 1987).

6. Richard D. Lamm and Gary Imhoff, *The Immigration Time Bomb: The Fragmenting of America* (New York: E. P. Dutton, 1985), p. 90.

7. National Association of Counties Research, Inc., "Analysis of San Diego and San Francisco County Data on the Length of Time Indochinese Refugees Have Been in the U.S. Prior to Application for Public Assistance" (Washington, D.C.: NACo, September 1981), p. 1. Quoted in Lamm and Imhoff, *Immigration Time Bomb*, p. 163.

8. A recent overview of the literature on female labor supply is given by Mark R. Killingsworth and James J. Heckman, "Female Labor Supply: A Survey," in Orley C. Ashenfelter and Richard Layard, editors, *Handbook of Labor Economics*, vol. 1 (Amsterdam: North-Holland, 1986), pp. 103–204.

9. For preliminary studies of the experience of female immigrants in the U.S. labor market, see James E. Long, "The Effect of Americanization on Earnings: Some Evidence for Women," *Journal of Political Economy* 88 (June 1980): 620–29; Paul M. Ong, "Immigrant Wives' Labor Force Participation," *Industrial Relations* 26 (Fall 1987): 296–303; and Cordelia Reimers, "Cultural Differences in Labor Force Participation Among Married Women," *American Economic Review* 65 (May 1985): 251–55.

10. The classic treatise on the assimilation hypothesis is Milton Gordon, *Assimilation and American Life* (New York: Oxford University Press, 1964).

11. Differences in skills among the various cohorts can also arise because of the selective emigration of the foreign-born in the United States. The census only enumerates persons who reside in the United States as of census week. Many immigrants returned to their birthplace (or migrated elsewhere) prior to 1980 and are not counted by the census. If this emigration is nonrandom (only a certain type of person emigrates), more recent cohorts will vary systematically from earlier cohorts.

12. This methodological problem is well known in the demography literature. See John Hobcraft, Jane Menken, and Samuel Preston, "Age, Period and Cohort Effects in Demography: A Review," *Population Index* 48 (Spring 1982): 4–43. The argument that "cohort effects" play an important role in determining the labor market experiences of immigrants was made and

Notes

elaborated in George J. Borjas, "Assimilation, Changes in Cohort Quality, and the Earnings of Immigrants," *Journal of Labor Economics* 3 (October 1985): 463–89.

13. See Jacob Mincer, *Schooling, Experience, and Earnings* (New York: Columbia University Press, 1974); and Giora Hanoch, "An Economic Analysis of Earnings and Schooling," *Journal of Human Resources* 2 (Summer 1967): 310–29.

14. See Mark R. Killingsworth, *Labor Supply* (New York: Cambridge University Press, 1983), for a comprehensive discussion of labor supply trends in the United States.

15. George J. Borjas, "Immigration and Self-Selection," in Richard B. Freeman and John M. Abowd, eds., *Immigration, Trade, and the Labor Market* (Chicago: University of Chicago Press, 1990), table 2.

Chapter 4

1. For a classic economic analysis of the decision to engage in illegal activity, see Gary S. Becker, "Crime and Punishment: An Economic Approach," *Journal of Political Economy* 76 (March–April 1968): 169–217.

2. Richard W. Cuthbert and Joe B. Stevens, "The Net Economic Incentive for Illegal Mexican Migration: A Case Study," *International Migration Review* 15 (Fall 1981): 543–50.

3. An interesting history of the bracero program is given by Ernesto Galarza, *Merchants of Labor: The Mexican Bracero Story* (Charlotte, N.C.: McNally and Loftin, 1964). Various legislative aspects of the bracero program are discussed by E. P. Hutchinson, *Legislative History of U.S. Immigration Policy, 1798–1965* (Philadelphia: University of Pennsylvania Press, 1981). Vernon M. Briggs, Jr., "Mexican Workers in the United States Labour Market: A Contemporary Dilemma," *International Labor Review* 112 (November 1975): 351–68, presents a discussion of the presumed impact of the bracero program on the U.S. economy.

4. U.S. Immigration and Naturalization Service, *Statistical Yearbook of the Immigration and Naturalization Service, 1987* (Washington, D.C.: Government Printing Office, 1988), p. 108.

5. S. J. Torok and Wallace E. Huffman, "U.S.–Mexican Trade in Winter Vegetables and Illegal Immigration," *American Journal of Agricultural Economics* 68 (May 1986): 246–60.

6. George J. Borjas, Richard B. Freeman, and Kevin Lang, "Undocumented Mexican-Born Workers in the U.S.: How Many, How Permanent?" in Richard B. Freeman and John M. Abowd, eds., *Immigration, Trade, and the Labor Market* (Chicago: University of Chicago Press, 1990).

7. Although it may seem patently ridiculous simply to assume that one illegal alien sneaks through for every one who gets caught (particularly as there is no evidence supporting the assumption), this type of assertion continues to be made. For instance, in a recent article in the *Washington Post*, Congressman Daniel Lungren noted that because 2 million persons were apprehended by the Border Patrol in a recent period, this fact implied that at least 4 million illegal aliens entered in that period; see Kenneth Hill, "Illegal Aliens: An Assessment," in Daniel B. Levine, Kenneth Hill, and Robert Warren, editors, *Immigration Statistics: A Story of Neglect* (Washington, D.C.: National Academy Press, 1985), p. 240.

8. Quoted in Elliott Abrams and Franklin S. Abrams, "Immigration Policy—Who Gets in and Why?" *Public Interest* 38 (Winter 1975): 21.

9. Borjas, Freeman, and Lang, "Undocumented Mexican-Born Workers."

10. An excellent (and critical) survey of the available studies is given by Hill, "Illegal Aliens: An Assessment."

11. Robert Warren and Jeffrey S. Passel, "A Count of the Uncountable: Estimates of Undocumented Aliens Counted in the 1980 United States Census," *Demography* 24 (August 1987): 375–93. Due to rounding error, the statistics presented in the Warren–Passel article differ slightly from those summarized in table 4.1. If one were to add their reported number of total foreign-born persons and subtract the number of persons naturalized and the number of legal aliens, the predicted number of illegal aliens is 2.055 million and not 2.057 million, as they report. Table 4.1 resolves this trivial discrepancy by adding in the missing 2,000 persons to the total number of foreign-born persons.

12. See U.S. Bureau of the Census, *The Coverage of Housing in the 1980 Census. Census of Population and Housing: 1980*, Evaluation and Research Reports, PHC80-E1 (Washington, D.C.: Government Printing Office, 1985).

13. This very brief description of the approach correctly describes the "flavor," but the ingredients are much more complicated. See Warren and Passel, "Count of the Uncountable," for details.

14. The second largest illegal-alien population originated in Iran. Approximately 58,000 "excess" Iranians were found in the 1980 Census (or about 6 percent of the non-Mexican illegal population). See Warren and Passel, "Count of the Uncountable," table 2.

15. The idea that mortality data provide information on the number of illegal aliens in the United States is due to J. Gregory Robinson, "Estimating the Approximate Size of the Illegal Alien Population in the United States by the Comparative Trend Analysis of Age-Specific Death Rates," *Demography* 17 (May 1980): 159–76. An updating of the methodology, using the data on mortality by country of birth and age available since 1984, is given by Borjas, Freeman, and Lang, "Undocumented Mexican-Born Workers," table 2.

16. Frank D. Bean, Allan G. King, and Jeffrey S. Passel, "The Number of Illegal Migrants of Mexican Origin in the United States: Sex Ratio–Based Estimates for 1980," *Demography* 20 (February 1983): 99–109. A related study by Hill, "Illegal Aliens: An Assessment," shows that the comparison of population counts between the 1970 and 1980 Mexican censuses leads to a very small number of persons "missing" from the 1980 census, which would suggest that the illegal-alien flow over the decade was relatively small. It may also suggest, however, that coverage and enumeration procedures used in the Mexican census vary widely over time.

17. Bean, King, and Passel, "The Number of Illegal Migrants," table 4.

18. See Jeffrey Passel, "Undocumented Immigration," *The Annals of the American Academy of Political and Social Science* 487 (September 1986): 181–200.

19. Josh Reichert and Douglas S. Massey, "Patterns of U.S. Migration from a Mexican Sending Community: A Comparison of Legal and Illegal Migrants," *International Migration Review* 13 (Winter 1979): 599–623.

20. Warren and Passel, "Count of the Uncountable," table 2. For further analysis of this point, see Frank D. Bean, Harley L. Browning, and W. Parker Frisbie, "The Sociodemographic Characteristics of Mexican Immigrant Status Groups: Implications for Studying Undocumented Mexicans," *International Migration Review* 18 (Fall 1984): 672–91.

21. Jeffrey S. Passel and Karen A. Woodrow, "Geographic Distribution of Undocumented Immigrants: Estimates of Undocumented Aliens Counted in the 1980 Census by State," *International Migration Review* 18 (Fall 1984): 658.

22. Warren and Passel, "Count of the Uncountable," table 3.

23. Borjas, Freeman, and Lang, "Undocumented Mexican-Born Workers," table 5.

24. Ibid., table 6.

25. Douglas S. Massey, "Do Undocumented Migrants Earn Lower Wages than Legal Immigrants? New Evidence from Mexico" *International Migration Review* 21 (Summer 1987): 236–74.

26. See also Susan I. Ranney and Sherrie A. Kossoudji, "Profiles of Temporary Mexican Labor Migrants to the United States," *Population and Development Review* 9 (September 1983): 475–93, for a complementary description of the illegal-alien population.

27. J. Edward Taylor, "Selectivity of Undocumented Mexico–U.S. Migrants and Implications for U.S. Immigration Reform," The Urban Institute, Working Paper no. PDS-85-4 (December 1985). For related work, see Sherrie A. Kossoudji and Susan I. Ranney, "Legal Status as Union Membership: Legal and Illegal Wage Rates of Mexican Immigrants" (mimeograph, University of Michigan, Ann Arbor, September 1986).

28. Barry R. Chiswick, *Illegal Aliens: Their Employment and Employers* (Kalamazoo, Mich.: W. E. Upjohn Institute for Employment Research, 1988).

29. Ibid., p. 43.

30. Ibid., p. 131.

31. Briggs, "Mexican Workers in the United States," p. 362.

32. Massey, "Do Undocumented Migrants Earn Lower Wages?"; see also idem, "The Settlement Process Among Mexican Migrants to the United States," *American Sociological Review* 51 (October 1986): 670–84.

33. Massey, "Do Undocumented Migrants Earn Lower Wages?" A related study by Barry R. Chiswick, "Illegal Aliens in the United States Labor Market: An Analysis of Occupational Attainment and Earnings," *International Migration Review* 18 (Fall 1984): 714–32, analyzes the earnings-determination process of illegal aliens, but his data do not allow any comparisons between legal and illegal aliens. See also David S. North and Marion F. Houstoun, *The Characteristics and*

Role of Illegal Aliens in the United States Labor Market: An Exploratory Study (Washington, D.C.: Linton and Co., 1976).

34. See the extensive discussion of this point in Chiswick, "Illegal Aliens in the United States Labor Market," and in idem, *Illegal Aliens.*

35. A clear and detailed description of the various provisions in IRCA is given by Thomas J. Espenshade, Frank D. Bean, Tracy Ann Goodis, and Michael J. White, "Immigration Policy in the United States: Future Prospects for the Immigration Reform and Control Act of 1986" (mimeograph, The Urban Institute, October 1988). A very useful how-to manual designed for potential amnesty applicants was published by the *Los Angeles Times,* "Becoming Legal," on June 30, 1987. See also Barry R. Chiswick, "Illegal Immigration and Immigration Control," *Journal of Economic Perspectives* 2 (Summer 1988): 101–15; and Clark W. Reynolds and Robert K. McCleery, "The Political Economy of Immigration Laws: Impact of Simpson–Rodino on the United States and Mexico," *Journal of Economic Perspectives* 2 (Summer 1988): 117–31.

36. Chiswick, "Illegal Immigration and Immigration Control," p. 109.

37. There is some concern that because employers must now check the legal status of job applicants, many firms will find it easier to discriminate against immigrants or ethnic minorities. This type of discrimination is specifically prohibited by IRCA. See General Accounting Office, *Immigration Reform: Status of Implementing Employer Sanctions After Second Year,* GAO/ GGD-89-16 (Washington, D.C.: Government Printing Office, 1988).

38. U.S. Immigration and Naturalization Service, statistical analysis branch, "Provisional Legalization Application Statistics," Washington, D. C., May 12, 1989; and "A Million Late Arrivals," *Time,* December 12, 1988, p. 33. The *Time* magazine article also reports on allegations of large-scale fraud among applicants applying for entry under the SAW program.

39. U.S. Immigration and Naturalization Service, "Provisional Legalization Application Statistics."

40. Larry Rohter, "Immigration Law Is Failing to Cut Flow From Mexico," *New York Times,* June 24, 1988, p. 1.

41. Espenshade, Bean, Goodis, and White, "Immigration Policy in the United States"; and "INS Reported Deficient in Checking Employers," *Santa Barbara News Press* March 19, 1989, p. 1.

42. The history of employer compliance with the minimum-wage and overtime provisions of the Fair Labor Standards Act is instructive. Recent studies indicate that at least one-third of all persons who qualify to receive the minimum wage get paid less than the minimum, and that about 10 percent of persons who work overtime do not receive the mandated overtime premium. See Orley Ashenfelter and Robert S. Smith, "Compliance with the Minimum Wage Law," *Journal of Political Economy* 87 (April 1979): 333–50; and Ronald G. Ehrenberg and Paul L. Schumann, "Compliance with the Overtime Pay Provisions of the Fair Labor Standards Act," *Journal of Law and Economics* 25 (April 1982): 159–81.

Chapter 5

1. John Higham, *Strangers in the Land: Patterns of American Nativism 1869–1925* (New York: Atheneum, 1955), presents a fascinating account of how economic fears of job displacement and unemployment interacted with nativist feelings and led to ever-increasing restrictions on immigration.

2. Joan Didion, *Miami* (New York: Pocket Books, 1987), pp. 47–48.

3. Michael J. Greenwood and John M. McDowell, "The Factor Market Consequences of Immigration," *Journal of Economic Literature* 24 (December 1986): 1750.

4. The methodological problem of estimating the extent of labor market competition among the various labor and capital inputs is clearly discussed by Daniel S. Hamermesh, "The Demand for Labor in the Long Run," in Orley C. Ashenfelter and Richard Layard, editors, *Handbook of Labor Economics,* vol. 1 (Amsterdam: North-Holland, 1987), pp. 429–71. A more technical discussion of the theory of production is given by Melvyn Fuss and Daniel McFadden, editors, *Production Economics: A Dual Approach to Theory and Applications,* vols. 1 and 2 (Amsterdam: North-Holland, 1978).

5. Greenwood and McDowell, "Factor Market Consequences," review the various arguments and conjectures. See also the discussion in George J. Borjas and Marta Tienda, "The Economic

Notes

Consequences of Immigration," *Science* 235 (February 6, 1987): 645–51; and Frank D. Bean, Edward E. Telles, and B. Lindsay Lowell, "Undocumented Migration to the United States: Perceptions and Evidence," *Population and Development Review* 13 (December 1987): 671–90.

6. Vernon M. Briggs, "Mexican Workers in the United States Labour Market: A Contemporary Dilemma," *International Labour Review* 112 (November 1975): 358. Quoted in Greenwood and McDowell, "Factor Market Consequences," pp. 1746–47.

7. An alternative argument that leads to the same conclusion assumes that immigrants are better qualified than natives, but that they get paid lower wage rates. In this view, employers would still prefer to hire immigrants over natives.

8. The impact of labor market discrimination on the wages and employment of minority groups is the focus of a large and growing literature in economics. The basic approach to the study of discrimination is due to Gary S. Becker, *A Theory of Discrimination*, 2d ed. (Chicago: University of Chicago Press, 1971). A recent survey of the voluminous literature is given by Glen G. Cain, "The Economic Analysis of Discrimination: A Survey," in Ashenfelter and Layard, editors, *Handbook of Labor Economics*, vol. 1, pp. 693–785.

9. For instance, it may be that the earnings of Hispanic immigrants are lower than those of white natives because of their "Hispanicity." Nonetheless, the study of earnings determination for persons of Hispanic origin born in the United States reveals that they have roughly the same earnings as white natives after controlling for differences in observable demographic characteristics, such as age, education, and English proficiency. See Cordelia Reimers, "Labor Market Discrimination Against Hispanic and Black Men," *Review of Economics and Statistics* 65 (November 1983): 570–79.

10. Michael J. Piore, *Birds of Passage: Migrant Labor and Industrial Societies* (New York: Cambridge University Press, 1979), p. 3.

11. James J. Heckman and V. Joseph Hotz, "An Investigation of the Labor Market Earnings of Panamanian Males: Evaluating the Sources of Inequality," *Journal of Human Resources* 21 (Fall 1986): 507–42, argue that it is impossible to develop unambiguous tests of the segmented labor market hypothesis. An opposing viewpoint is given by William Dickens and Kevin Lang, "A Test of Dual Labor Market Theory," *American Economic Review* 75 (September 1985): 792–805.

12. Sherwin Rosen, "The Theory of Equalizing Differences," in Ashenfelter and Layard, editors, *Handbook of Labor Economics*, vol. 1, pp. 641–92, presents an excellent survey of the economic theory of compensating differentials: how wages in jobs that contain bad working conditions adjust in order to attract persons willing to work in those jobs.

13. Examples of these types of models are George Johnson, "The Labor Market Effects of Immigration," *Industrial and Labor Relations Review* 33 (April 1980): 331–41; and Jean Baldwin Grossman, "Illegal Immigrants and Domestic Employment," *Industrial and Labor Relations Review* 37 (January 1984): 240–51.

14. Although this simple description of the empirical insight is correct, the actual methodological approach followed by most of the studies in the literature is far more complex. Immigrants affect the economic opportunities of natives through their effect on the demand for native labor. What is required, therefore, is the estimation of the firm's demand function for the various inputs. To estimate the system of demand equations (which includes one demand function for each of the inputs used in the production process), a functional form for the firm's production technology must be specified. This technical assumption, combined with the behavioral assumption that firms maximize profits, leads to a system of equations that can be estimated using data on the quantities and prices of the inputs. The econometric methodology estimates all of the equations in this demand system jointly, and it is from these demand functions that the impact of immigrants on the native labor market is calculated. For details, see Hamermesh, "Demand for Labor."

15. George J. Borjas, "Immigrants, Minorities, and Labor Market Competition," *Industrial and Labor Relations Review* 40 (April 1987): 382–92.

16. Robert J. LaLonde and Robert H. Topel, "Labor Market Adjustments to Increased Immigration," in Richard B. Freeman and John M. Abowd, eds., *Immigration, Trade, and the Labor Market* (Chicago: University of Chicago Press, 1990).

17. U.S. Department of Commerce, *Statistical Abstract of the United States, 1988* (Washington, D.C.: Government Printing Office, 1988), p. 365. A classic study of the increase in the labor force participation rate of women is given by Jacob Mincer, "Labor Force Participation of Married Women: A Study of Labor Supply," in *Aspects of Labor Economics* (Princeton, N.J.: Princeton University Press, 1962), pp. 63–105.

18. U.S. Department of Commerce, *Statistical Abstract of the United States, 1988*, p. 13. See Finis Welch, "Effects of Cohort Size on Earnings: The Baby Boom Babies' Financial Bust," *Journal of Political Economy* 87 (October 1979): S65–S98, for an empirical study of the impact that the baby-boom cohort had on its own earnings.

19. John M. Abowd and Richard B. Freeman, "The Internationalization of the U.S. Labor Market," in Freeman and Abowd, eds., *Immigration, Trade, and the Labor Market*, table 1.

20. Quoted in Thomas Muller, "Economic Effects of Immigration," in Nathan Glazer, editor, *Clamor at the Gates: The New American Immigration* (San Francisco: Institute for Contemporary Studies, 1985), p. 110.

21. For details, see Jeffrey S. Passel and Karen A. Woodrow, "Geographic Distribution of Undocumented Immigrants: Estimates of Undocumented Aliens Counted in the 1980 Census by State," *International Migration Review* 18 (Fall 1984): 642–71.

22. Frank D. Bean, B. Lindsay Lowell, and Lowell J. Taylor, "Undocumented Mexican Immigrants and the Earnings of Other Workers in the United States," *Demography* 25 (February 1988): 35–52. This study was further expanded in Lowell J. Taylor, Frank D. Bean, James B. Rebitzer, Susan Gonzalez Baker, and B. Lindsay Lowell, "Mexican Immigrants and the Wages and Unemployment Experience of Native Workers," mimeograph, The Urban Institute, September 1988.

23. Bean, Lowell, and Taylor, "Undocumented Mexican Immigrants," table 4.

24. There is, however, substantial variation in the estimates. Part of this variation is due to technical problems encountered when estimating "own effects" in some systems of demand equations. See George J. Borjas, "The Demographic Determinants of the Demand for Black Labor," in Richard B. Freeman and Harry J. Holzer, editors, *The Black Youth Employment Crisis* (Chicago: University of Chicago Press, 1986): 191–230.

25. Recent work by Taylor, Bean, Rebitzer, Gonzalez Baker, and Lowell, "Mexican Immigrants," suggests that illegal immigration substantially *reduces* the unemployment rate of natives.

26. The studies include Joseph Altonji and David Card, "The Effects of Immigration on the Labor Market Outcomes of Natives," in Freeman and Abowd, eds., *Immigration, Trade, and the Labor Market;* George J. Borjas, "The Sensitivity of Labor Demand Functions to Choice of Dependent Variable," *Review of Economics and Statistics* 68 (February 1986): 58–66; and LaLonde and Topel, "Labor Market Adjustments."

27. Borjas, "Sensitivity of Labor Demand Functions," tables 1–3.

28. David Card, "The Impact of the Mariel Boatlift on the Miami Labor Market" (mimeograph, Princeton University, May 1989).

29. Ibid., p. 4.

30. The technical problem is that a system of supply-and-demand functions for the various types of labor must be estimated jointly. See Altonji and Card, "Effects of Immigration"; Bean, Lowell, and Taylor, "Undocumented Mexican Immigrants"; and Borjas, "Sensitivity of Labor Demand Functions."

31. See Thomas R. Bailey, *Immigrant and Native Workers: Contrasts and Competition* (Boulder, Colo.: Westview Press, 1987); Sheldon L. Maram, "Hispanic Workers in the Garment and Restaurant Industries in Los Angeles County," mimeograph, University of California, San Diego, 1980; and Roger Waldinger, "Ethnic Enterprise and Industrial Change: A Case Study of the New York Garment Industry," Ph.D. diss., Harvard University, 1983.

32. David Hensley, "The Economic Consequences of Mexican Immigration to California," mimeograph, University of California, Los Angeles, May 1988.

33. The impact of Mexican immigration in California is also analyzed by Kevin F. McCarthy and R. Burciaga Valdez, *Current and Future Effects of Mexican Immigration in California* (Santa Monica, Calif.: Rand Corporation, 1986).

Chapter 6

1. For an interesting discussion of these views, see Richard D. Lamm and Gary Imhoff, *The Immigration Time Bomb: The Fragmenting of America* (New York: E. P. Dutton, 1985).

2. The classic presentation of the assimilation hypothesis is contained in Milton Gordon, *Assimilation and American Life* (New York: Oxford University Press, 1964).

Notes

3. Doubts about the generality of the assimilation experience were first raised by observers who noted that many immigrant groups retain language and cultural habits well beyond the first and second generations. See Nathan Glazer and Daniel P. Moynihan, *Beyond the Melting Pot: The Negroes, Puerto Ricans, Jews, Italians, and Irish of New York City* (Cambridge, Mass.: M.I.T. Press, 1963); and Andrew Greely, *Why Can't They Be Like Us? America's White Ethnic Groups* (New York: E. P. Dutton, 1971).

4. Glazer and Moynihan, *Beyond the Melting Pot*, p. xcvii.

5. A clear discussion of the historical evidence on the extent of economic assimilation experienced by immigrants is given by John Bodnar, *The Transplanted: A History of Immigration in Urban America* (Bloomington: Indiana University Press, 1985), pp. 169–75.

6. Ibid., pp. 170–71.

7. For the most part, the literature focuses on the rate of economic mobility experienced by first-generation immigrants, not on the experiences of the children and grandchildren of immigrants. The important question of intergenerational transfers of skills and financial resources within immigrant families has not been carefully analyzed, due mainly to the lack of data. For a theoretical analysis of these important issues, see Gary S. Becker, *A Treatise on the Family* (Cambridge, Mass.: Harvard University Press, 1981). Preliminary empirical studies of intergenerational mobility in immigrant households are given by Geoffrey Carliner, "Wages, Earnings, and Hours of First, Second, and Third Generation American Males," *Economic Inquiry* 18 (January 1980): 87–102; and Barry R. Chiswick, "Sons of Immigrants: Are They at an Earnings Disadvantage?" *American Economic Review, Papers and Proceedings* 67 (February 1977): 376–80.

8. For a study that jointly analyzes economic and cultural assimilation, see Douglas S. Massey, "The Settlement Process Among Mexican Migrants to the United States," *American Sociological Review* 51 (October 1986): 670–84.

9. The most influential study is by Barry R. Chiswick, "The Effect of Americanization on the Earnings of Foreign-Born Men," *Journal of Political Economy* 86 (October 1978): 897–921. Related studies include Francine Blau, "Immigration and Labor Earnings in Early Twentieth Century America," *Research in Population Economics* 2 (1980): 21–41; Carliner, "Wages, Earnings, and Hours"; Gregory DeFreitas, "The Earnings of Immigrants in the American Labor Market" (Ph.D. diss., Columbia University, 1980); and James E. Long, "The Effect of Americanization on Earnings: Some Evidence for Women," *Journal of Political Economy* 88 (June 1980): 620–29.

10. Chiswick, "Effect of Americanization." The age/earnings profiles illustrated in figure 6.1 refer to men aged twenty-five to sixty-four who are employed in the civilian, salaried sector. This data restriction, unless otherwise indicated, will be used throughout the empirical analysis reported in this chapter and in chapters 7 and 8. The study of the labor market experiences of self-employed immigrants is deferred until chapter 10.

11. This hypothesis is proposed by Chiswick, "Effect of Americanization." Basically, Chiswick assumes that immigrants have greater incentives to invest in human capital than natives. The greater investment rates by immigrants "explain" their steeper age/earnings profiles because, by assumption, earnings increase faster the greater the accumulation of human capital. The classic expositions of the human capital model are presented in Gary S. Becker, *Human Capital*, 2d ed. (New York: Columbia University Press, 1975); and Jacob Mincer, *Schooling, Experience, and Earnings* (New York: Columbia University Press, 1974).

12. Chiswick, "Effect of Americanization," pp. 900–901.

13. Michael J. Greenwood and John M. McDowell, "The Factor Market Consequences of U.S. Immigration," *Journal of Economic Literature* 24 (December 1986): 1738–72, survey this literature. The similarity of the findings among the many studies led some observers to conclude that perhaps a universal law was at work; see, for instance, Barry R. Chiswick, "The Economic Progress of Immigrants: Some Apparently Universal Patterns," in William Fellner, editor, *Contemporary Economic Problems* (Washington, D.C.: American Enterprise Institute, 1979), pp. 375–99. This consensus, however, was greatly affected by the fact that most of the studies were studying the same historical period, namely, the postwar years. A recent study by Barry Eichengreen and Henry A. Gemery, "The Earnings of Skilled and Unskilled Immigrants at the End of the Nineteenth Century," *Journal of Economic History* 46 (June 1986): 441–54, also uses a cross-section data set but analyzes a very different time period. The Eichengreen–Gemery results differ greatly from those obtained by Chiswick and others, in that they conclude that immigrants in the late 1800s experienced relatively small assimilation rates and had significantly lower earnings than comparable natives throughout their entire working lives.

14. The methodological problem with the cross-sectional analysis was noted by George J. Borjas, "Assimilation, Changes in Cohort Quality, and the Earnings of Immigrants," *Journal of Labor Economics* 3 (October 1985): 463–89.

15. Robert Warren and Jennifer Marks Peck, "Foreign-Born Emigration from the United States: 1960 to 1970," *Demography* 17 (February 1980): 71–84; Guillermina Jasso and Mark R. Rosenzweig, "Estimating the Emigration Rates of Legal Immigrants Using Administrative and Survey Data: The 1971 Cohort of Immigrants to the United States," *Demography* 19 (August 1982): 279–90; and Kit Chum Lam, "An Analysis of the Outmigration of Foreign Born Members in a Population" (Ph.D. diss., Harvard University, 1987).

16. Two recent studies attempt to determine the type of selectivity that characterizes the emigrant population. See George J. Borjas, "Immigrant and Emigrant Earnings: A Longitudinal Study," *Economic Inquiry* 27 (January 1989): 21–37; and Guillermina Jasso and Mark R. Rosenzweig, "How Well Do U.S. Immigrants Do? Vintage Effects, Emigration Selectivity, and Occupational Mobility," *Research in Population Economics* 6 (1988): 229–53. Neither of these studies, however, truly observes emigration, but instead infers the return-migration propensities of immigrants either from sample attrition or from naturalization behavior. Moreover, they reach contradictory conclusions. The Jasso–Rosenzweig study concludes that emigrants are successes, while my study concludes the opposite.

17. For examples of this type of analysis, see Borjas, "Assimilation"; idem, "Self-Selection and the Earnings of Immigrants," *American Economic Review* 77 (September 1987): 531–53; idem, "Immigration and Self-Selection," in Richard B. Freeman and John M. Abowd, eds., *Immigration, Trade, and the Labor Market* (Chicago: University of Chicago Press, 1990); idem, "Immigrant and Emigrant Earnings"; Jasso and Rosenzweig, "How Well Do U.S. Immigrants Do?"; and Barry R. Chiswick, "Is the New Immigration Less Skilled than the Old?" *Journal of Labor Economics* 4 (April 1986): 168–92. The technical problem addressed by these studies—namely, the identification of aging, period, and cohort effects—is well known in the demography literature. See John Hobcraft, Jane Menken, and Samuel Preston, "Age, Period, and Cohort Effects in Demography: A Review," *Population Index* 48 (Spring 1982): 4–43; and James J. Heckman and Richard Robb, "Using Longitudinal Data to Estimate Age, Period, and Cohort Effects in Earnings Equations," in H. Winsborough and O. Duncan, eds., *Analyzing Longitudinal Data for Age, Period, and Cohort Effects* (New York: Academic Press, 1983).

18. Of course, the results obtained by tracking immigrant cohorts across censuses are biased by the existence of emigration. As long as the emigrants are nonrandomly selected from the immigrant population, the extent of wage growth exhibited by a specific immigrant cohort across censuses depends on who the emigrants are. The biases introduced by this problem are discussed in detail below.

19. See Borjas, "Assimilation"; idem, "Self-Selection and the Earnings of Immigrants"; and idem, "Immigration and Self-Selection." The emphasis on the earnings determination of immigrant and native men (as opposed to women) is quite common in the literature; for an exception, see Long, "Effect of Americanization." This emphasis is due to the fact that average earnings of working immigrant women are affected not only by the assimilation process but also by their intermittent labor force participation. As women enter, exit, and reenter the labor market over the life cycle, the skill composition of the sample of working women is shifting over time, and earnings comparisons of women at different ages must account for these shifts. This problem raises difficult technical issues. See James J. Heckman, "Shadow Prices, Market Wages, and Labor Supply," *Econometrica* 42 (July 1974): 188–94; idem, "Sample Selection Bias as a Specification Error with an Application to the Estimation of Labor Supply Functions," in James P. Smith, ed., *Female Labor Supply: Theory and Estimation* (Princeton: Princeton University Press, 1980), pp. 206–48; and James J. Heckman and Thomas MaCurdy, "A Life Cycle Model of Female Labor Supply," *Review of Economic Studies* 47 (January 1980): 47–74.

20. In principle, the rate of economic assimilation will vary among the various waves. An important technical assumption in the empirical analysis summarized in figure 6.2 is that the percentage rate of wage growth is the same for all immigrant cohorts. This assumption greatly simplifies the estimation procedure and leads to more statistically reliable estimates of the underlying parameters. For a discussion of differences in the rate of economic assimilation among cohorts, see Borjas, "Assimilation." A second problem with the statistical analysis is that the skill composition of an immigrant cohort changes over time due to the emigration of the foreign-born. Because a large number of immigrants decide to return home or migrate elsewhere, the typical person in the 1965–1969 cohort surveyed by the 1970 Census differs from the typical cohort member who

Notes

remained until the 1980 Census enumeration. The tracking of the labor market performance of that cohort across censuses, therefore, can be seriously contaminated by the selective emigration of some of the cohort members. Suppose that many of the return migrants are likely to have relatively low earnings (in other words, they are labor market failures). In that case, tracking the immigrant wave's earnings across censuses gives too high an assimilation rate. The data available in the 1970 Census reveal a low average wage because the cohort includes a number of individuals who are not doing well and who will eventually emigrate. By 1980, this cohort's average wage increases not only because of assimilation but also because a large number of low-wage persons vanished from the sample. Thus, the average wage growth calculated from census data overestimates the true rate of labor market assimilation. To the extent that failures leave the United States, the assimilation rates reported here are biased not because they are too low but because they are too high.

21. This discussion is based on the analysis of the variation in assimilation rates among forty-one national origin groups. The forty-one countries account for more than 90 percent of all immigration to the United States in the 1951–1980 period. See Borjas, "Self-Selection and the Earnings of Immigrants," table 6.

22. Jacob Mincer and Solomon W. Polachek, "Family Investments in Human Capital: Earnings of Women," *Journal of Political Economy* 82 (March–April 1974 Supplement): S76–S108; and Mary Corcoran and Greg Duncan, "Work History, Labor Force Attachment, and Earnings Differences Between the Races and the Sexes," *Journal of Human Resources* 14 (Winter 1979): 3–20. The applicability of this hypothesis to other groups who enter the labor market at relatively late stages of their life is illustrated by the work of George J. Borjas and Finis Welch, "The Post-Service Earnings of Military Retirees: Evidence from the Air Force," *Research in Labor Economics* 8 (1986): 57–83, who study the adaptation experience of retired military personnel in the civilian labor market. See also Matthew S. Goldberg and John T. Warner, "Military Experience, Civilian Experience, and the Earnings of Veterans," *Journal of Human Resources* 22 (Winter 1987): 62–81.

23. George J. Borjas, "The Earnings of Male Hispanic Immigrants in the United States," *Industrial and Labor Relations Review* 35 (April 1982): 343–53.

24. See Alejandro Portes and Robert L. Bach, *Latin Journey: Cuban and Mexican Immigrants in the United States* (Berkeley: University of California Press, 1985); and Robert L. Bach and Rita Carroll-Seguin, "Labor Force Participation, Household Composition, and Sponsorship Among Southeast Asian Refugees," *International Migration Review* 20 (Summer 1986): 381–404, for studies of the refugee experience.

25. This argument also implies that persons who originate in countries that are very distant from the United States should have higher assimilation incentives than persons originating in nearby countries. The closer the home country, the lower the costs of return migration, hence the less the incentives to adapt quickly to the host country's labor market. Because of the modern advances in transportation, however, mobility costs may not vary sufficiently to create differential incentives among national-origin groups, and the empirical evidence on this point is mixed. The work of Oscar Lewis, however, suggests that back-and-forth migration between Puerto Rico and New York City is an important factor in explaining the relatively poor labor market performance of Puerto Ricans in the United States; see *La Vida* (New York: Random House, 1965).

26. Labor market assimilation rates also depend on the age at which the immigrants arrive in the United States. Persons who migrate during their childhood and go through the U.S. educational system closely resemble the typical native by the time they enter the labor market, hence there is little reason to expect any further assimilation to take place. Immigrants arriving in the United States as adults, by contrast, have the most to gain from learning about the U.S. labor market and tend to have the highest rates of labor market assimilation.

27. Chiswick, "Effect of Americanization," p. 908.

28. Walter S. McManus, William Gould, and Finis Welch, "Earnings of Hispanic Men: The Role of English Language Proficiency," *Journal of Labor Economics* 1 (April 1983): 101–30. See also Gilles Grenier, "The Effects of Language Characteristics on the Wages of Hispanic-American Males," *Journal of Human Resources* 19 (Winter 1984): 35–52; and Sherrie A. Kossoudji, "English Language Ability and the Labor Market Opportunities of Hispanic and East Asian Men," *Journal of Labor Economics* 6 (April 1988): 205–228.

29. Walter S. McManus, "Labor Market Costs of Language Disparity: An Interpretation of Hispanic Earnings Differences," *American Economic Review* 75 (September 1985): 818–27.

30. See Walter S. McManus, "Labor Market Effects of Ethnic Enclaves: Hispanic Men in the United States" (mimeograph, University of Florida, April 1987); and Guillermina Jasso and Mark R. Rosenzweig, "English Language Skill Acquisition, Locational Choice and Labor Market Returns Among the Major Foreign-Born Language Groups in the United States in 1900 and 1980," mimeograph, University of Minnesota, October 1987.
31. Alejandro Portes, "The Social Origins of the Cuban Enclave Economy in Miami," *Sociological Perspectives* 30 (October 1987): 340–72, table 2. A thoughtful discussion of the sociology of enclaves is given in Alejandro Portes and Robert D. Manning, "The Immigrant Enclave: Theory and Empirical Examples," in J. Nagel and S. Olzak, editors, *Competitive Ethnic Relations* (Orlando, Fla.: Academic Press, 1986), pp. 47–64.
32. Borjas, "Assimilation," table A2.
33. Ann P. Bartel, "Location Decisions of the New Immigrants to the United States," National Bureau of Economic Research Working Paper no. 2049 (October 1986); and Ann P. Bartel and Marianne J. Koch, "Internal Migration of U.S. Immigrants," in Freeman and Abowd, eds., *Immigration, Trade, and the Labor Market.*
34. An additional source of wage differentials between the two groups is the fact that American employers are likely to attach different values to the demographic characteristics of immigrants and natives.

Chapter 7

1. The contrast between the new immigrants and earlier immigrant waves has a long history in the debate over immigration policy. See, for instance, the work of Paul H. Douglas, "Is the New Immigration More Unskilled than the Old?" *Journal of the American Statistical Association* 16 (June 1919): 393–403; and C. C. Brigham, *A Study of American Intelligence* (Princeton, N. J.: Princeton University Press, 1923).
2. This assumption implies that labor supply differences between immigrants and natives, as well as within the immigrant population, are being held constant, so that differences in lifetime earnings among the groups only reflect the impact of variations in the wage rate. Chapter 8 presents a complementary analysis of differences in the labor market attachment of the various groups.
3. Future earnings are discounted because $1 received next year is worth less than $1 received today. After all, $1 received today can be put in the bank and, at a 5-percent interest rate, will be worth $1.05 next year. Hence, a future payment of $1 is discounted so that its present value is really only 95.2 cents (that is, the deposit of 95.2 cents in the bank today leads to a $1 payment next year).
4. See George J. Borjas, "Immigration and Self-Selection," in Richard B. Freeman and John M. Abowd, eds., *Immigration, Trade, and the Labor Market* (Chicago: University of Chicago Press, 1990), tables 3 and 6; and idem, "Self-Selection and the Earnings of Immigrants," *American Economic Review* 77 (September 1987): 531–53.
5. For a discussion of these changes in the national-origin composition of the immigrant flow, see George J. Borjas, "Immigrants in the U.S. Labor Market: 1940–1980" (mimeograph, University of California, Santa Barbara, September 1988).
6. Barry R. Chiswick, "Is the New Immigration as Skilled as the Old?" *Journal of Labor Economics* 4 (April 1986), table 4.
7. Borjas, "Immigration and Self-Selection," table 2.
8. The private rate of return to higher education characterizing the source country of the typical immigrant in the 1950s was .17, and .19 in the 1970s. International differences in the rate of return to schooling are documented by George Psacharopoulos, *Returns to Education: An International Comparison* (San Francisco: Jossey-Bass, 1973).
9. Borjas, "Immigration and Self-Selection."
10. See Gary S. Becker, *Human Capital,* 2d ed. (New York: Columbia University Press, 1975).
11. Borjas, "Immigration and Self-Selection," table 5; and Guillermina Jasso and Mark R. Rosenzweig, "What's in a Name? Country-of-Origin Influences on the Earnings of Immigrants in the United States," *Research in Human Capital and Development* 4 (1986): 75–106.

Notes

12. The economics of the brain drain are discussed in Walter Adams, *The Brain Drain* (New York: Macmillan, 1968), and in Jagdish N. Bhagwati and Martin Partington, *Taxing the Brain Drain: A Proposal* (Amsterdam: North-Holland, 1976). A recent theoretical analysis of the brain drain which resembles the immigration market approach is given by Viem Kwok and Hayne Leland, "An Economic Model of the Brain Drain," *American Economic Review* 72 (March 1982): 91–100. Empirical studies of the migration of professionals to the United States include Vinod B. Agarwal and Donald R. Winkler, "Migration of Professional Manpower to the United States," *Southern Economic Journal* 50 (January 1984): 814–30; and Wei-Chiao Huang, "A Pooled Cross-Section and Time-Series Study of Professional Indirect Immigration to the United States," *Southern Economic Journal* 54 (July 1987): 95–109.

13. Borjas, "Immigration and Self-Selection."

14. J. Edward Taylor, "Undocumented Mexico–U.S. Migration and the Returns to Households in Rural Mexico," *American Journal of Agricultural Economics* 69 (August 1987): 626–38.

15. World Bank, *World Development Report, 1988* (New York: Oxford University Press, 1988), pp. 272–73.

16. The typical person who migrated in the 1950s originated in a country in which the ratio of income accruing to the top 10 percent of the households to the income accruing to the bottom 20 percent of the households was 11.2. The typical person who migrated in the 1970s originated in a country in which this measure of income inequality was 16.1.

17. Borjas, "Immigration and Self-Selection," table 5.

18. Ibid.

19. See the studies in Richard B. Freeman and David A. Wise, editors, *The Youth Labor Market Problem: Its Nature, Causes, and Consequences* (Chicago: University of Chicago Press, 1982); and Richard B. Freeman, *The Overeducated American* (New York: Academic Press, 1976).

20. This approach seems to be quite common in studies of the refugee experience. See, for instance, the studies included in "Refugees: Issues and Directions," *International Migration Review* 20 (Summer 1986).

21. Borjas, "Self-Selection and the Earnings of Immigrants."

22. Borjas, "Immigration and Self-Selection," table 6. An excellent analysis of the Cuban refugee experience is given by Alejandro Portes and Robert L. Bach, *Latin Journey: Cuban and Mexican Immigrants in the United States* (Berkeley: University of California Press, 1985).

23. Gary S. Becker, *The Economics of Discrimination*, 2d ed. (Chicago: University of Chicago, 1974). A recent survey of the voluminous literature on employment discrimination is given by Glen S. Cain, "The Economic Analysis of Labor Market Discrimination: A Survey," in Orley C. Ashenfelter and Richard Layard, editors, *Handbook of Labor Economics*, vol. 1 (Amsterdam: North-Holland, 1986), pp. 693–785.

24. For a discussion of the many flaws in this interpretation of the empirical evidence, see George J. Borjas, "Discrimination in HEW: Is the Doctor Sick or Are the Patients Healthy?" *Journal of Law and Economics* 21 (April 1978): 97–110.

25. See Cain, "Economic Analysis," p. 762, for a review of this literature.

26. Cordelia W. Reimers, "Labor Market Discrimination Against Hispanic and Black Men," *Review of Economics and Statistics* 65 (November 1983), table 1. See also James D. Gwartney and James E. Long, "The Relative Earnings of Blacks and Other Minorities," *Industrial and Labor Relations Review* 31 (April 1978): 336–46; and Walter S. McManus, William Gould, and Finis Welch, "Earnings of Hispanic Men: The Role of English Language Proficiency," *Journal of Labor Economics* 1 (April 1983): 101–30.

27. Barry R. Chiswick, "An Analysis of the Earnings and Employment of Asian-American Men," *Journal of Labor Economics* 1 (April 1983): 197–214.

28. A number of variations of this basic assumption are used in the studies. Some net out the impact of the cycle on immigrant wages by using the wage growth experienced by white natives, while others allow different national-origin groups to have different period effects and define the period effect experienced by the immigrant in terms of the period effect experienced by a native group with the same ethnic background. See Borjas, "Immigration and Self-Selection," for details.

29. See Richard B. Freeman, "Black Economic Progress After 1964: Who Has Gained and Why?" in Sherwin Rosen, editor, *Studies in Labor Markets* (Chicago: University of Chicago Press, 1981), pp. 247–94; James J. Heckman and Brook S. Payner, "Determining the Impact of Federal Antidiscrimination Policy on the Economic Status of Blacks: A Study of South Carolina,"

American Economic Review 79 (March 1989): 138–77; and Jonathan Leonard, "The Effectiveness of Equal Employment Law and Affirmative Action Regulations," *Research in Labor Economics* 8 (1986, Part B): 319–50.

30. Douglas, "Is the New Immigration More Unskilled?" p. 403.

Chapter 8

1. See Richard D. Lamm and Gary Imhoff, *The Immigration Time Bomb: The Fragmenting of America* (New York: E. P. Dutton, 1985), p. 159.

2. The labor force participation rate is defined as the fraction of individuals in the population who are either employed or actively looking for work in the census week. The unemployment rate gives the fraction of labor force participants who are not employed but are instead actively looking for work. Only persons who are in the labor force are included in the calculation of the unemployment rate. Finally, annual hours of work are given by the average number of hours worked in the calendar year prior to the census, where the average is calculated in the subsample of workers.

3. See Mark R. Killingsworth, *Labor Supply* (New York: Cambridge University Press, 1983), for a comprehensive survey of the voluminous economic literature that analyzes the labor supply decision.

4. There are relatively few studies of immigrant labor supply. See George J. Borjas, "The Labor Supply of Male Hispanic Immigrants in the United States," *International Migration Review* 17 (Winter 1983/1984): 653–71; Geoffrey Carliner, "Wages, Earnings, and Hours of First, Second, and Third Generation Immigrants," *Economic Inquiry* 18 (January 1980): 87–102; and Barry R. Chiswick, *The Employment of Immigrants in the United States* (Washington, D.C.: American Enterprise Institute, 1982), who also presents an extensive discussion of the way the assimilation process affects employment outcomes.

5. Kim Clark and Lawrence H. Summers, "Demographic Differences in Cyclical Employment Variation," *Journal of Human Resources* 16 (Winter 1981): 61–79; and Ronald G. Ehrenberg, "The Demographic Structure of Unemployment Rates and Labor Market Transition Probabilities," *Research in Labor Economics* 3 (1980): 241–93.

6. The analysis of labor supply reported here is restricted to immigrant and native men. It is well known that the employment experiences of men differ from those of women. Women tend to have much lower participation rates and are more likely to be engaged in part-time work than men. Of course, the key factor creating gender differences in labor supply is that many women withdraw from the labor force in order to raise children, and, if they work, they tend to be in part-time jobs while the children are relatively young. Differences in labor supply behavior between immigrant and native women (as well as within the female immigrant population) reflect not only the differences in labor force attachment but also the impact of differential fertility behavior among the groups. The employment histories of immigrant and native men, by contrast, are not complicated by the frequency and timing of the household's fertility history, and they provide a clearer description of the differences in work incentives that arise solely because of the immigrant experience. For general discussions of female labor supply, see Killingsworth, *Labor Supply*, and Mark R. Killingsworth and James J. Heckman, "Female Labor Supply: A Survey," in Orley C. Ashenfelter and Richard Layard, editors, *Handbook of Labor Economics*, vol. 1 (Amsterdam: North-Holland, 1986), pp. 103–204. Preliminary studies of the labor supply decision of immigrant women include Paul M. Ong, "Immigrant Wives' Labor Force Participation," *Industrial Relations* 26 (Fall 1987): 296–303; and Cordelia Reimers, "Cultural Differences in Labor Force Participation Among Married Women," *American Economic Review* 65 (May 1985): 251–55.

7. U.S. Bureau of the Census, *Statistical Abstract of the United States, 1986* (Washington, D.C.: Government Printing Office, 1985), p. 392.

8. There is a problem with the data on annual hours of work reported by the census for the most recent immigrant cohorts, for the data refer to hours of work in the calendar year prior to the census. Some of the men in the most recent immigrant cohort arrived sometime during that calendar year. Hence they were unable to work a full year, which may bias some of the results.

9. Labor market conditions deteriorated substantially between 1970 and 1980, and immigrants may be particularly sensitive to adverse economic conditions. The comparisons among successive immigrant cohorts reported in table 8.1 may be biased if the impact of business-cycle

fluctuations on immigrants' employment opportunities are not properly accounted for. To determine the sensitivity of the results to differential period effects, I also allowed the period effects experienced by immigrants to be the same as those of blacks or Hispanic natives, groups who are presumably more sensitive to the worsening labor market conditions, instead of white natives (which is the group used in the calculations presented in the table). The results of these experiments indicate that the most recent immigrant cohort has lower labor force participation rates and lower annual hours of work even if the business cycle affected immigrant labor supply to the same extent that it affected the labor supply of black or Hispanic natives.

10. George J. Borjas, "Immigrants in the U.S. Labor Market: 1940–1980" (mimeograph, September 1988), table 7.

11. The reason is that immigrants work many fewer hours than natives in the first few years after immigration. The annual earnings of immigrants in these years are likely to be quite low, particularly because these are also the years in which immigrant wage rates are at their minimum. By discounting future earnings, present value calculations attach a greater weight to earnings soon after immigration and a lesser weight to earnings in the future. These calculations thus lead to a substantial worsening of immigrant labor market performance.

12. In particular, at a 5-percent rate of discount, the present value of an earnings stream of $5,000 per year for forty-five years (from ages twenty to sixty-five) is approximately $90,000.

13. Approximately 1.14 million men entered the United States legally between 1975 and 1979, and an additional 514,000 male illegal aliens were enumerated in the 1980 Census. See U.S. Immigration and Naturalization Service, *Statistical Yearbook of the Immigration and Naturalization Service* (Washington, D.C.: Government Printing Office, annual); and Robert Warren and Jeffrey S. Passel, "A Count of the Uncountable: Estimates of Undocumented Aliens Counted in the 1980 United States Census," *Demography* 24 (August 1987): table 3.

14. Approximately 1.3 million women entered the United States legally between 1975 and 1979, and Warren and Passel report the entry of an additional 400,000 undocumented women.

15. The empirical evidence in chapter 5 also indicates that new immigrants have a negative impact on the earnings of earlier immigrant waves. This effect will reduce national income somewhat, but in view of the relatively small fraction of the population that is foreign-born, the required adjustment is minor.

16. U.S. Bureau of the Census, *Statistical Abstract . . . 1988*, p. 411.

17. Tax Foundation, Inc., *Allocating Tax Burdens and Government Benefits by Income Class, 1972–73 and 1977*, Government Finance Brief No. 31 (Washington, D.C., February 1981), p. 3. See also James R. Hines, Jr., "What is Benefit Taxation?" (mimeograph, Princeton University, March 1988); and Peter J. Lambert and Wilhelm Pfahler, "On Aggregate Measures of the Net Redistributive Impact of Taxation and Government Expenditure," *Public Finance Quarterly* 16 (April 1988): 198–202.

18. For interesting discussions of poverty in the United States, see Sheldon H. Danziger and Daniel H. Weinberg, eds., *Fighting Poverty: What Works and What Doesn't* (Cambridge, Mass.: Harvard University Press, 1986); and David T. Ellwood, *Poor Support: Poverty in the American Family* (New York: Basic Books, 1988).

19. The poverty rates are calculated using all persons surveyed by the censuses. Therefore, they include men and women in all age groups. For a detailed analysis of poverty in the immigrant population, see Leif Jensen, "Poverty and Immigration in the United States: 1960–1980," in Gary D. Sandefur and Marta Tienda, *Divided Opportunities: Minorities, Poverty, and Social Policy* (New York: Plenum Press, 1988): 117–37.

Chapter 9

1. There are now available a number of important studies of the economic and social impacts of entitlement programs. They include George Gilder, *Wealth and Poverty* (New York: Basic Books, 1981); Charles Murray, *Losing Ground: American Social Policy, 1950–1980* (New York: Basic Books, 1984); and David Ellwood, *Poor Support: Poverty in the American Family* (New York: Basic Books, 1988). A recent survey of the voluminous academic literature on poverty and income-transfer programs is given by Isabel V. Sawhill, "Poverty in the U.S.: Why Is It So Persistent?" *Journal of Economic Literature* 26 (September 1988): 1073–119. None of these studies analyzes the extent to which immigrants participate in entitlement programs.

2. The analysis reported throughout this chapter originates in George J. Borjas and Stephen J. Trejo, "Immigrant Participation in the Welfare System" (mimeograph, University of California, Santa Barbara, September 1988).

3. A few systematic studies of this important problem exist. They include Francine D. Blau, "The Use of Transfer Payments by Immigrants," *Industrial and Labor Relations Review* 37 (January 1984): 222–39; Borjas and Trejo, "Immigrant Participation"; Marta Tienda and Leif Jensen, "Immigration and Public Assistance Participation: Dispelling the Myth of Dependency," *Social Science Research* 15 (December 1986): 372–400; Leif Jensen, "Patterns of Immigration and Public Assistance Utilization, 1970–1980," *International Migration Review* 22 (Spring 1988): 51–83; and Lenna Kennedy and Jack Schmulowitz, "SSI Payments to Lawfully Resident Aliens, 1978–79," *Social Security Bulletin* 43 (March 1980): 3–10. A survey of the literature and a discussion of the key policy issues are given by George J. Borjas and Marta Tienda, "The Economic Consequences of Immigration," *Science* 235 (February 6, 1987): 645–51.

4. Quoted in Blau, "Use of Transfer Payments," p. 222.

5. Tienda and Jensen, "Immigration and Public Assistance Participation," p. 373; Richard D. Lamm and Gary Imhoff, *The Immigration Time Bomb: The Fragmenting of America* (New York: E. P. Dutton, 1985), p. 159.

6. Lamm and Imhoff, *The Immigration Time Bomb*, p. 185.

7. For a formal development of a theoretical model that incorporates the welfare system into the immigration decision, see Borjas and Trejo, "Immigrant Participation."

8. U.S. Bureau of the Census, *Statistical Abstract of the United States, 1986* (Washington, D.C.: Government Printing Office, 1985), p. 842.

9. This argument ignores the fact that the welfare system must be funded through taxation and that progressive income taxation will adversely affect the immigration incentives of highly skilled workers.

10. I use the census definition of a "household"—a group of persons living in the same housing unit—throughout. Clearly this definition allows for the possibility that the household contains a number of persons who are unrelated to the household head. The results presented in this chapter are not affected by this fact. See Borjas and Trejo, "Immigrant Participation."

11. The census also provides information on the household's participation in the Social Security system. The household's receipt of Social Security income, however, is mainly a function of the age of its members and is not means-tested. Differences between the participation of immigrants and natives in the system, therefore, almost completely depend on the age distribution of the two groups. Because a large fraction of immigrants are sixty-five years or older, it is not surprising that the typical immigrant household is much more likely to be receiving Social Security than the typical native household (see chapter 3). For a discussion of immigrant participation in social insurance programs, see Blau, "Use of Transfer Payments."

12. The household head's country of birth determines whether the household is an immigrant or a native one. Further, the head's country of birth and year of immigration also determine the household's national-origin and cohort classifications.

13. The fraction of female-headed households is 28 percent in both the immigrant and the native populations.

14. E. P. Hutchinson, *Legislative History of American Immigration Policy* (Philadelphia: University of Pennsylvania Press, 1981), p. 450.

15. Milton D. Morris, *Immigration—The Beleaguered Bureaucracy* (Washington, D.C.: The Brookings Institution, 1985), p. 46.

16. Of course, these recent legal restrictions on immigrant participation in the welfare system cannot explain the empirical results, because the data refer to the pre-1980 period.

17. In particular, the differences in welfare participation rates among cohorts become much smaller after controlling for the immigrant's country of origin. See Borjas and Trejo, "Immigrant Participation," table 3. It would also be useful to study differences in the duration of welfare spells between immigrants and natives, as well as within the immigrant population. This type of analysis would help determine whether the same immigrant households remain on welfare over time or there is a lot of mobility into and out of welfare. Unfortunately, longitudinal surveys with relatively large samples of immigrants are required for this type of analysis, and such surveys are not yet in existence.

18. Borjas and Trejo, "Immigrant Participation," table 3.

Notes

19. Unfortunately, this is the question that has dominated much of the econometric research on the problem. See, for instance, Blau, "Use of Transfer Payments"; and Tienda and Jensen, "Immigration and Public Assistance Participation."

20. Borjas and Trejo, "Immigrant Participation," table 6.

21. The skill composition of the immigrant flow also depends on the extent of inequality in the source country's income distribution. The immigrant flow entering the United States is likely to be relatively skilled when it originates in a country with an egalitarian income distribution, because the United States then offers a higher price for skills than the source country does. Alternatively, the immigrant flow is likely to be relatively unskilled when it originates in a country with substantial income inequality, because economic opportunities in the source country are particularly favorable to skilled workers. This correspondence suggests that the bigger the differences in earnings inequality between the source country and the United States, the bigger the differential in skill prices between the countries, and the more likely immigration is to be a result of individuals searching for better employment opportunities, not searching for relatively generous welfare payments. See Borjas and Trejo, "Immigrant Participation."

22. U.S. Social Security Administration, Office of Refugee Resettlement, *Refugee Resettlement Program, Annual Report, FY 1982* (Washington, D.C.: Government Printing Office, 1983), p. 25.

23. Borjas and Trejo, "Immigrant Participation," table 6.

24. Ibid., table 5 shows that controlling for demographic characteristics accounts for most of the differences in welfare incomes between immigrant and native households.

25. U.S. Department of Commerce, *Statistical Abstract of the United States, 1982–1983* (Washington, D.C.: Government Printing Office, 1982), p. 319.

26. U.S. Department of Commerce, *Statistical Abstract of the United States, 1988* (Washington, D.C.: Government Printing Office, 1987), p. 334.

27. Julian Simon, "Immigrants, Taxes, and Welfare in the United States," *Population and Development Review* 10 (March 1984): 55–69. For related work, see Sidney Weintraub, "Illegal Immigrants in Texas: Impact on Social Services and Related Considerations," *International Migration Review* 18 (Fall 1984): 733–47.

Chapter 10

1. Until very recently, the study of the self-employment sector, whether of immigrants or of natives, has been basically ignored by labor economists. Among the few studies that contain analyses of various aspects of the self-employment decision are David M. Blau, "A Time-Series Analysis of Self-Employment in the United States," *Journal of Political Economy* 95 (June 1987): 445–67; George J. Borjas, "The Self-Employment Experience of Immigrants," *Journal of Human Resources* 21 (Fall 1986): 485–506; George J. Borjas and Stephen G. Bronars, "Consumer Discrimination and Self-Employment," *Journal of Political Economy* 97 (June 1989): 581–605; David S. Evans and Linda S. Leighton, "Some Empirical Aspects of Entrepreneurship," *American Economic Review*, 79 (June 1989): 519–35; Edward P. Lazear and Robert L. Moore, "Incentives, Productivity, and Labor Contracts," *Quarterly Journal of Economics* 99 (May 1984): 275–95; and Andrew M. Yuengert, "Self-Employment and the Earnings of Male Immigrants" (mimeograph, Yale University, November 1988). The sociological literature, by contrast, has traditionally been more attentive to the important role played by self-employment in the labor market, and particularly of the role played by ethnic enclaves in determining the self-employment propensities and incomes of immigrants. For examples of this approach, see Ivan Light, *Ethnic Enterprise in America* (Berkeley: University of California Press, 1972); Edna Bonacich and John Modell, *The Economic Basis of Ethnic Solidarity: Small Business in the Japanese-American Community* (Berkeley: University of California Press, 1980); and Alejandro Portes and Robert D. Manning, "The Immigrant Enclave: Theory and Empirical Examples," in J. Nagel and S. Olzak, eds., *Competitive Ethnic Relations* (Orlando, Fla.: Academic Press, 1986), pp. 47–64.

2. Borjas, "Self-Employment Experience," table 2.

3. See Borjas and Bronars, "Consumer Discrimination and Self-Employment"; Evans and Leighton, "Some Empirical Aspects of Entrepreneurship"; and Lazear and Moore, "Incentives, Productivity, and Labor Contracts."

Notes

4. Borjas and Bronars, "Consumer Discrimination and Self-Employment," table 3.
5. Ibid.
6. Ibid.
7. The impact of assimilation on self-employment rates is determined by tracking the self-employment propensities of a specific immigrant cohort between the 1970 and 1980 Censuses after controlling for any changes in self-employment rates due to changes in economic conditions (namely, the change in self-employment rates experienced by the native population). For details, see Borjas, "Self-Employment Experience."
8. For studies of other immigrant enclaves, see Bonacich and Modell, *Economic Basis of Ethnic Solidarity;* Illsoo Kim, *New Urban Immigrants: The Korean Community in New York* (Princeton, N.J.: Princeton University Press, 1981); Moses Rischin, *The Promised City: New York Jews, 1870–1914* (Cambridge, Mass.: Harvard University Press, 1962); William I. Thomas and Florian Znaniecki, *The Polish Peasant in Europe and America* (New York: Knopf, 1927); and Kenneth L. Wilson and W. Allen Martin, "Ethnic Enclaves: A Comparison of the Cuban and Black Economies in Miami," *American Journal of Sociology* (September 1982): 135–60. For an interesting discussion of many aspects of Miami's Cuban enclave and its impact on the surrounding community, see Joan Didion, *Miami* (New York: Pocket Books, 1987).
9. Alejandro Portes and Robert L. Bach, *Latin Journey: Cuban and Mexican Immigrants in the United States* (Berkeley: University of California Press, 1985); Portes and Manning, "The Immigrant Enclave"; Alejandro Portes and Alex Stepick, "Unwelcome Immigrants: The Labor Market Experiences of 1980 (Mariel) Cuban and Haitian Refugees in South Florida," *American Sociological Review* 50 (August 1985): 493–514; Alejandro Portes, "The Social Origins of the Cuban Enclave Economy of Miami," *Sociological Perspectives* 30 (October 1987): 340–72; and Alejandro Portes and Joszef Borocz, "Contemporary Immigration: Theoretical Perspectives on Its Determinants and Modes of Incorporation," *International Migration Review,* forthcoming.
10. Portes, "Social Origins of the Cuban Enclave Economy," p. 351.
11. Borjas, "Self-Employment Experience." A related study of the economic effects of ethnic enclaves, though it does not directly address the interaction between enclaves and self-employment, is given by Walter S. McManus, "Labor Market Effects of Ethnic Enclaves: Hispanic Men in the United States" (mimeograph, University of Florida, April 1987).
12. Borjas, "Self-Employment Experience," p. 503. I should add that although the Hispanic immigrant population is composed of a number of different national-origin groups, these groups are much more homogeneous in culture and in language than immigrants from other areas, and thus the concept of a "Hispanic enclave" has economic and social relevance.
13. Borjas and Bronars, "Consumer Discrimination and Self-Employment," table 2.
14. Portes, "Social Origins of the Cuban Enclave Economy," table 2.
15. Alejandro Portes and Robert L. Bach, "Immigrant Earnings: Cuban and Mexican Immigrants in the United States," *International Migration Review* 14 (Fall 1980): table 2.
16. This result is obtained from a regression estimated in the sample of working immigrants in the 1980 Census. The dependent variable is the logarithm of annual incomes, and the regression holds constant education, age, marital status, and year of immigration. The statistic reported in the text is the percentage differential in annual incomes implied by the coefficient of the variable indicating self-employment status.
17. The fact that self-employed workers earn less than salaried workers, even among natives, has been noted in the literature. See Lazear and Moore, "Incentives, Productivity, and Labor Contracts."
18. An excellent discussion of the theory of compensating differentials is given by Sherwin Rosen, "The Theory of Equalizing Differences," in Orley C. Ashenfelter and Richard Layard, *Handbook of Labor Economics,* vol. 1 (Amsterdam: North-Holland, 1986), pp. 641–92.
19. This argument is developed at length in Borjas and Bronars, "Consumer Discrimination and Self-Employment."
20. Ibid., table 4.
21. Alan B. Krueger and Lawrence H. Summers, "Efficiency Wages and the Inter-Industry Wage Structure," *Econometrica* 56 (March 1988): 259–93.
22. Internal Revenue Service, *Estimates of Income Unreported on Individual Income Tax Returns* (Washington, D.C.: Government Printing Office, 1979).
23. For an analysis of the misreporting of wages in the Current Population Surveys, see Lee Lillard, James P. Smith, and Finis Welch, "What Do We Really Know about Wages? The

Notes

Importance of Nonreporting and Census Imputation," *Journal of Political Economy* 94 (June 1986): 489–506.

24. For evidence of the very high transition rates of individuals between the self-employment and salaried sectors, see Evans and Leighton, "Some Empirical Aspects of Entrepreneurship."

Chapter 11

1. In addition, the visas allocated to the skill or occupational preferences include visas not just for the principals (the persons qualifying under the skill and occupational restrictions) but also for the spouses and children of the principals.

2. The value of these information flows within the family network is stressed in the work of Douglas S. Massey, "Social Structure, Household Strategies, and the Cumulative Causation of Migration" (mimeograph, University of Chicago, May 1988).

3. U.S. Select Commission on Immigration and Refugee Policy, *Final Report: U.S. Immigration Policy and the National Interest* (Washington, D.C.: Government Printing Office, 1981), pp. 335–41.

4. For an interesting analysis of the way that family ties among persons in a population can quickly multiply across successive generations, see B. Douglas Bernheim and Kyle Bagwell, "Is Everything Neutral?" *Journal of Political Economy* 96 (April 1988): 308–38.

5. U.S. Department of State, *1984 Report of the Visa Office* (Washington, D.C.: Government Printing Office, 1986), p. 112.

6. U.S. Bureau of the Census, *Statistical Abstract of the United States, 1986* (Washington, D.C.: Government Printing Office, 1985), p. 87.

7. Guillermina Jasso and Mark R. Rosenzweig, "Family Reunification and the Immigration Multiplier: U.S. Immigration Law, Origin-Country Conditions, and the Reproduction of Immigrants," *Demography* 23 (August 1986): 291–311.

8. U.S. Immigration and Naturalization Service, *Annual Report of the Immigration and Naturalization Service, 1965* (Washington, D.C.: Government Printing Office, 1965), p. 34.

9. U.S. Bureau of the Census, *1970 Census of Population, Characteristics of the Population* (Washington, D.C.: Government Printing Office, 1972), p. 600.

10. The long-run multiplier is a geometric sum, and the formula for the long-run multiplier is $m/(1-m)$, where m is the short-run multiplier.

11. Jasso and Rosenzweig, "Family Reunification and the Immigration Multiplier," p. 298.

12. Ibid., pp. 291–311.

13. Ibid., tables 5 and 6.

14. A classic discussion of the social and economic behavior of the family unit is given by Gary S. Becker, *A Treatise on the Family* (Cambridge, Mass.: Harvard University Press, 1981). The role of the family network in motivating international migration decisions is stressed by Douglas S. Massey and Felipe Garcia España, "The Social Process of International Migration," *Science* 237 (August 14, 1987): 733–38; and George J. Borjas and Stephen G. Bronars, "Immigration and the Family," mimeograph, University of California, Santa Barbara, January 1989.

15. Josh Reichert and Douglas S. Massey, "Patterns of U.S. Migration from a Mexican Sending Community: A Comparison of Legal and Illegal Migrants," *International Migration Review* 11 (Winter 1979): 599–623.

16. Massey and España, "Social Process of International Migration."

17. For details on the construction of these data, see Borjas and Bronars, "Immigration and the Family."

18. Ibid., table 4. The estimates of the incidence of chain immigration discussed in the text are likely to underestimate the true extent for two reasons. First, these data are constructed by comparing the immigration dates of relatives residing in the same household as of the census week. In effect, this comparison creates a "household immigration history" that portrays the extent to which immigrants living in the same household belong to different cohorts. It is likely, however, that many immigrant families migrated together but over time formed new family relationships and dissolved old ones, and members of the original family unit dispersed over the United States and set up separate residences. By the time of the census, therefore, there are many chain immigrants who will not reside with their original sponsors, and the frequency of chain immigra-

tion may be much higher than the census statistics indicate. Second, census data only allow the identification of the year of immigration within five-year intervals. It is likely that minichains of immigrant households arriving within the same five-year period exist. The statistics discussed in the text do not account for the existence of these additional chains.

19.   Part of the differences in chain-immigration propensities among national-origin groups may be due to the fact that, for a number of cultural and economic reasons, some immigrant groups are more likely to reside in extended households.

20.   The conceptual framework of the family's immigration decision presented here, along with the empirical evidence summarized below, are due to Borjas and Bronars, "Immigration and the Family." The theoretical model assumes that the earnings of the various household members follow a multivariate normal distribution. It can be shown, however, that the theoretical insights can be derived under various alternative assumptions about the structure of family earnings. Related studies of the family's role in the migration of households within the United States are Jacob Mincer, "Family Migration Decisions," *Journal of Political Economy* 86 (October 1978): 749–73; Julie DaVanzo, *Why Families Move: A Model of the Geographic Mobility of Married Couples*, Rand Corporation Report R-1972-DOL, September 1976; and Steven Sandell, "Women and the Economics of Family Migration," *Review of Economics and Statistics* 59 (November 1977): 406–14.

21.   This approach was introduced into the social-science literature by Gary Becker. Using this key hypothesis, Becker shows that such phenomena as fertility, marriage, divorce, intergenerational income-transfers, love, and even altruism in the animal kingdom can be understood within a single analytical framework. See Gary S. Becker, "A Theory of Social Interactions," *Journal of Political Economy* 82 (December 1974): 1063–91; idem, "A Theory of Marriage," in T. W. Schultz, ed., *Economics of the Family: Marriage, Children, and Human Capital* (Chicago: University of Chicago Press, 1975): 299–344; and idem, *Treatise on the Family.*

22.   The example can be easily extended to the case in which the husband and the wife consider the option of dissolving the family unit. See Gary S. Becker, Elizabeth M. Landes, and Robert T. Michael, "An Economic Analysis of Marital Instability," *Journal of Political Economy* 85 (December 1977): 1141–87; and Borjas and Bronars, "Immigration and the Family."

23.   Mincer, "Family Migration Decisions."

24.   Borjas and Bronars, "Immigration and the Family."

25.   It is well known that married men, regardless of whether they are immigrants, earn more than single men; see Lawrence W. Kenny, "The Accumulation of Human Capital During Marriage by Males," *Economic Inquiry* 21 (April 1983): 223–31; and Sanders Korenman, "Empirical Explorations in the Economics of the Family" (Ph.D. diss., Harvard University, 1988). This wage differential arises because married men can specialize in the labor market, hence they are more likely to accumulate marketable human capital. The differential in earnings between immigrants who were married and those who were single at the time of migration includes the returns to this specialization and may not be indicating anything about the impact of family ties on the skill composition of the immigrant flow. Subtracting out the gains to specialization, however, does not change the basic result: persons who migrated as part of a husband-wife unit are more skilled and are more successful in the U.S. labor market than persons who did not. See Borjas and Bronars, "Immigration and the Family."

26.   Borjas and Bronars, "Immigration and the Family," table 5. The implication of the conceptual framework that single immigrants tend to do relatively better than family immigrants if the immigrant flow originates in countries with egalitarian income distributions is also confirmed by the data.

27.   The fact that immigrants remit large sums of money to family members back in the source countries suggests that indeed incomes in both countries are part of the same "pot." For an analysis of the determinants of remittances by immigrants to households in the source countries, see Sharon Stanton Russell, "Remittances from International Migration: A Review in Perspective," *World Development* 14 (June 1986): 677–96; and Juan Diez-Canedo, "Migration, Return, and Development in Mexico" (Ph.D. diss., Massachusetts Institute of Technology, 1979).

28.   Borjas and Bronars, "Immigration and the Family."

29.   Ibid., table 7.

30.   The conceptual framework also suggests that the first links of immigration chains originating in countries with less income inequality than the United States will be much more successful

Notes

than later links, while the opposite is true for chains originating in countries with more. The empirical evidence suggests that this is indeed the case. For details, see Borjas and Bronars, "Immigration and the Family," table 8.

31. J. Edward Taylor, "Undocumented Mexico–U.S. Migration and the Returns to Households in Rural Mexico," *American Journal of Agricultural Economics* 69 (August 1987): 626–38.

Chapter 12

1. United Nations, *Demographic Indicators of Countries* (New York: United Nations, 1982), p. 44. The 5 million transnational migrants do not include the large (and presumably temporary) population flows from Ethiopia to Somalia in the late 1970s or the movement of guest workers into oil-producing countries in the Middle East.

2. Recent studies that specifically compare the size and composition of the foreign-born population in each of these three host countries include George J. Borjas, *International Differences in the Labor Market Performance of Immigrants* (Kalamazoo, Mich.: W. E. Upjohn Institute for Employment Research, 1988); and Barry R. Chiswick, "Immigration Policies, Source Countries, and Immigrant Skills: Australia, Canada, and the United States" (mimeograph, University of Illinois at Chicago, 1987).

3. Borjas, *International Differences*, table 1.1.

4. Detailed discussions of Canadian immigration policy are given by Monica Boyd, "Immigration Policies and Trends: A Comparison of Canada and the United States," *Demography* 13 (February 1976): 83–104; Charles B. Keely and Patricia J. Elwell, "International Migration: The United States and Canada," in Mary M. Kritz, Charles B. Keely, and Silvano M. Tomasi, editors, *Global Trends in Migration* (New York: Center for Migration Studies, 1981), pp. 181–207; Daniel Kubat, "Canada," in Daniel Kubat, editor, *The Politics of Migration Policies* (New York: Center for Migration Studies, 1979), pp. 19–36; Department of Manpower and Immigration, *The Immigration Program* (Ottawa: Immigration Canada, 1974); and Department of Manpower and Immigration, *The Revised Selection Criteria for Independent Immigrants* (Ottawa: Immigration Canada, 1985).

5. Boyd, "Immigration Policies and Trends," p. 85.

6. Borjas, *International Differences*, table 2.3.

7. Detailed discussions of Australian immigration policy are given by Robert Birrell, "A New Era in Australian Migration Policy," *International Migration Review* 18 (Spring 1984): 65–84; Charles Price, "Australia," in Kubat, editor, *The Politics of Migration Policies*, pp. 3–18; and Jerzy Zubrzycki, "International Migration in Australasia and the South Pacific," in Kritz, Keely, and Tomasi, editors, *Global Trends in Migration*, pp. 158–180.

8. Price, "Australia," p. 4.

9. Ibid., p. 6.

10. In the 1980s, Australian immigration policy also began to emphasize family reunification in its visa-allocation system. For a discussion, see Birrell, "A New Era in Australian Migration Policy."

11. Borjas, *International Differences*, table 2.4.

12. A number of recent studies analyze the labor-market performance of immigrants in Australia or Canada. See John J. Beggs and Bruce J. Chapman, "Immigrant Wage and Unemployment Experience in Australia," in Richard B. Freeman and John M. Abowd, eds., *Immigration, Trade, and the Labor Market* (Chicago: University of Chicago Press, 1990); David E. Bloom and Morley K. Gunderson, "An Analysis of the Earnings of Canadian Immigrants," in Freeman and Abowd, eds., *Immigration, Trade, and the Labor Market;* Borjas, *International Differences;* Chiswick, "Immigration Policies, Source Countries, and Immigrant Skills"; Barry R. Chiswick and Paul Miller, "Immigrant Generation and Income in Australia," *Economic Record* 61 (June 1985): 540–53; Robert G. Gregory, R. Anstie, and E. Klug, "Why Are Low Skilled Immigrants in the U.S. Poorly Paid Relative to Their Australian Counterparts?" in Freeman and Abowd, eds., *Immigration, Trade, and the Labor Market;* Paul Miller, "Immigrant Unemployment in the First Year of Australian Labor Market Activity," *Economic Record* 62 (March 1986): 82–87; and B. B. Tandon, "Earnings Differentials Among Native Born and Foreign Born Residents of Canada," *International Migration Review* 12 (Fall 1978): 406–10.

13. The Australian 1981 Census and the Canadian 1971 Census contain a 1-percent random sample of the population, while the Canadian 1981 Census contains a 2-percent random sample of the population. The empirical analysis reported in the text is based on these sampling proportions. The study uses data on annual earnings as opposed to wage rates because that is the income measure commonly available in the various censuses. Unfortunately, the Australian census only reports total income in the year prior to the census, as opposed to total labor earnings, and it provides no information on the number of hours worked in that calendar year. Further, the income comparisons reported in this chapter are between immigrants and the typical native. Hence the results for the United States differ slightly from those presented in chapters 7 and 8, which focus on the estimation of earnings differentials between immigrants and white natives. For a discussion of data problems encountered in the comparative analysis of the various data sets, see Borjas, *International Differences*, chapter 5.

14. There are, of course, major differences in the labor market institutions of the three host countries, and these institutional differences are likely to have a major impact on the wage-setting process for immigrants and natives. Unionization and centralized wage-setting policies, for instance, are much less important in the United States than in the other host countries. For an interesting discussion of international differences in labor market institutions, see Richard B. Freeman, "Labor Market Institutions, Constraints, and Performance," National Bureau of Economic Research Working Paper no. 2560, Cambridge, Mass., April 1988; and Keith Whitfield, *The Australian Labor Market* (Sydney: Harper & Row, 1987).

15. The methodological approach tracks immigrant cohorts across censuses to estimate the rate of growth experienced by each of the immigrant cohorts. Because the Australian census data are available only for 1981, it is impossible to track cohorts over time, and instead I use the assumption that the extent of labor market assimilation experienced by the typical immigrant in Australia is the same as the average labor market assimilation rate experienced by a comparable immigrant in Canada or the United States. The calculations were not very sensitive to alternative assumptions. See Borjas, *International Differences*, chaps. 4 and 7, for details.

16. These numbers are tabulated from the 1980 and 1981 census data available in each of the host countries.

17. For evidence on the earnings differential among demographically comparable national-origin groups, see Borjas, *International Differences*, table 7.4.

18. This discussion implicitly assumes that there were similar trends in the skills of the native populations in each of the host countries. Although this assumption is not empirically verifiable, it does not seem unreasonable in view of the similarity in economic development among the three countries.

19. A detailed discussion of these trends, including the role played by the migration of Vietnam draft evaders, is given in Borjas, *International Differences*, chap. 9.

20. For an analysis of the standardized earnings differentials between American immigrants in Canada and Canadian natives, see Borjas, *International Differences*, chap. 9.

21. U.S. Department of Commerce, *Statistical Abstract of the United States, 1986* (Washington, D.C.: Government Printing Office, 1986), pp. 842, 848.

22. Borjas, *International Differences*, p. 92.

Chapter 13

1. Elliott Abrams and Franklin S. Abrams, "Immigration Policy—Who Gets in and Why?" *Public Interest* 38 (Winter 1975): 28.

2. For a preliminary assessment, see Thomas J. Espenshade, Frank D. Bean, Tracy Ann Goodis, and Michael J. White, "Immigration Policy in the United States: Future Prospects for the Immigration Reform and Control Act of 1986" (mimeograph, The Urban Institute, October 1988).

3. Barry R. Chiswick, "Illegal Immigration and Immigration Control," *Journal of Economic Perspectives* 2 (Summer 1988): 101–15.

4. Larry Rohter, "Immigration Law Is Failing to Cut Flow from Mexico," *New York Times*, June 24, 1988, p. 1.

5. The Select Commission on Immigration and Refugee Policy summarizes its recommendations in *U.S. Immigration Policy and the National Interest* (Washington, Government Printing

Notes

Office, 1981). More innovative proposals include Gary S. Becker, "Why Not Let Immigrants Pay for Speedy Entry," *Business Week,* March 2, 1987, p. 20; Gary S. Becker, "Hong Kong's Best and Brightest: Ours for the Asking," *Business Week,* October 17, 1988, p. 20; and Barry R. Chiswick, "Legal Aliens: Toward a Positive Immigration Policy," *Regulation* 12 (1988): 17–22. A review of the current policy debate is given by Constance Holden, "Debate Warming up on Legal Migration Policy," *Science* 241 (July 15, 1988): 288–290.

6. See the discussion in Holden, "Debate Warming up," p. 289.

7. For a discussion of immigration's impact on economic growth, see Edward Denison, *The Sources of Economic Growth in the United States and the Alternatives Before Us* (Washington, D.C.: Committee for Economic Development, 1962), pp. 177–79. Denison's calculations imply that a 1-percent increase in the labor force due to immigration increases national income by about 1 percent, assuming that the immigrant work-force is as skilled as the native work-force. But if immigrants are less skilled than natives, per capita income in the United States may fall, and the impact of immigration on economic growth is reduced.

8. There are many other costs associated with the entry of unskilled immigrants that are extremely difficult to quantify. For example, the birth of an immigrant underclass and the presence of large numbers of unassimilated immigrants living in segregated ghettos may be a potential source of serious political and social problems in the future. Many participants in the debate over immigration policy perceive these costs to be extremely large, for nothing less than our national identity is at stake. See, for example, Richard D. Lamm and Gary Imhoff, *The Immigration Time Bomb: The Fragmenting of America* (New York: E. P. Dutton, 1985).

9. A particular program to sell visas in the open market is proposed by Becker, "Why Not Let Immigrants Pay?"

10. "Capitalism's Last Frontier," *Newsweek,* May 16, 1988, 53–55; and Becker, "Hong Kong's Best and Brightest."

INDEX

Index

1965, 27–29; and the importation of Mongolians, 26; national-origins quota system, 28–30, 31, 228; power of, over immigration, Supreme Court decision on, 27; and refugee entries, 33; and welfare participation of immigrants, 155–56
Contagious diseases, 29
Convicts, 27
Coolidge, Calvin, 29
Coolie-trade, 26
Corcoran, Mary, 250n22
Crime: the employment of illegal aliens as a, 73–74; and grounds for deportation, 29; and the growth of the unassimilated underclass, 4–5
Criminals, career, 94
Cuba, immigrants from, 4, 12, 33, 128–29; assimilation of, 108–9, 111–12; the Mariel boatlift (1980), 43, 94–95; in Miami, 43, 80, 94–95, 170–73; poverty rates for, 148; welfare participation of, 153
Cultural heritage, attachment to, 98
Cuthbert, Richard W., 244n2

Danziger, Sheldon H., 255n18
DaVanzo, Julie, 260n20
Debt repayment subsidies, 22
DeFreitas, Gregory, 87, 249n9
Democratic Party, 26
Denison, Edward, 263n7
Denmark, 34
Dennis, Barbara D., 87
Deportation, 26, 27; grounds for, and Congress, 29; of illegal aliens, 57, 58, 62, 70, 74, 219–20
Desegregation, 80
Dickens, William, 247n11
Didion, Joan, 79–80, 246n2
Diez-Canedo, Juan, 260n27
Dinnerstein, Leonard, 241n4
Discrimination, against immigrants, 82, 83, 129–30, 172–73
Diseases, 29
Dominican Republic, immigrants from, 37; assimilation of, 108–9, 140; poverty rates among, 148; welfare participation of, 153
Douglas, Paul, 133, 252n1, 254n30
Downs, Anthony, 239n10
Drug addiction, 29
Duncan, Greg, 250n22
Duncan, O., 250n17

Econometrics, 80–81, 88, 93, 102, 105
Economic: conditions, in competing countries, 9, 126, 127; growth, 103; policies, 22, 23. *See also* Economy
Economy: Canadian, 215; free-enterprise, 8; Mexican, 68–69
—United States: 52, 79–196, 225–26; and the business cycle, 126–27, 131–32; and the Canadian economy, comparison of, 215; fixed number of jobs in, notion of, 82; and illegal aliens, 56, 60–61, 69, 75; and inflation, 142; and IRCA, impact of, 74. *See also* Economic; GNP (gross national product); National income
Education, 52–53, 72, 82, 86, 96; higher levels of, and higher earnings, 15–16, 49–50, 110–11, 117, 124; of and immigration to Australia, 209; and immigration to Canada, 209, 211–12, 214, 215; of immigrant men, average years of, 231; lower levels of, in recent immigration waves, 20, 45–46, 121–22, 126; of natives and immigrants, comparison of, 41–42, 100–101; and point systems, 209, 211–12, 214, 215, 224; and self-employment, 166–67
Ehrenberg, Ronald G., 246n42, 254n5
Eichengreen, Barry, 249n13
Ellwood, David T., 255n18, 255n1
Elwell, Patricia J., 261n4
Emigration, 213–17; flow, skill composition of, 12, 104, 213–17; of the foreign born, 35, 103–4, 109, 132, 143; policy, 12, 35
Employer-sanctions provisions, 75
Enclaves, immigrant, 21, 24–25, 112; crowding of, and social conflict, 42–43; economy of, 169–74; and ethnic and cultural goods, demand for, 163
English language, 4, 67, 72, 82, 83; proficiency in, and assimilation, 97, 110–12, 173; requirements, IRCA, 73; training, 35. *See also* Self-employment
Entrepreneurs, immigrant, 21, 24–25, 163–76
Entry penalties, 13
España, Felipe Garcia, 185, 259n14, 259n16
Espenshade, Thomas J., 87, 246n35, 246n41, 262n2
Europe, Western, 20, 36–37, 118; decrease in immigrants from, 119; democracies in, immigrants originating in, 109. *See also* specific countries
Evans, David S., 257n1, 257n3, 259n24

267

Index

Illegal aliens, 56–75, 219; apprehension of, 58, 59, 61–62, 74; Briggs on, 71–72, 81; conventional wisdom regarding, 5; as criminals, accusation of, 4; deportation of, 57, 58, 62, 70, 74, 219–20; employment of, 58, 70–72, 73–75, 81–83, 220; exploitation of, 71, 82–83; and the INS, 57, 58, 63–64, 70–71, 75; and native labor markets, 5, 81–82, 88–90; number of, in the U.S., 19, 62–66, 142; skill composition of, 24, 120, 121; statistical portrait of, 66–70; wages of, 67–68, 71–72; and the welfare state, 134–35

Illinois: Chicago, 70–71; geographic concentration of immigrants in, 42; illegal aliens in, 66, 70–71

Imhoff, Gary, 4, 43, 239n6, 243n6, 243n7, 248n1, 254n1, 256n6, 263n8

Immigration Act (1976), 202

Immigration and Nationality Act of 1952, 29 —1965 amendments to, 30–32, 34, 36–39, 220; Canadian version of, 202; and changes in immigrant flow, 51, 217; family-reunification provisions, 31–32, 177–96, 228; lifetime wealth prior to, 116

Immigration market, 7–25, 26, 35–39; and illegal aliens, 57–58, 75. *See also* Illegal aliens; Israel and, 34; nature of, 9–18; and poverty, 149; and welfare, 150–52 —competitiveness in, 7–8, 9, 13, 18–25, 39, 197–228; Australian, 11, 19, 22, 25, 124, 199–213, 216–17; Canadian, 11, 22, 25, 124, 199–217; and economic conditions, 9, 126, 127 —sorting generated by, 40–42, 45, 47–48, 55, 69; and the economy, 79–196; and education, 122; and the skill composition of immigrant flows, 14–25, 45–52, 124, 126–27, 139, 149, 191–92

Immigration multiplier, 179–84, 188

Immigration policy. *See* Family-reunification policy; Immigration market; Visa-allocation system

Immigration Reform and Control Act of 1986 (IRCA), 32–33, 56, 58, 60, 72–75; amnesty program, 67, 70, 73–74; effectiveness of, 71, 219–20; enactment of, impetus behind, 89–90; impact of, on the U.S. economy, 74; and the skill composition of the illegal-alien flow, 69

Import restrictions, 22, 225

Income distributions, egalitarian, 16–17, 20, 124–25, 190, 193; in the U.S. and Canada, comparison of, 215

Income inequality, 16–18, 125, 126, 130, 191, 193

Incomes, per-capita, 38

India, 37, 108–9, 148, 153, 165

Indo-Chinese refugees, 43

Industrialization, 123

Industries: automobile, 216; business services, 166; construction, 166; "immigrant-intensive" and "native-intensive," 95–96; restaurant, 70, 95, 163; retail-trade, 166, 175

Inflation, 142

INS (Immigration and Naturalization Service), 3, 23, 63–64, 89, 242n36; and family reunification, 183; and illegal aliens, 57, 58, 63–64, 70–71, 75; and Iranian students in the U.S., 5; Record of Deportable Alien form, 70

Internal Revenue Service, 175

International Monetary Fund, 22

International trade, 7

Iran, 245n14

Iran hostage crisis, 5

Ireland, 202

Irish immigrants, 99

Israel, 34

Italy, 28, 108, 148, 153, 204

Jamaica, immigrants from, 14, 37, 38; assimilation of, 108, 140; poverty rates among, 148; self-employment rates for, 164, 165; welfare participation of, 153.

Japan, 108, 148, 153, 171, 204, 216

Jasso, Guillermina, 183–84, 242n33, 242n37, 250n15, 250n16, 252n30, 252n11, 259n7, 259n11–13

Jencks, Christopher, 240n20

Jensen, Leif, 255n19, 256n3, 256n5

Jews, Soviet, 34

Job displacement, 7, 24

Johnson, George, 247n13

Johnson, Lyndon B., 31

Jones, Maldwyn Allen, 239n2, 239n4

Katzenbach, Nicholas, 32

Keely, Charles B., 261n4, 261n7

Kennedy, Lenna, 256n3

Kennedy, Robert F., 32

Kenny, Lawrence W., 260n25

Killingsworth, Mark R., 243n8, 244n14, 254n3, 254n6

269

Index